GODDESS LIFE DE

THE POWERFUL

MANIFESTATION RITUAL

DESIGN YOUR LIFE

& EVOLVE YOUR SOUL

IN ALIGNMENT WITH THE MOON

Hello, beautiful soul, I am grateful we have been aligned.

THE GODDESS LIFE DESIGNER FORMULA APPLIES
THE S.M.A.R.T. GOAL ACHIEVEMENT FORMULA,
THE 12 UNIVERSAL LAWS,
AND QUANTUM PHYSICS.
A JOURNAL PROMPT GUIDE FOR
PASSIONATELY DESIGNING
AND MANIFESTING
THE LIFE DESIGN YOU DESIRE.

UNVEIL, EMBRACE AND ALIGN
YOUR INFINITE CREATIVE MAGICK POTENTIAL.
EXTRACT YOUR DEEPEST LIFE PASSIONS
& HARNESS YOUR INTERNAL POWER
ALONGSIDE
THE ALIGNING POWER OF
MOON PHASE & CYCLE PLANNING.

EST. 2017
THIS IS THE 2019 EDITION.

EXTERIOR AND INTERIOR
DESIGNED BY

ZAEYLIN SATYA

May your
life journey be
infinitely blessed
and all of your
desires manifest,
for the highest
good of all souls.

EXTRACT
YOUR DEEPEST PASSIONS & DESIRES
THEN PUT THEM TO USE,
BY YOUR OWN DESIGN.
THIS IS THE
GODDESS LIFE DESIGNER
POWERFUL MANIFESTATION RITUAL.
YOUR DESIRES MANIFESTED
THROUGH
DEFINING,
DESIGNING
&
A
L
I
G
N
I
N
G

TO **FEEL**,
LIVE,
AND RADIATE
ABUNDANCE OF LOVE AND LIFE.

WHEN YOU MOVE THE ENTIRE UNIVERSE MOVES WITH YOU,
TO SUPPORT YOU.

THIS IS MY OWN LIFE DESIGNER SCRIPT
WHICH I ABIDE BY WHILE JOURNALING AND MANIFESTING.
THIS FORMULA RESONATES WITH MY OWN LIFE VERY WELL.
I LOVE THAT IT IS A 'DESIGNER', RATHER THAN A PLANNER,
BECAUSE THAT IS EXACTLY WHAT I FEEL
WHEN I THINK ABOUT MY GOALS AND MY LIFE--

I am passionately designing each moment.

DESIGNED TO PROVIDE AN INCREASE IN BLISSFUL, BEAUTIFUL LIVING,
DEEPENED GODDESS ENERGY, AND SUCCESSFUL MANIFESTATION
THROUGHOUT THE 13 MOON CYCLES.
WE WILL EXTRACT OUR INNERMOST PASSIONS AND DESIRES,
THEN ALIGN THOSE PASSIONS AND DESIRES WITH
THE MOON CYCLES AND PHASES,
WHILE ALSO APPLYING THE S.M.A.R.T. GOAL ACHIEVEMENT FORMULA.
MANIFESTING WITH THE MOON.
THIS COMBINATION CONJURES AN APPRECIATION
AND ACKNOWLEDGMENT OF OUR UNIVERSE
WHILE LOOKING INTO THE SKY AND TRACKING OUR DESIRES
WITH BLISS AND EASE,
MOMENT BY MOMENT, ONE DAY AT A TIME,
TO COMPOSE EACH MOON CYCLE, AND YEAR OF
THIS LIFE [100 YEAR DREAM].
WE ARE INCREASING OUR COMPREHENSION OF
TRULY SURRENDERING TO A POWER GREATER THAN OURSELF,
ALLOWING OUR DIVINE LIFE AND POWER SOURCE
TO MOVE IN AND MANIFEST OUR DESIRES INTO TRUE FORM,
IN ALIGNMENT WITH OUR PRODUCTIVE, INSPIRED ACTIONS
AND PURE FEELINGS - WHICH CANNOT BE DISGUISED, BUT TRAINED AND
HARNESSED FOR MANIFESTING WHAT WE EACH PERSONALLY DESIRE.

THIS IS MY OWN GODDESS LIVING RECIPE
INCLUDING THINGS I HAVE SPENT YEARS LEARNING AND APPLYING.
DESIGNED FOR MY SELF LOVE RITUALS AND LIFE DESIGN THIS YEAR.
AS AN OVERFLOW I AM SHARING WITH EVERYONE ELSE.
I AM GRATEFUL AND BLESSED, I AM TRULY IN LOVE WITH MY LIFE DESIGN.
MAY YOU BE BLESSED WITH DIVINE, LOVING ENERGY
AS YOU MOVE THROUGHOUT EACH OF THESE WORDS AND PAGES.

Zaeylin Satya

READ ENTIRELY, FROM FRONT TO BACK., DO NOT SKIP AROUND.
THIS GUIDEBOOK IS DESIGNED AS A FORMULA.
YOU MUST FOLLOW THE FORMULA COMPLETELY, EACH DAY,
IN ORDER TO SUCCESSFULLY MANIFEST YOUR OWN DESIRED RESULTS.

↓

IN YOUR JOURNAL,
WRITE IN CORRESPONDENCE WITH
ALL QUESTIONS, PROMPTS & LISTS.
YOU MAY ALSO USE THE SPACES PROVIDED ON SELECT PAGES,
THEY ARE PROVIDED FOR EASY REFLECTION
AS YOU PROGRESSIVELY MANIFEST YOUR DESIRED LIFE DESIGN THIS YEAR.

↓

SET YOUR LONG TERM GOALS USING THE BLUEPRINT FOR MANIFESTING LONG TERM GOALS PAGES

↓

SET YOUR 3, 6 & 9 MONTH GOALS FOR THE SOLAR YEAR.

↓

FOLLOW THE SPECIFIC NEW MOON PAGE FOR THIS PRESENT DATE IN TIME.

↓

ALWAYS FOLLOW THE CURRENT MOON PHASE.
EACH SPECIFIC MOON CYCLE PAGE PROVIDES DATES FOR WHEN THE 8 PHASES WILL
OCCUR, GUIDING YOU EFFORTLESSLY THROUGH EACH OF THE 13 CYCLES..

↓

FOLLOW & COMPLETE EACH OF THE STEPS LISTED ABOVE. THEN,
UTILIZE THE DAILY JOURNALING PAGES EVERY SINGLE DAY IN ORDER TO
SUCCESSFULLY MANIFEST YOUR OWN DESIRED LIFE DESIGN.

GOD IS LOVE,

AND LIVES WITHIN.

I NOW UNDERSTAND MY BEING,

I AM SIMPLY

GOD COVERED IN SKIN.

THE ART OF CHANGING PERSPECTIVE.

FROM FOCUSING ON THE PHYSICAL REALM AS TRUTH IN DEFINING WHAT IS REAL ..
MY REALITY .. TO HAVING AN AWAKENING OF TRUTH ~ I AM PURE ENERGY, I AM NOT
JUST THIS PHYSICAL BODY. IN MY PUREST FORM I AM NOT VISIBLE TO THE HUMAN
EYE ~ AT ALL. I AM AN EXPRESSION OF MY DIVINE LIFE SOURCE. I AM A PART OF THE
WHOLE, ALL TRULY IS ONE. I AM ALWAYS CONNECTED TO MY DIVINE LIFE SOUCE ~
THE ORGANIZED INTELLIGENCE THAT PERMEATES THROUGHOUT THE ENTIRE
UNIVERSE ~ PURE CONSCIOUSNESS AND UNCONDITIONAL LOVE ~ THE
CONSCIOUSNESS THAT CREATES REALITY ~ WITH THIS KNOWINGNESS I AM CAPABLE
OF HARNESSING MY OWN CONSCIOUS POWER, MY FREE WILL TO DESIGN AND
MANIFEST THE LIFE DESIGN I DESIRE ~ OR SOMETHING EVEN
BETTER. I ACKNOWLEDGE THAT THE SOURCE OF MY EXISTENCE [MY DIVINE LIFE
SOURCE] IS THE INFINITE, ORGANIZED INTELLIGENCE THAT IS ALL AROUND
ME, ALBEIT INVISIBLE TO THE HUMAN EYE. THE HUMAN MIND IS NOT CAPABLE OF
COMPREHENDING OR DEFINING HOW INFINITE, IMMENSE AND POWERFUL THIS
FORCE TRULY IS. THIS FORCE IS THE SOURCE I HAVE COME FROM AND WILL ONE DAY
RETURN TO. ALTHOUGH, IN ACTUALITY I HAVE NOT EVER SEPARATED FROM SOURCE,
BUT RATHER, THE HUMAN MIND AND PHYSICAL EYES SERVE AS A BLINDFOLD - ONLY
ALLOWING A SMALL PERCENTAGE OF WHAT TRULY EXISTS TO BE SEEN AND KNOWN
BY THE HUMAN MIND - SO THAT THE CREATIVE, SOUL EVOLVING HUMAN
EXPERIENCE CAN BE ENJOYED FULLY FOR WHAT IT IS BEFORE RETURNING TO OUR
PUREST FORM ONCE AGAIN. SOURCE ALLOWS US THE FREE WILL TO EMBODY THE
THOUGHTS AND FEELINGS WE PERSONALLY DESIRE THROUGHOUT THIS HUMAN
EXPERIENCE. WE CAN BELIEVE LIFE IS HAPPENING TO US, OR WE CAN RECOGNIZE
LIFE IS RESPONDING TO US. THE FREE WILL WITHIN EACH OF US ALLOWS US EACH TO
LIVE WITHIN OUR OWN DESIRED LIFE DESIGN - IF WE CONSCIOUSLY CHOOSE TO
HARNESS OUR INNATE POWER AND DESIGN OUR OWN MOST FULFILLING,
SOUL EVOLVING JOURNEY FOR THIS HUMAN LIFETIME.
THE GODDESS LIFE DESIGNER SERVES AS A GUIDE FOR
EMBRACING AND IMPLEMENTING THIS TRUTH.
I AM CONSISTENTLY STRENGTHENING MY INNER POWER
AND EMANATING THE VIBRATIONAL ENERGY FREQUENCIES
I DESIRE TO MANIFEST MORE OF WITHIN MY LIFE.
I AM GENUINELY GRATEFUL IN ALL MOMENTS.
THUS, I AM ALWAYS ATTRACTING MORE AND MORE TO BE GRATEFUL FOR IN MY
LIFETIME. MORE UNCONDITIONAL LOVE, MORE PASSION AND MORE BLISS.
I AM THRIVING WITHIN MY OWN PATH OF PASSIONATE BLISS FIRST,
THEN ACCENTUATING LIFE WITH PHYSICAL THINGS
THE WORLD HAS TO OFFER.
I FULLY RECOGNIZE I AM NOT TAKING THINGS WITH ME WHEN I LEAVE.
IT IS ABOUT THE WORTH I GIVE WHILE I AM HERE,
AND THE JOY AND ADVENTURES I CREATE.
IN GIVING I DO RECEIVE,
MORE THAN I COULD HAVE
THROUGH RECEIVING ALONE.
DESIRES EXPOSE PASSION AND BLISS,
PASSION AND BLISS NURTURE DESIRES.

CONTENT REFERENCE GUIDE: BY PAGE NUMBER

GODDESS LIFE DESIGNER

CONTENT REFERENCE GUIDE: BY PAGE NUMBER

GODDESS LIFE DESIGNER

OVERVIEW OF
THE 5 AGREEMENTS
FROM DON MIGUEL RUIZ
A GROUNDING FORMULA FOR THIS LIFE
[100 YEAR DREAM].

BE IMPECCABLE WITH YOUR WORD:
SPEAK WITH INTEGRITY. SAY ONLY WHAT YOU MEAN. AVOID USING
WORDS TO SPEAK AGAINST YOURSELF OR TO GOSSIP ABOUT OTHERS.
USE THE POWER OF YOUR WORD IN THE DIRECTION OF TRUTH & LOVE.

DO NOT TAKE ANYTHING PERSONALLY:
NOTHING OTHERS DO IS BECAUSE OF YOU. WHAT OTHERS SAY AND
DO IS A PROJECTION OF THEIR OWN REALITY, THEIR OWN DREAM.
WHEN YOU ARE IMMUNE TO THE OPINIONS & ACTIONS OF OTHERS,
YOU WON'T BE THE VICTIM OF NEEDLESS SUFFERING.

DO NOT MAKE ASSUMPTIONS:
FIND THE COURAGE TO ASK QUESTIONS & TO EXPRESS WHAT YOU
REALLY WANT. COMMUNICATE WITH OTHERS AS CLEARLY AS YOU CAN
TO AVOID MISUNDERSTANDINGS, SADNESS & DRAMA. WITH JUST THIS
ONE AGREEMENT, YOU CAN COMPLETELY TRANSFORM YOUR LIFE.

ALWAYS DO YOUR BEST:
YOUR BEST IS GOING TO CHANGE FROM MOMENT TO MOMENT; IT
WILL BE DIFFERENT WHEN YOU ARE HEALTHY AS OPPOSED TO SICK.
UNDER ANY CIRCUMSTANCE, SIMPLY DO YOUR BEST,
& YOU WILL AVOID SELF-JUDGEMENT, SELF-ABUSE & REGRET.

BE SKEPTICAL, BUT LEARN TO LISTEN:
DO NOT BELIEVE YOURSELF OR ANYBODY ELSE.
USE THE POWER OF DOUBT TO QUESTION EVERYTHING YOU HEAR.
IS IT REALLY THE TRUTH?
LISTEN TO THE INTENT BEHIND WORDS
& YOU WILL UNDERSTAND THE REAL MESSAGE.

YOU COME FIRST.
MAKE CERTAIN TO LOVE YOURSELF,
GODDESS

**KEEP A LIST OF THINGS YOU LOVE ABOUT
YOURSELF:
ALWAYS ADD TO IT.**

**KEEP A LIST OF THINGS YOU ARE
GRATEFUL FOR:
ALWAYS ADD TO IT.**

SELF CARE IS SELF LOVE

SELF LOVE IS SELF CARE

TAKE SOME DEEP BREATHS

EAT WELL & HYDRATE

TAKE A WALK

GET IN THE SUN

TAKE A SHOWER

WATCH CLOUDS

JOURNAL

GET A MANICURE/PEDICURE

GO FOR A DRIVE

I Am Worthy

**LISTEN TO MUSIC,
AN AUDIOBOOK
OR A PODCAST**

WAKE UP TO WATCH THE SUNRISE

APPLY A FACE MASK

**LISTEN TO 432 HERTZ OR 528 HERTZ
ON YOUTUBE**

GET COSY

TAKE A NAP

GO TO A FARMERS MARKET

BE YOUR PUREST FORM

WATCH SUNSETS

WATCH TUTORIALS ON
YOUTUBE FOR WHAT
INTERESTS YOU

GET A MASSAGE

**TAKE A BATH
WITH ESSENTIAL OILS,
DEAD SEA SALT/HIMALAYAN SALT,
CANDLES,
HERBS
& MEDITATION MUSIC/SOUNDS.**

**READ A BOOK,
OR A BLOG**

**GET YOUR BODY MOVING.
OUR BODIES CRAVE MOVEMENT
& RELEASE ENDORPHINS TO ENJOY**

**BRING TEA, LEMON-MINT WATER OR
LEMON-CUCUMBER WATER TO DRINK.**

**CREATE AN I AM AFFIRMATION TO
REPEAT.**

The most fulfilling & abundant feeling
I've ever experienced... I feel that now.
This is how I feel when praying,
meditating & in every other moment
that I remind myself to.

I MOVE MY BODY
BECAUSE I LOVE &
RESPECT MY BODY.

**BE ABOUT THE SOLUTION,
NOT THE PROBLEM**

WATCH A RIVER FLOW

**ALLOW YOURSELF TO DAY DREAM
& JOURNAL YOUR DAYDREAMING**

FOLLOW THE LIFE DESIGN PLAN YOU CREATE.
IN EACH MOMENT,
TO CREATIVELY DESIGN EACH DAY,
INTO EACH MONTH & EACH YEAR.

**PRAY
THROUGH
GIVING THANKS IN ADVANCE
FOR WHAT YOU DESIRE,
'THANK YOU FOR ____, OR SOMETHING BETTER'
USE SUPERIOR CLARITY IN DESCRIBING THE THINGS WHICH YOU DO DESIRE,
IGNITE ALL YOUR SENSES IN THE FEELING OF THE DESIRE FULFILLED.
TRUST YOUR DESIRES ARE ALREADY BEING FULFILLED.**

WEAR WHAT MAKES YOUR
VIBRATION
FEEL BEST

IN SHOWER MEDITATION:

VISUALIZE WASHING AWAY YOUR STRESS
& ANXIETY. CONCENTRATE ON THE FEEL
OF THE WATER UPON YOUR SKIN.
ENVISION THE POWER OF THE WATER
WASHING AWAY YOUR NEGATIVE
THOUGHTS. FEEL SADNESS, REGRET,
ANGER, AND DEPRESSION
WASHING RIGHT OFF YOU.
LET IT ALL GO DOWN THE DRAIN.
FEEL THE LIGHTNESS IN YOUR BODY.
ENJOY THE CLARITY OF YOUR MIND.
YOUR SOUL IS FREE OF ALL THAT DOES
NOT SERVE YOUR HIGHEST GOOD.
YOU ARE READY FOR A NEW BEGINNING.

**I'LL BELIEVE IT WHEN I SEE IT,
SWITCHED TO
I'LL SEE IT WHEN I BELIEVE IT.**

GO TO BED EARLY

WHO DO I SPEND MY TIME AROUND?
ARE THEY MOTIVATING, OR NOT?
ARE THEIR GOALS/DESIRES ALIGNED WITH MINE?
WHAT IS THEIR ROLE IN MY LIFE?

**MEDITATE
TO RECEIVE GUIDANCE,
OBSERVE THOUGHTS & FEELINGS THAT ARISE.
[THEY ARE YOUR INTUITION SPEAKING]**

RECOGNIZE, WE EACH CHOOSE
WHAT WE LET IN OUR MINDS AS TRUTH.

DO YOU LET YOUR HIGHER SELF OR
LOWER SELF TALK TO YOU?
ARE YOU SELF-LOVING, OR ARE YOU
SELF-CRITICIZING
WE CHOOSE WHAT WORDS (FROM
BOTH OURSELVES & OTHERS)
WE ALLOW TO
DEFINE OUR DESIGN & TRUTH.

**DAILY RITUAL:
MY AFFIRMATION WHENEVER I
LOOK INTO A MIRROR:
I AM BEAUTIFUL,
MY LIFE IS BLISSFUL.**

**MEDITATION ISN'T
ABOUT GETTING RID OF YOUR THOUGHTS,
IT IS ABOUT OBSERVING THEM
& TRAINING YOURSELF TO
RECOGNIZE YOU CAN
DESIGN THEM IN EACH MOMENT.
RECOGNIZE YOU ARE THINKING [IN THIS MOMENT].
THERE YOU GO, YOU MEDITATED.
PRACTICE NON JUDGEMENT, PURE OBSERVATION OF YOUR THOUGHTS.**

THE SEVEN ENERGY CENTERS

CHAKRA ALIGNMENT

MEDITATE ON EACH AREA WITHIN YOUR OWN BODY,
INHALE HEALING ENERGY INTO THESE SPACES,
EXHALE ALL THAT DOES NOT SERVE YOUR HIGHEST SELF.

[THOUGHTS ORIGINATE IN THE CROWN, 3RD EYE & THROAT CHAKRAS]

[VIOLET]
CROWN CHAKRA
I AM DIVINE
[THE TOP OF HEAD]
YOUR CONNECTION TO THE DIVINE, UNIVERSE & YOUR SOUL
BLISS
[CENTRAL NERVOUS SYSTEM]

[INDIGO]
3RD EYE CHAKRA
I AM CONNECTED
[ABOVE BROW, CENTERED BETWEEN EYES]
INTUITION & PSYCHIC SENSES
[EYES & PINEAL GLAND]

[BLUE]
THROAT CHAKRA
I AM EXPRESSIVE
COMMUNICATION & PERSONAL TRUTH
[EARS & THROAT]

**[THE COMBINATION OF THOUGHTS & EMOTIONS
ACTIVATE FEELING STATES
WHICH ARE EMBODIED WITHIN & EMANATE FROM THE HEART CHAKRA]**

[GREEN]
HEART CHAKRA
I AM LOVED
LOVE & RELATIONSHIPS
BALANCE
[LUNGS & HEART]

[YELLOW]
SOLAR PLEXUS CHAKRA
I AM STRONG
[ABDOMEN, ABOVE BELLY BUTTON]
CONFIDENCE & PERSONAL POWER
CREATIVITY
[DIGESTIVE SYSTEM]

[ORANGE]
SACRAL CHAKRA
I AM CREATIVE
CREATIVITY, EMOTIONS, & SELF-EXPRESSION
SEXUALITY
[REPRODUCTIVE AREA]

[RED]
ROOT CHAKRA
I AM SAFE
YOUR POWER BASE
CENTERING
[LEGS, SPINE & ADRENAL GLANDS]

[THOUGHTS IGNITE EMOTIONS IN THE SOLAR PLEXUS, SACRAL & ROOT CHAKRAS]

ALIGNING HEALING CRYSTALS WITH CHAKRAS IS AS SIMPLE AS COLOR MATCHING

AURA CLEANSING

MOST PEOPLE HAVE BEEN TAUGHT, OR SIMPLY BELIEVE, THAT EVERYTHING IS SOLID.
HOWEVER, THE TRUTH IS THAT EVERY SINGLE PERSON AND THING IN OUR REALITY
IS COMPOSED OF ATOMS, AND THE ATOMS ARE NOTHING BUT ENERGY.

QUANTUM PHYSICS PROVES TO US THAT IN THE DEPTHS OF THE ATOM,
AT THE ATOM'S VERY CORE, IT IS PURELY AND ENTIRELY COMPOSED OF ENERGY WAVES.
AN ATOM IS A TORNADO OF ENERGY THAT IS CONSTANTLY EMITTING WAVES OF
ELECTRICAL ENERGY. ENERGY TRAVELS IN CIRCULAR, SPIRAL MOVEMENTS.
EVERY SINGLE THING IS COMPOSED OF ATOMS [ENERGY],
EACH WITH ITS OWN UNIQUE VIBRATION,
YOU AND I ARE 99.9999999% ATOMS, WE ARE 99.9999999% ENERGETIC VIBRATION,
EVERYONE YOU KNOW, EVEN THE STRANGERS YOU ENCOUNTER,
ARE ALSO 99.9999999% ATOMS [ENERGY] AND THEY ALL HAVE THEIR OWN UNIQUE VIBRATION.

THE AURA IS A MAGNETIC ENERGY FIELD,
[APPROXIMATELY A 3 FOOT RADIUS]
AROUND EACH HUMAN.
THE ENERGY WE EMBODY WE EMIT,
AND THEREFORE WE MAGNETIZE THAT SAME ENERGY FREQUENCY
BACK INTO OUR BEING AND OUR LIFE.
THE AURA IS COLOR COORDINATED WITH THE SEVEN CHAKRAS.
EACH PERSON WILL HAVE THEIR OWN MOST PROMINENT AND VIBRANT COLOR(S)
DEPENDING ON THEIR OWN UNIQUE SOUL, MIND, PERSONALITY
AND THEIR LIFESTYLE THEY ARE RIGHT NOW LIVING WITHIN.

PARTAKE IN AURA CLEANSING AS OFTEN AS EVERYDAY.

MAKE IN DEPTH AURA CLEANSING
[SUCH AS A SALT BATH / PROFESSIONAL ENERGY HEALING]
A RITUAL YOU PARTAKE IN AT VERY LEAST ONCE A MONTH.
[FOR EXAMPLE: EVERY SUNDAY EVENING OR EVERY NEW MOON / FULL MOON]
IF YOU DO NOT HAVE A TUB, TAKE A SHOWER AND SCRUB YOUR BODY
WITH THE INGREDIENTS YOU WOULD HAVE PLACED IN THE BATH.

PARTAKE IN AURA CLEANSING WITH THE EMBODIMENT OF FAITH AND LOVE.
YOU ARE INFUSING YOUR BEING WITH ENERGY,
YOU WANT THAT ENERGY TO BE ONLY OF THE HIGHEST VIBRATIONAL FREQUENCIES.

THE FOLLOWING PAGES CONTAIN TIPS/RECOMMENDATIONS
IN REGARDS TO AURA CLEANSING RITUALS
AS WELL AS MAINTAINING A RADIANT, GLOWING AND PROTECTIVE AURA.

BREATHE DEEPLY INTO YOUR BEING, PAUSE AND EXHALE FROM ALL FIBERS OF YOUR BEING.
AS YOU DO THIS ENVISION WHITE LIGHT OR A VOILET FLAME INFUSING EVERY SINGLE
FIBER OF YOUR BEING AND RADIATING OUTWARD ~ CLEANSING YOUR AURA ~
FEEL YOURSELF GLOWING AND RADIATING DIVINE ENERGY, YOUR INTERNAL POWER.
ENJOY THIS FOR A FEW MOMENTS, OR MINUTES.
THEN, THANK YOUR DIVINE LIFE SOURCE, HIGHEST SELF,
AND HIGHEST VIBRATIONAL ANGELS AND SPIRIT GUIDES
FOR CONTINUOUS GUIDANCE, PROTECTION AND SUPPORT.

BURN PALO SANTO, SAGE OR DIFFUSE ESSENTIAL OILS SUCH AS LAVENDER, LEMON, ROSE
[THESE ARE JUST A FEW EXAMPLES—USE ANY OTHERS YOU DESIRE TO!]

LISTEN TO 432 HZ OR 528 HZ FREQUENCIES [YOUTUBE HAS MANY OPTIONS]

LISTEN TO AUDIO RECORDINGS OF **SINGING BOWLS** OR **SHAMANIC DRUMMING**
[OR USE YOUR OWN IF YOU HAVE THEM!]

CLEAN YOUR MIND SPACE AND YOUR LIVING SPACE(S) REGULARLY.
CHOOSE DECOR THAT PROMOTES A STRONG, PURE AURA.
EXAMPLES: HIMALAYAN SALT LAMP, BEESWAX CANDLES, LIVE HERBS & PLANTS

HAVE A SACRED SPACE OF YOUR OWN.
ALLOW YOUR SPACE TO BE A REFLECTION OF YOUR SOUL,
REMINDING YOU OF YOUR PUREST SELF AND YOUR DEEPEST DESIRES.

AURA CLEANSING BATH
WATER IS NATURALLY PURIFYING, CLEANSING AND HEALING.
SHOWER OFF BEFORE SO THAT YOUR WATER IS NOT ABSORBING
ALL OF YOUR LOTIONS, PERFUMES, SWEAT, ETC.
[SHOWERING ALSO PUTS YOU IN THE CREATIVE THETA BRAIN WAVE STATE]
DISSOLVE A CUP OR TWO OF DEAD SEA SALT, HIMALAYAN SALT, EPSOM SALT OR SEA SALT
IN THE BATH. YOU MAY ALSO DESIRE TO ADD ROSE PETALS,
AS THE VIBRATIONAL FREQUENCY OF THE ROSE IS VERY HIGH.
MOST ESSENTIAL OIL FREQUENCIES START AT 52HZ AND REACH A MAXIMUM VIBRATION OF
320HZ--WHICH IS THE VIBRATION OF DAMASK ROSE OIL.
ADD ANY HERBS AND/OR HEALING CRYSTALS OR ESSENTIAL OILS YOU ARE DRAWN TO.
LIGHT WHITE CANDLES [OR ANY COLOR YOU ARE DRAWN TO AT THIS TIME].
AS YOU MEDITATE WITHIN THIS CLEANSING BATH. EMBODY THE INTENTION OF CLEANSING
YOUR AURA AND DISSOLVING ANY DENSE OR HEAVY ENERGY CORDS AS YOU FOCUS ON THE
FLAME(S). THEN, EMBODY THE INTENTION THAT YOU ARE ESTABLISHING A PROTECTIVE ENERGY
SHIELD AROUND YOUR ENTIRE BEING AND AURA. DO SO BY ENVISIONING
A PURIFIED WHITE ORB OR VIOLET FLAME INFUSING EVERY FIBER OF YOUR BEING AND AURA.
VISUALIZE IT EVER-INCREASINGLY BECOMING STRONGER WHILE BEING INFUSED WITH PURIFIED
SOURCE ENERGY AND LOVE DIRECTLY FROM YOUR DIVINE LIFE SOURCE
AND HIGHEST VIBRATIONAL ANGELS AND GUIDES.
[WHEN YOU EXTINGUISH CANDLE FLAMES DO SO WITHOUT USING THE BREATH OF LIFE]

GO INTO NATURE & CONNECT AS YOU PLEASE. **WALK BAREFOOT ON EARTH OR LAY ON HER.**
IT HAS BEEN SCIENTIFICALLY PROVEN THAT WHEN OUR BARE SKIN IS IN CONTACT WITH THE
EARTH WE ABSORB ELECTRONS. THIS IS SIGNIFICANT BECAUSE THESE ELECTRONS ARE NATURE'S
PURE AND POWERFUL ANTIOXIDANTS. THEY NEUTRALIZE FREE RADICALS,
[FREE RADICALS LEAD TO INFLAMMATION / DISEASE].
THIS HEALS OUR PHYSICAL BODY, AS WELL AS OUR AURA.

CONNECT YOUR ENERGY FIELD WITH **HEALING CRYSTALS** THAT RESONATE WITH YOU PERSONALLY.
— YOU AND I ARE ENERGETIC VIBRATION — HEALING CRYSTALS ARE ALSO ENERGETIC VIBRATION,
JUST LIKE EVERYTHING ELSE IN OUR ENTIRE REALITY — BUT, HEALING CRYSTALS NATURALLY HAVE A
VERY HIGH VIBRATIONAL FREQUENCY — WHEN WE ARE IN CONTACT WITH OR NEARBY HEALING
CRYSTALS OUR OWN VIBRATIONAL FREQUENCY IS IMPACTED BY THE HEALING CRYSTAL(S)
IN A VERY POSITIVE WAY [SINCE THEY NATURALLY VIBRATE AT A HIGH FREQUENCY]
— OUR ENERGY IS UNIQUELY OUR OWN, BUT WE ARE ALSO IMPACTED BY
WHATEVER ENERGY FREQUENCIES WE ARE SURROUNDED BY OR NEAR.
THIS IS HOW HEALING CRYSTALS WORK TO RAISE OUR OWN VIBRATIONAL FREQUENCY,
TO CLEAR AND HEAL OUR ENERGY [OUR BODY, OUR CHAKRAS AND OUR AURA].

INVEST IN AN ACUPRESSURE MAT / MASSAGE PILLOW /
HIMALAYAN SALT BLOCKS FOR THE FEET
[ALL OF THESE ARE GREAT, VERY AFFORDABLE, LONG-LASTING INVESTMENTS]

GET A PROFESSIONAL REIKI ENERGY HEALING / ANY OTHER HIGH QUALITY ENERGY HEALING

BE PRESENT, INDULGE IN YOUR SENSES IN EACH MOMENT.
CLARIFY YOUR BOUNDARIES [SEE THE BOUNDARIES PAGES]
KEEP YOUR DISTANCE FROM THINGS / PEOPLE / PLACES / ENVIRONMENTS / TOPICS
THAT LOWER YOUR MINDSET / FEELINGS / OVERALL VIBRATION.
[SEE THE POWER IN CLEAN & TIDY PAGES]
DO THE THINGS / GO TO THE PLACES / BE AROUND THE PEOPLE
THAT HARMONIZE WITH YOU IN YOUR PERSONAL VIBRATIONAL FREQUENCY OF PEACE.
REDUCE SOCIAL MEDIA, ALL OTHER MEDIA, NEWS, ELECTRONICS, ETC.
[SLEEP WITH YOUR PHONE ON AIRPLANE MODE, ACROSS THE ROOM OR IN ANOTHER ROOM ENTIRELY]
HAVE A BEDTIME FOR YOUR PHONE, TV .. ETC.

BE CONSCIOUS OF WHAT YOU ARE **FUELING & HYDRATING** YOUR TEMPLE WITH.
[THE NEXT COUPLE PAGES COVER THIS IN MORE DETAIL]

FOLLOWING AURA CLEANSING [ESPECIALLY DEEP AURA CLEANSING] TAKE PART IN
A SELF-LOVE / BEAUTY RITUAL TO FILL YOUR PURIFIED AURA WITH
ENERGY THAT BLESSES YOU IN THE WAYS YOU PERSONALLY DESIRE TO BE BLESSED.
THIS IS ALSO WHY AN AURA CLEANSE BEFORE INTENTION SETTING IS SO POWERFUL.
DO AN AURA CLEANSE BEFORE BEAUTY RITUALS.
A BEAUTY RITUAL CAN BE AS SIMPLE AS WRITING YOURSELF A SELF-LOVE LETTER.
A BEAUTY RITUAL BATH:
1-3 CUPS MILK [WHICHEVER TYPE YOU PREFER], ROSE ESSENTIAL OIL, ROSE PETALS, HIBISCUS PETALS,
CANDLES AND GENUINE, HEARTFELT GRATITUDE FOR THE DESIRED BEAUTY RECEIVED.
THESE ARE A FEW EXAMPLES, SIMPLY CREATE YOUR BEAUTY BATH WITH
WHATEVER MAKES YOU FEEL HOW YOU DESIRE TO FEEL.

I AM VIBRATING WITHIN A TEMPLE OF PURE LOVE, COVERED IN SKIN.

GODDESS,
BE CONSCIOUS WHEN PROVIDING FUEL AND HYDRATION TO YOUR TEMPLE.
EVERYTHING YOU PLACE INTO YOUR BODY SHOULD BE
THE HIGHEST OF QUALITY.
THAT WHICH IS CONSUMED BY THE HUMAN BODY HOLDS IMPACT ON
ENERGY LEVELS, EMOTIONS, THE AURA AND OVERALL VIBRATIONAL FREQUENCY.

WHAT ENERGIES ARE YOU WELCOMING INTO YOUR TEMPLE?

**HEALTHY EATING CAN BE SIMPLE OR COMPLEX.
SIMPLY, ALWAYS CHOOSE THE MOST PURE AND WHOLE FORM AVAILABLE
FOR EACH FOOD YOU DESIRE TO CONSUME.**

AN ARTICLE PUBLISHED BY THE AMERICAN PSYCHOLOGICAL ASSOCIATION EXPLAINS
THAT GUT BACTERIA MANUFACTURE 95 PERCENT OF THE HUMAN BODY'S SUPPLY OF SEROTONIN,
AN IMPORTANT NEUROCHEMICAL THAT CAN AFFECT MOOD, DIGESTION, AND SLEEP.
RESEARCHERS DISCOVERED THAT BRAIN CHEMISTRY CAN BE ALTERED
BY MANIPULATING THE BALANCE OF BENEFICIAL AND HARMFUL BACTERIA FOUND IN THE GUT.

PROBIOTIC RICH FOODS AND SUPPLEMENTS ARE A WONDERFUL ADDITION TO ANY DIET. THEY ARE
BENEFICIAL BACTERIA FOR THE GUT, WHILE ALSO REDUCING HARMFUL BACTERIA IN THE GUT. THERE
IS A LOT OF INFORMATION AVAILABLE ON WHICH PROBIOTIC RICH FOODS AND SUPPLEMENTS
PROVIDE THE MOST BENEFITS, RESEARCH AS MUCH AS YOU PLEASE. INCORPORATING PLENTY OF
PLANT BASED FOODS INTO YOUR DIET WILL ALSO BENEFIT GUT HEALTH.

PLANTS OBTAIN THEIR ENERGY DIRECTLY FROM THE SUNLIGHT, PROVIDING HIGH VIBRATIONAL
ENERGY TO THE BODY. FRUITS, VEGETABLES, BEANS, LEGUMES, NUTS, SEEDS, GRAINS AND WILD RICE
ARE ALL GREAT OPTIONS. ROOT VEGETABLES ARE GREAT FOR GROUNDING
AND ATTUNING THE BODY TO THE ENERGY OF MOTHER EARTH.
CONSIDERING THE ENERGY EACH FOOD SOURCE EATS OR ABSORBS PROVIDES IS A GREAT WAY TO
EASILY DETERMINE THE ENERGY FREQUENCY YOU ARE INFUSING YOUR TEMPLE WITH
THROUGH CONSUMING IT. THUS, YOU ARE BETTER ABLE TO DETERMINE
WHAT WILL MAKE YOU PERSONALLY FEEL YOUR BEST.
THE ENERGY OF QUALITY ANIMAL PRODUCTS ARE A STEP FURTHER FROM THE DIRECT ENERGY OF THE
SUN, AS THEY EAT THE PLANTS AND DO NOT RECEIVE THEIR ENERGY FOR GROWTH FROM THE
SUNLIGHT ALONE. OTHER PRODUCTS ARE OFTEN PROCESSED MUCH MORE, DEPLETING THE QUALITY
OF ENERGY WITHIN THEM. HIGHLY SENSITIVE PEOPLE OFTEN FIND BENEFIT IN CONSUMING A FULLY
PLANT BASED DIET, OR A MAINLY PLANT BASED DIET. WHEN CHOOSING ANY KIND OF FOOD PRODUCT
CONSIDER OPTING FOR SUSTAINABLY SOURCED PRODUCTS.

USE HERBS AND SPICES WHEN COOKING, THEY CONTAIN MAGICKAL AND HEALING PROPERTIES
FOR THE BODY AND ENTIRE BEING. HERBS ARE THE LEAVES OF THE PLANT, SPICES COME FROM THE
ROOTS, BARK, AND SEEDS. STUDY THEM, GET TO KNOW THEIR PURPOSES AND THE COMBINATIONS
THAT TASTE AMAZING TOGETHER. YOU MAY COME TO FIND THAT YOUR FAVORITE MEALS ARE YOUR
FAVORITE NOT ONLY BECAUSE OF THE MAIN COMPONENTS USED, BUT BECAUSE OF THE HERBS AND
SPICES USED, CREATING THE OVERALL FLAVOR THAT YOU LOVE SO MUCH. WHEN TRYING NEW FOODS
IMPLEMENT THOSE HERBS AND SPICES TO BRING THE FLAVORS YOU LOVE INTO NEW DISHES!
THESE PLANTS CAN ALSO BE PURCHASED AND GROWN AS HOUSEPLANTS OR WITHIN THE GARDEN.

HYDRATION

WATER IS NATURALLY PURIFYING, CLEANSING AND HEALING.

AIM FOR AT LEAST EIGHT 8-OUNCE GLASSES,

WHICH IS THE SAME AS 2 LITERS,

OR 1 HALF-GALLON OF WATER PER DAY

BENEFITS:

AIDS DIGESTION

ENERGY AND STAMINA

ELEVATES MOOD AND VIBRATION

SUPPLE, CLEAR AND GLOWING SKIN

PROMOTES CARDIOVASCULAR HEALTH

QUALITY MUSCLE AND JOINT FUNCTION

CLEANSES YOUR BODY

WATER DETOXES THE BODY,

THUS IT WORKS TO CLEANSE THE AURA

[ADD 1 TBSP LEMON OR APPLE CIDER VINEGAR TO 8 OZ OF WATER 1X PER DAY]

HERBAL TEAS ARE ALSO WONDERFUL FOR THE HUMAN BODY TO CONSUME.

BLESSING ALL FOOD AND BEVERAGES IS A VERY POWERFUL PRACTICE
SINCE YOU WILL BE CONSUMING THE ITEM(S)
YOU ARE PLACING THE BLESSING / INTENTION UPON.

EXAMPLE:
I AM GRATEFUL FOR THIS FOOD AND DRINK.
THIS FOOD AND DRINK I AM NOW GOING TO CONSUME
WILL HEAL, ENERGIZE AND BLESS EVERY SINGLE FIBER OF MY BEING.

AS WITH OUR BODIES,
OUR MINDS & MANIFESTING POWERS
DESERVE A WARM UP
BEFORE WE START USING THEM FULL FORCE.

BEGIN BY
STATING YOUR INTENTION
[PRAYER/AFFIRMATION]
ALWAYS IN THE PRESENT TENSE
OF YOUR SOLUTION / DESIRE COMPLETELY MANIFESTED.
EXAMPLE: I AM GRATEFUL FOR ALL OF THE INSIGHT
I HAVE RECEIVED IN MY MEDITATION.
I AM NOW EFFORTLESSLY ABLE TO DEFINE
MY OWN PASSIONS AND DESIRES.
I KNOW THAT IN EACH MOMENT
I AM CREATING
MY DESIRED LIFE DESIGN.

THEN RECEIVE
[MEDITATE]
THIS IGNITES THE EFFORTLESSLY CREATIVE THETA BRAIN WAVE STATE,
ALLOWING IDEAS AND INSPIRATIONS TO FLOW
INTO YOUR MIND [SEEMINGLY FROM 'NOWHERE']

GO TO A PLACE YOU LOVE,
WHERE YOU REALLY **FEEL** YOU ARE YOUR MOST RELAXED, SINCERE SELF.
SOMETIMES YOU WILL RECEIVE INSIGHT OR INTUITION DURING MEDITATION,
OTHER TIMES IT COMES SHORTLY AFTER MEDITATION
WHEN YOU ARE STILL RELAXED,
OR IT MAY ALSO COME IN A MOMENT FURTHER DOWN THE ROAD.
REMEMBER:
INSIGHTS AND INTUITIONS CAN SINK INTO YOUR MIND AT ANY MOMENT.
DAY OR NIGHT.
THEY ARRIVE MOST OFTEN WHEN WE ARE RELAXED AND
PRESENT IN THE MOMENT, NOT OVER-STIMULATED OR OVERTHINKING.
CREATE YOUR OWN FAVORITE WAY(S) TO MEDITATE AND RECEIVE.

UTILIZE THESE NEXT FEW MEDITATIVE PAGES I HAVE CREATED
AND
CREATE YOUR OWN DESIGN WITH SIMILAR STRUCTURE.
I FIND THEM TO BE A VISION BOARD OF WORDS.
DO CREATE A VISION BOARD OF YOUR OWN,
OR A VISION BOARD SLIDESHOW ON YOUR PHONE,
OUT OF IMAGES REPRESENTING YOUR DESIRES,
THAT IGNITE THE FEELING STATES OF YOUR DESIRES FULFILLED.
SET AN ALARM TO VIEW YOUR IMAGES LEAST ONCE A DAY.

LET'S BEGIN EXTRACTING YOUR PERSONAL *passions & desires*

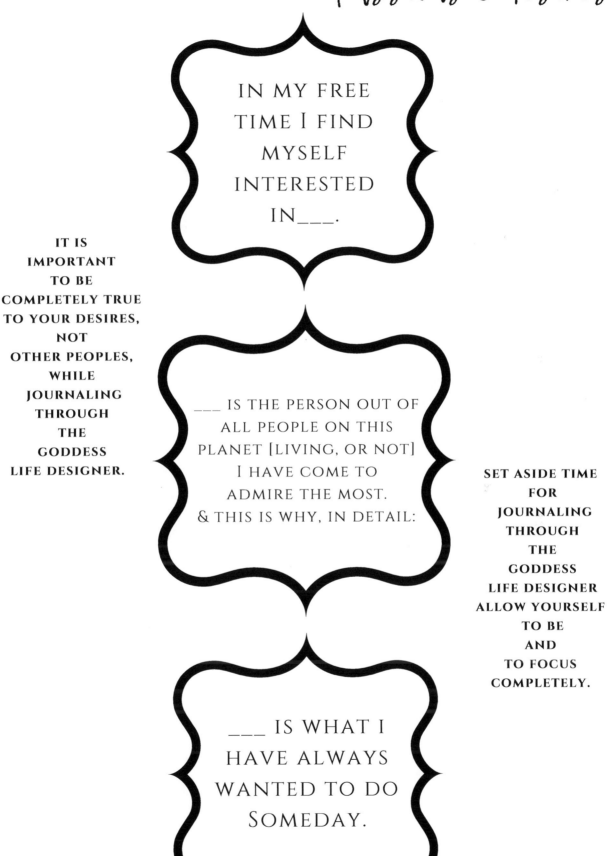

IN MY FREE TIME I FIND MYSELF INTERESTED IN___.

IT IS IMPORTANT TO BE COMPLETELY TRUE TO YOUR DESIRES, NOT OTHER PEOPLES, WHILE JOURNALING THROUGH THE GODDESS LIFE DESIGNER.

___ IS THE PERSON OUT OF ALL PEOPLE ON THIS PLANET [LIVING, OR NOT] I HAVE COME TO ADMIRE THE MOST. & THIS IS WHY, IN DETAIL:

SET ASIDE TIME FOR JOURNALING THROUGH THE GODDESS LIFE DESIGNER ALLOW YOURSELF TO BE AND TO FOCUS COMPLETELY.

___ IS WHAT I HAVE ALWAYS WANTED TO DO SOMEDAY.

TO FURTHER EXPOSE
YOUR INNERMOST *passions & desires*

I SPEND MY TIME DOING ___ BECAUSE I KNOW, FOR CERTAIN, I ALREADY HAVE ACCESS TO UNLIMITED FINANCIAL ABUNDANCE FOR LIFE.

MEDITATTE ON THESE &/OR SIMILAR QUESTIONS. CREATE YOUR OWN LIST OF QUESTIONS. REFLECT ON THEM OFTEN, IN ORDER TO STAY A L I G N E D

WRITE DOWN ALL THE DEAILS OF HOW YOU DESIRE YOUR LIFE TO BE IN THESE AREAS:

I HAVE MORE THAN I WILL EVER NEED FINICALLY FOR MY ENTIRE LIFETIME. THIS IS HOW I CHOOSE TO GIVE BACK:

_____

HEALTH
LOVE
WEALTH
ADVENTURE

I ALWAYS FOLLOW WHAT MAKES ME FEEL GOOD. I KNOW WHAT IS IT ABOUT CERTAIN THINGS THAT MAKES ME FEEL SO GOOD PARTAKING IN THEM. THESE THINGS LISTED:

_____

Your passions & desires are already inside of you, they always have been.

JOURNAL ON THESE PROMPTS:

I FEEL WARM, LOVED AND AT PEACE WHEN I AM:

I LOVE LEARNING ABOUT___/ I DESIRE TO KNOW MORE ABOUT___:

IN THE MORNING I AM INSPIRED TO WAKE UP BECAUSE I REMEMBER I AM GOING TO ___ TODAY:

**IF I WERE TO SUDDENLY FIND MYSELF AT THE END OF THIS LIFETIME
I WOULD HAVE WISHED I HAD THESE EXPERIENCES AND ADVENTURES:**

LIST ALL OF YOUR SKILLS AND ABILITIES:

LIST ANY SPECIFIC DRIVE(S) YOU HAVE FELT / DO FEEL WITHIN YOUR HEART:

THINK OF A SPORTS TEAM, OR GROUP OF ANY KIND.
ALL INDIVIDUALS OF THE TEAM / GROUP PLAY A ROLE IN THE OVERALL FUNCTION AND
SUCCESS. IF YOU WERE WILLINGLY ON A TEAM OR IN A GROUP YOU WOULD FEEL
THE INNATE DESIRE TO HAVE A PURPOSE,
TO CONTRIBUTE IN YOUR OWN UNIQUE WAY TO BOOST
YOUR TEAM'S / GROUP'S FUNCTION AND SUCCESS.
DOING SO FULFILLS A DEEP SENSE OF WORTH.
SEE LIFE IN THIS WAY.
HOW YOU ARE UNIQUELY CONTRIBUTING AND IMPACTING THE WORLD GENERATES A
SENSE OF WORTH AND FULFILLMENT
IN THE DEPTHS OF YOUR SOUL.
THE RESULT IS A FEELING OF GENUINE PURPOSE WITHIN YOUR LIFE.
THIS DOES NOT MEAN YOU MUST DO SOMETHING HUGE,
YOUR UNIQUENESS IS EXACTLY WHAT THE WORLD NEEDS MORE OF.
SO, DO WHAT MAKES YOU FEEL ALIVE, ENERGIZED AND EMPOWERED EACH DAY.
DIVERSITY IS BEAUTIFUL, IT ALLOWS HUMANITY TO TRULY THRIVE.
NOT A SINGLE PASSION IS INSIGNIFICANT.
ALSO RECOGNIZE THAT EACH INDIVIDUAL CAN HAVE MANY DIFFERENT PASSIONS AND
PURPOSES THROUGHOUT THEIR LIFETIME.
YOU DO NOT NEED TO KNOW ALL OF YOUR PASSIONS AND PURPOSES RIGHT NOW. SIMPLY
START WHERE YOU ARE WITH WHAT YOU ARE PASSIONATE ABOUT RIGHT NOW. AS YOU
MOVE FORWARD YOU WILL SOON BE ABLE TO REFLECT AND OBSERVE YOUR PASSIONS
AND YOURSELF EVOLVING AND CHANGING IN WAYS YOU WOULD NOT HAVE BEEN ABLE
TO PREDICT AT AN EARLIER TIME,
THERE IS IMMENSE BEAUTY EMBEDDED WITHIN
THE EVERY-CHANGING JOURNEY OF THIS HUMAN LIFETIME.

IF YOU HAVE MORE THAN ONE THING YOU FEEL PULLED TOWARDS
[WHETHER NOW OR AT A LATER TIME]:
PRIORITIZE. WRITE THEM ALL OUT ON A PIECE OF PAPER AND
SIT WITH YOUR OPTIONS ~ FEEL INTO THE ORDER OF IMPORTANCE.
~ ASK FOR GUIDANCE FROM YOUR HIGHEST VIBRATIONAL ANGELS AND GUIDES ~
YOU DO NOT HAVE TO THROW ANY OF THE OPTIONS AWAY,
JUST PRIORITIZE THEN, SO THAT YOU CAN WORK WITH ONE AT A TIME.
OR AT LEAST DIVIDE YOUR TIME APPROPRIATELY BETWEEN A SELECT FEW.
THIS ORDER OF IMPORTANCE CAN CHANGE AS YOU PLEASE,
THIS IS YOUR LIFE DESIGN ~ YOU ARE THE CREATOR ~
YOU MAKE THE CHANGES AS YOU DESIRE TO,
BUT DO HAVE A WRITTEN ORDER OF IMPORTANCE TO WORK WITH.
WHEN DECIDING YOUR ORDER OF IMPORTANCE THINK ON WHAT IS MOST IMPORTANT
TO YOU AND YOUR LIFE RIGHT NOW: IS IT FREEDOM? ADVENTURE?TIME? FINANCES?
HEALTH? LOVE? SECURITY? HOME LIFE? OTHER THINGS?

REVIEW ALL YOU HAVE JOURNALED IN REGARDS TO YOUR PASSIONS AND DESIRES.

SIT WITH THESE GOOD FEELINGS FOR A FEW MOMENTS OF BREATHING.

USE THE SPACE BELOW TO SUMMARIZE AND PRIORITIZE YOUR PREVIOUS JOURNALING.

PASSION [PLUS] GIVING VALUE TO OTHERS = TRUE BLISS AND ETERNAL SOUL FULFILLMENT.

RECOGNIZE THIS TRUTH:

IF SOMEONE [NO MATTER WHO IT IS] IS RESPONDING TO YOU, YOUR DREAMS, YOUR IDEAS, CHOSEN PATH, WHAT YOU ARE DOING IN LIFE, WHAT YOU DESIRE TO DO IN LIFE ETC. WITH EVEN THE SLIGHTEST AMOUNT OF DOUBT, FEAR, LOGICAL REASONS WHY THIS WILL NOT WORK, OR SIMPLY DO NOT BELIEVE IN YOU - THEY ARE HALTING YOUR GROWTH, YOUR HAPPINESS AND YOUR SOUL'S OPTIMAL FULFILLMENT. DO NOT TAKE THEIR OPINIONS PERSONALLY. THIS IS IN NO WAY A REFLECTION OF YOU, IT IS ENTIRELY A REFLECTION OF THEM. RECOGNIZE THAT IF YOU ARE SOMEONE WHO IS DEEPLY CONNECTED TO YOUR INNER VISIONS, AND YOU LOVE TO DREAM WITHOUT LIMITS, YOU MUST SURROUND YOURSELF WITH OTHERS WHO FULLY SUPPORT YOU. IF YOU CANNOT STAY AWAY FROM UNSUPPORTIVE SOURCES THEN DO NOT EXPOSE YOUR DREAMS AND IDEAS TO THEM. THIS IS OFTEN DISGUISED AS 'I JUST WANT TO PROTECT YOU FROM LOSSES OR PAIN' AND OTHER 'LOGICAL REASONS'. ALSO RECOGNIZE THAT WHEN ANY PERSON EXPRESSES THESE THINGS TO YOU OR DOES NOT BELIEVE IN YOU AND YOUR DREAMS IT IS SOLEY BECAUSE THEY ARE INCAPABLE OF DOING / ACHIEVING THIS THING. THIS ISN'T IMPLYING THAT THEY ARE 'LESS THAN' YOU OR ANYTHING ALONG THOSE LINES. IT IS SIMPLY BECAUSE WE ARE EACH SO UNIQUE, AND THEY MAY NOT UNDERSTAND YOUR UNIQUENESS BECAUSE IT IS NOT WITHIN THEM. THIS UNIQUENESS IS YOUR POWER. THE THINGS IN YOUR HEART ARE NOT RANDOM, THEY ARE YOUR CALLING. THESE ARE THE THINGS THAT WILL PROVIDE YOU WITH THE DEEPEST LEVELS OF SATISFACTION AND HAPPINESS IN LIFE. YOU MUST TAKE THE RISKS AND BE SELF-EMPOWERED ON YOUR JOURNEY. YOU MUST BELIEVE YOU WILL BE SUPPORTED BY YOUR DIVINE LIFE SOURCE IN ACHIEVING ALL YOU ENVISION, AND YOU WILL BE. BE CONSCIOUS AND AWARE, DO NOT ALLOW OTHERS' OPINIONS TO DICTATE YOUR LIFE JOURNEY AND YOUR SOUL'S EVOLUTION. YOU ARE PURE MAGICK AND POWER. EVERY SINGLE THING ABOUT YOU IS SIGNIFICANT, STOP PLAYING SMALL. CHOOSE TO PERSIST IN THE DIRECTION OF YOUR DREAMS. YOUR SELF-EMPOWERMENT WILL ONLY GROW STRONGER IN THE PROCESS, AND THEN GUESS WHAT? NO ONE WILL EVER BE ABLE TO MOVE YOU OR IMPACT YOU WITH THEIR PERSONAL OPINIONS BECAUSE AT THIS POINT YOU WILL HAVE BECOME SO SOLID WITHIN YOUR OWN SELF THAT YOU SIMPLY WILL NOT CARE WHAT ANY LOWER VIBRATIONS MAY HAVE TO SAY. AND NOT ONLY THAT, BUT YOU WILL ALWAYS SEE THE TRUTH FOR WHAT IT IS: EACH PERSON'S OPINION IS ONLY A REFLECTION OF THEIR INNERMOST SELF. YOU WILL BEGIN TO FEEL A LEVEL OF COMPASSION TOWARDS THEM BECAUSE NOW YOU REALIZE THIS IS HOW THEY TALK TO THEMSELVES, THIS IS HOW THEY LIVE LIFE ALL THE TIME. THESE ARE THEIR LIMITS, NOT YOURS. OTHERS ARE ONLY ABLE TO PERCEIVE YOU FROM THEIR PERSONAL LEVEL OF AWARENESS, THIS HAS NOTHING TO DO WITH YOU OR YOUR PERSONAL LEVEL OF AWARENESS. ALWAYS KEEP THIS IN MIND AND DO NOT TAKE ANYTHING PERSONALLY. IF YOU ARE IN A POSITION WHERE A PERSON OR GROUP OF OTHERS IS SPEAKING THEIR LOW VIBRATIONAL OPINION, JUST REPLY WITH A SIMPLE: THANK YOU FOR YOUR OPINION. MEANWHILE REMIND YOURSELF THAT THEIR OPINION IS ONLY A REFLECTION OF THEM, EVEN IF IT IS DIRECTED AT YOU. IF THEY CONTINUE ON AFTER THIS: CALMLY ASK THEM WHAT THEIR INTENTION IS. RESPOND WITH ANOTHER THANK YOU FOR YOUR OPINION, LETS AGREE TO DISAGREE AND CLOSE THE CONVERSATION WITH THAT. DISAGREEMENTS REQUIRE A RESPONSE IN ORDER TO CONTINUE. IT IS A HEALTHY SIGN OF TRUE INNER STRENGTH TO BE ABLE TO AGREE TO DISAGREE AND CLOSE THE CONVERSATION WITHOUT THE NEED TO RESPOND, WITHOUT THE NEED TO HAVE THE LAST WORDS, WHILE REMAINING TRUE TO YOUR OWN SOUL AND UNAFFECTED BY ANOTHER'S OPINION. CALM IS A SUPERPOWER. REMEMBER THAT.

Manifesting Explained

Manifestation is the innate inner power constantly operating within each human. No one is exempt, it does not need to be turned on and it cannot be shut off. It can be explained completely through all 12 universal laws. These laws are each explained in detail at the end of this book. The current reality you are living in is the physical manifestation of all your predominant thoughts, emotions and feelings you have embodied throughout your entire life, up to this point in time. Your future will inevitably take its manifested form based upon all of your predominant thoughts, emotions and feelings you are experiencing right now. Yes, you are creating your future through thought, emotion and feeling right now. The universal laws do not skip a beat or wait for your recognition. You can predict your future by designing it. You can design it by defining what exactly you want, and then ever-increasingly embodying the thoughts, emotions and feelings that are in harmony with the outcome you have decided you desire to have manifest into your physical reality. Manifestation is not limited to a single area or few areas of life, although many times we hear of it in correlation with money or love, it is not bound to just these things. It is applicable to every area of life. The Goddess Life Designer is formulated around extracting your deepest desires and most authentic self. When you are truly at your most authentic and purely fulfilled state you will attract into your life a greater quality of everything you desire. Far greater than you would have in a state of forced positivity or through following a path that does not truly resonate with the depths of your own soul. You do not need to gain anything in order to manifest your dream life, but rather get rid off all the things that are not serving your own unique and powerful soul. Manifesting your best life is not about becoming better than anyone else. Ever. Period. It is about choosing to reveal your own authenticity. Choosing to fulfill your own deepest passions and desires so that you can live your own unique desired life design. When you are living within your desired life design you are also able to give quality and value to others, and the entire world as a collective, simply through being you. Your most authentic version of you. The most fulfilled version of you. This is because you are highlighting your strengths and evolving your divine, unique gifts. Recognize that this does not mean you need to accumulate anything in order to be your most authentic and fulfilled version of you. It is, paradoxically, more so about the removal of all things that are not truly you. Which will allow you to realize that your most authentic and fulfilled self thrives when you are surrounded only by what you love and not distracted by excess of other things that do not fulfill you at the core of your being. The frequency of your desires fulfilled is not hard to match. In your most pure and true state you are the highest vibrational frequency there is. The vibrational frequency of peace is in fact one of the highest vibrational frequencies a human can embody. High energy does not equate to high vibrational frequencies - this is important to realize! High energy can also be the result of low vibrational frequencies. Your truest embodiment of satisfaction and peace is your highest vibrational frequency. This will provide you with energy at your core ~ true inspiration ~ this will be a pure, balanced, harmonious energy - not a chaotic and unbalanced or forced energy. The only thing holding your vibrational frequency down during this human experience is resistance [often in the form of limiting beliefs]. So, give yourself permission to release resistance when it begins to arise. In simply holding the intent to do so [and following through when the opportunities arise] you will gradually let go of all resistance and ever-increasingly become a harmonious vibrational match with your desires fulfillment.

MASTERING YOUR INNATE MANIFESTATION POWER IS A HUGE INVESTMENT IN YOURSELF, A LIFE CHANGING INVESTMENT, THE MOST POWERFUL INVESTMENT YOU WILL EVER MAKE.

IT TAKES DEDICATION, PATIENCE AND PERSEVERANCE TO MASTER HARNESSING THE POWER THAT IS ALREADY [AND ALWAYS HAS BEEN] WORKING WITHIN YOUR LIFE, BUT IS WELL WORTH IT AS THE POWER OF YOUR MIND IS MUCH STRONGER THAN THE CONCEPT OF TIME, OR ANY AMOUNT OF HARD WORK / WORK HOURS YOU COULD EVER POSSIBLY PUT IN, EVEN IF YOU SPENT YOUR ENTIRE LIFETIME WORKING. SO, BLESS YOUR LIFETIME THROUGH MASTERING YOUR INNATE POWER OF MANIFESTATION. UTILIZING THE GODDESS LIFE DESIGNER GUIDEBOOK EACH DAY WILL KEEP YOU ALIGNED AND EMPOWERED IN YOUR JOURNEY OF MASTERING YOUR POWER OF MANIFESTATION. AREAS OF LIFE TO CONSIDER WHILE EMBARKING ON YOUR JOURNEY OF HARNESSED INTENTION AND MANIFESTATION: HEALTH, WEALTH, LOVE, RELATIONSHIPS, MONEY, CAREER, ADVENTURE, GROWTH, CREATIVITY, ENVIRONMENT. THESE ARE JUST A FEW OF THE MAIN CATEGORIES, HARNESSED INTENTION AND MANIFESTATION CAN BE APPLIED TO ANY AREA OF LIFE YOU CAN THINK OF. THE MOON WILL NOW BE YOUR FOCAL POINT AS YOU TRANSFORM AND EMBODY YOUR DESIRED EVOLUTION FOR THIS LIFETIME. THE GODDESS LIFE DESIGNER IS FORMULATED TO ALIGN EACH OF US WITH THE 8 MOON PHASES, FORMING A 30 DAY MANIFESTATION CYCLE [EACH MOON CYCLE IS APPROXIMATELY 29.5 DAYS]. THERE ARE 13 MOON CYCLES PER YEAR. THE GODDESS LIFE DESIGNER PROVIDES ENJOYABLE, EFFORTLESS ALIGNMENT IN SUPPORT OF YOUR OWN MOST FULFILLING LIFE DESIGN. THE 8 MOON PHASES ARE EACH COVERED IN DETAIL AND THE 13 MOON CYCLES OF THE YEAR ARE ALSO COVERED, WITH DATES FOR EACH PHASE DURING THAT CYCLE. PROVIDING YOU WITH EFFORTLESS ALIGNMENT. DAILY PAGES ARE ALSO PROVIDED FOR MORNING AND END OF DAY REFLECTION, TO KEEP YOU ALIGNED EACH DAY.

THE FOLLOWING PAGES WILL REQUIRE YOUR COMPLETE FOCUS AND ATTENTION. THEY ARE DESIGNED TO GUIDE YOU AS YOU ESTABLISH A STRONG FOUNDATION FOR MANIFESTING YOUR DESIRED LIFE DESIGN. SET ASIDE ENOUGH TIME TO FULLY IMMERSE YOURSELF IN EACH EXERCISE. DO NOT SKIP OVER THEM! THEY ARE A VERY CRUCIAL STEP IN THE PROCESS OF HARNESSING YOUR INNATE POWER OF MANIFESTATION.

IT IS IMPORTANT TO NOTE:
WE CANNOT FORCE OTHERS TO CHANGE OR DO INNER WORK. IT IS ENTIRELY A PERSONAL CHOICE AND SHOULD BE DONE ONLY WITH ONESELF, NEVER FOR ANYONE ELSE OR WITH ANYONE ELSE. INNER WORK IS MEANT TO BE PRIVATE SO THAT IT IS RAW, PURE AND TRUE. ATTEMPTING TO PERSUADE ANOTHER TO DO INNER WORK IS LIKELY TO ONLY PUSH THEM FURTHER AWAY FORM THE IDEA, THEIR JOURNEY WILL LEAD THEM INTO DOING INNER WORK WHEN THE TIMING IS RIGHT. IF ANOTHER ASKS FOR SUPPORT, BY ALL MEANS LOVE THEM UNCONDITIONALLY AND SUPPORT THEM. SHOW THEM YOU BELIEVE IN THEM AND SHOW THEM THE TOOLS THEY CAN USE TO GUIDE THEM INWARD, IN THE RIGHT DIRECTION. BUT MAKE SURE THEY RECOGNIZE THEIR PROGRESS IS ENTIRELY RELIANT ON THEIR OWN SELF-DISCIPLINE AND DESIRE TO CHANGE. WE SIMPLY CANNOT CHANGE ANOTHER BECAUSE WE CANNOT THINK AND FEEL FOR THEM. THEY HAVE FREE WILL AND THEY ARE THE CREATOR OF THEIR OWN REALITY. TELLING ANOTHER WE CAN CHANGE THEM WILL ONLY LEAD TO DISAPPOINTMENT AND EVEN ANGER. THIS IS ALSO LIKELY TO LEAD OURSELF INTO LOWER FREQUENCIES AS RESULT. IF SOMEONE TRULY DESIRES TO PARTAKE IN INNER WORK TO CHANGE THEIR LIFE THEY WILL RECOGNIZE THIS ON THEIR OWN AND EMBODY THE SELF DISCIPLE TO DO SO. FORCING THIS ON ANOTHER IS NOT RECOMMENDED AS THIS IS LIKELY TO PUSH THEM AWAY FROM PARTAKING IN INNER WORK FOR A LONG PERIOD OF TIME. BE A GUIDE WHEN ASKED. DO NOT ATTEMPT TO INTRODUCE THE CONCEPT WITHOUT BEING ASKED. IT IS ALSO NOT WISE TO ATTEMPT TO HELP ANOTHER WORK THROUGH THEIR INNER WORK, IT IS A VERY DEEP AND PERSONAL PRACTICE. NO MATTER HOW WELL WE BELIEVE WE KNOW SOMEONE WE WILL NEVER KNOW THEM LIKE THEY KNOW THEIR OWN SELF, AND LIKEWISE NO ONE WILL EVER TRULY KNOW AND UNDERSTAND OURSELF LIKE WE KNOW OURSELF. THAT IS PRECISELY WHY THIS SHOULD BE KEPT EXCLUSIVE AND PERSONAL. IF THIS IS ATTEMPTED FOR YOU BY ANOTHER, OR BY YOU FOR ANOTHER, THE RESULTS WILL NOT BE NEAR AS FULFILLING AND CAN LEAD ONE TO DISREGARDING THE POTENCY OF TRUE INNER WORK ALTOGETHER. SO, FOCUS ON YOURSELF ONLY. ALLOW OTHERS TO BE, JUST OBSERVE THEM WITHOUT JUDGEMENT, DO NOT ABSORB THEIR ENERGY OR THEIR JOURNEY.
WE ARE EACH ON OUR OWN JOURNEY WITH UNIQUE PURPOSE.
WE MUST RESPECT EACH OTHER'S JOURNEY AND BOUNDARIES.

WRITE DOWN EVERY SINGLE PROBLEM
YOU HAVE WITHIN YOUR LIFE.
BOTH BIG AND SMALL, WRITE THEM ALL.

WRITE DOWN THE IDEAL SOLUTION
TO EACH PROBLEM YOU HAVE LISTED.

NOW, CREATE A PRESENT TENSE THANK YOU STATEMENT FOR EACH IDEAL SOLUTION.
DO SO AS IF IT HAS ALREADY BEEN PERFECTLY ALIGNED WITH
AND FULLY MANIFESTED INTO YOUR LIFE.
WHAT ARE YOU THANKFUL THE SOLUTION HAS DONE FOR YOU AND YOUR LIFE?

TRULY FEEL SATISFIED AND AT PEACE WHILE WRITING EACH OF THESE STATEMENTS.
YOUR FEELING STATE CREATES THE VIBRATION YOU ARE EMANATING,
SO CREATE THE VIBRATION YOU DESIRE TO RECEIVE.
VISUALIZE AND REALLY FEEL INTO THIS.
EMBODY THIS FULFILLMENT WITHIN YOURSELF FULLY.

WORDS ON THEIR OWN ARE SYMBOLS. COMBINE WORDS WITH EMOTION AND FEELING.
FEEL THE GRATITUDE, JOY AND PEACE THESE STATEMENTS BRING TO YOUR LIFE. REFER TO THIS
LIST OFTEN, ESPECIALLY IF YOU ARE FEELING OVERWHELMED OR DOWN. IT WILL LIFT YOUR
VIBRATION AND SPEED UP YOUR MANIFESTATION PROCESS.

YOUR DEFINITION OF SUCCESS

KEEP IN MIND, SUCCESS DOES NOT ALWAYS MEAN MONEY, FAME, ETC.
KNOW YOUR OWN DEFINITION OF SUCCESS WELL.
EACH PERSON DESERVES TO HAVE THEIR OWN TRUE DEFINITION OF SUCCESS,
THAT DEFINITION IS WHAT THEY CONSIDER THEIR OPTIMAL SUCCESS IN LIFE.
THE DEFINITION OF THEIR DREAM LIFE, THE LIFE DESIGN THEY DESIRE TO LIVE WITHIN.
KNOW YOUR DEFINITION OF SUCCESS WELL SO THAT YOU KNOW THE EXACT DIRECTION YOU DESIRE YOUR LIFE
TO GO. DEFINE WHAT YOU WANT SO THAT YOU CAN MOVE TOWARDS THAT. WORK YOUR HARNESSED, INTERNAL
MAGICK THROUGHOUT THE PROCESS. ANY GIVEN DEFINITION OF SUCCESS IS NOT 'RIGHT' OR 'WRONG'
IT SIMPLY MUST BE TRUE AND FULFILLING FOR THE PERSON LIVING BY IT.
KNOW YOUR OWN DEFINITION OF SUCCESS,
AND LIVE BY YOUR OWN DEFINITION OF SUCCESS.
LET OTHERS LIVE IN THEIR OWN DEFINITION OF SUCCESS.
YOU ARE AN INFINITE BEING WITH INFINITE POSSIBILITIES.
TAKE THE TIME TO JOURNAL YOUR PERSONAL DEFINITION OF SUCCESS.
DO NOT ALLOW OTHER PEOPLE'S DEFINITIONS OF SUCCESS TO INFLUENCE YOUR OWN.
NO ONE'S DEFINITION OF SUCCESS IS WRONG.
SO, RESPECT OTHER PEOPLE'S DEFINITIONS.
THEY ARE NOT WRONG IN THEIR OWN PERSONAL DEFINITION.
ALSO, DO NOT BE PERSUADED TO CHANGE YOUR OWN. YOUR OWN IS ALWAYS RIGHT FOR YOU.
DO NOT LET OTHERS TELL YOUR THAT YOURS IS 'WRONG' AND/OR SHOULD BE ADJUSTED.
YOUR DEFINITION IS PERFECT.
EVERYONE IS DIFFERENT.
RESPECT THAT.
FOCUS ON STAYING TRUE TO YOUR OWN SELF.
MAYBE YOU DESIRE LARGE AMOUNTS OF FINANCIAL ABUNDANCE AND LAVISH THINGS.
MAYBE YOU DESIRE TO OWN VERY FEW THINGS AND TO LIVE IN THE WOODS FAR FROM ANYONE ELSE AT ALL.
MAYBE YOU DESIRE A COMBINATION, OR SOMETHING ENTIRELY DIFFERENT.
MAYBE YOU SIMPLY DESIRE FREEDOM TO SPEND ALL YOUR TIME WITH LOVED ONES.
MAYBE YOU DESIRE TO ALWAYS BE IN THE SUNSHINE.
MAYBE YOU DESIRE TO ALWAYS BE IN THE RAIN.
MAYBE YOU DESIRE TO TRAVEL THE EARTH.
MAYBE YOU DESIRE TO STAY HOME.
MAYBE YOU DESIRE _____ OR ____.
JUST KNOW THAT YOU ARE NOT WRONG FOR YOUR DESIRES
AS LONG AS THEY ARE TRULY THE MOST FULFILLING TO YOU.
THERE IS NO JUDGEMENT, YOU DESERVE ALL THE SUCCESS YOU DESIRE.
TAKE THE TIME TO DEFINE YOUR DEFINITION OF SUCCESS SO THAT YOU CAN
EVER-INCREASINGLY GET TO KNOW AND EMBODY THE FEELINGS
OF ALREADY HAVING YOUR DESIRED SUCCESS,
AND THEREFORE MANIFEST YOUR DESIRED LIFE DESIGN.

HAVE A WRITTEN COPY OF WHAT SUCCESS MEANS TO YOU,
SO THAT YOU CAN REFLECT ON IT WHEN YOU WANT TO / NEED TO.
THIS ALLOWS YOU TO MEASURE HOW CLOSE YOU ARE TO THAT DEFINITION,
AND KNOW WHEN YOU HAVE ACHIEVED IT.
IT ALSO ALLOWS YOU TO ALIGN EACH AREA OF YOUR LIFE ACCORDINGLY.

ASK YOURSELF:

WHAT WOULD THE VERSION OF MYSELF WHO HAS ACHIEVED MY DEFINITION OF SUCCESS
BE DOING EACH DAY THAT I AM NOT PRESENTLY DOING IN MY LIFE?
WHAT WOULD THIS SUCCESSFUL VERSION OF MYSELF NOT BE DOING ANYMORE
THAT I AM PRESENTLY DOING?
MAKE A LIST OF THE THINGS YOU DO IN YOUR PRESENT DAY TO DAY LIFE
AND THEN MAKE A LIST OF THE THINGS YOU WILL BE DOING IN YOUR LIFE WITH YOUR DEFINITION OF SUCCESS
ACHIEVED. ONCE YOU DO SO,
BEGIN TO TAKE ACTION IN ADJUSTING YOUR LIFE ACCORDINGLY WITHIN EACH MOMENT.
INCREASINGLY BECOME THAT PERSON NOW, NOT SOMEDAY DOWN THE ROAD. START NOW.
A YEAR FROM TODAY YOU WILL HAVE WISHED YOU STARTED TODAY.

SUBCONSCIOUS BELIEFS

IMAGINE THE MIND AS AN ICEBERG.

THE SUBCONSCIOUS MIND IS THE UNDERWATER POTION [95% OF THE MIND]
AND THE CONSCIOUS MIND IS THE ABOVE WATER PORTION [5% OF THE MIND].

THE CONSCIOUS MIND PERTAINS TO WHAT YOU ARE AWARE YOU ARE PERCEIVING AND THINKING, THE SUBCONSCIOUS IS OPERATING AS A FOUNDATION FOR THE CONSCIOUS THINKING WE DO. IT IS VERY WISE AND RECEPTIVE TO WHAT WE FEEL. IT IS CONSTANTLY AT WORK, SUPPORTING OUR THOUGHTS, EMOTIONS AND FEELINGS WE CONSCIOUSLY PERCEIVE OURSELVES EXPERIENCING. IT IS BUILD UPON THE BELIEFS OUR LIFE EXPERIENCES AND TEACHINGS HAVE CONDITIONED US TO PERCEIVE AS TRUE. EACH PERSON'S SUBCONSCIOUS MIND IS COMPOSED OF BOTH EMPOWERING AND LIMITING BELIEFS. THE PERCENTAGE OF EMPOWERING AND LIMITING BELIEFS THAT COMPOSE THE SUBCONSCIOUS MIND WILL VARY FOR EACH INDIVIDUAL. THESE SUBCONSCIOUS BELIEFS CAN EASILY GO UNRECOGNIZED FOR AN ENTIRE LIFETIME, BUT THEY CAN ALSO BE UNCOVERED AND TRANSFORMED AT THE WILL AND SELF DISCIPLINE OF THE INDIVIDUAL IN A VERY SHORT AMOUNT OF TIME. IT IS IMPORTANT TO RECOGNIZE THAT THE SUBCONSCIOUS MIND DOES NOT HAVE THE INTENTION OF SABOTAGING OUR LIFE, IT SIMPLY REINFORCES THE BELIEFS WE HAVE ABSORBED AS TRUE. THUS, OUR CONSCIOUS MIND PERCEIVES AND REACTS TO LIFE AS A RESULT OF OUR OWN SUBCONSCIOUS BELIEFS, OFTEN IN A WAY THAT SAYS 'THAT ISN'T POSSIBLE', [INSERT ANY LIMITING / EMPOWERING BELIEF]. IT IS THE REASON WHY WE EACH FEEL OUR BELIEFS ARE ABSOLUTELY CORRECT, AND SO WE GO ABOUT LIVING LIFE BASED UPON OUR BELIEFS BEING ABSOLUTELY CORRECT. THIS IS ALSO WHY WE ARE DRAWN TO AND RESONATE WITH PEOPLE WHO HAVE THE SAME OR SIMILAR BELIEFS, THEY REAFFIRM OUR OWN SUBCONSCIOUS BELIEFS AND THAT IS COMFORTING TO US. BE CONSCIOUS OF WHO YOU ARE SURROUNDING YOURSELF WITH, FOR WE UNDOUBTABLY [FULLY OR PARTIALLY] ABSORB / ARE INFLUENCED BY THE SUBCONSCIOUS BELIEFS OF THOSE AROUND US. ENJOY OTHERS AS THEY ARE. SAVOR THE MOMENTS WITH THEM, OBSERVE THEM, RATHER THAN ABSORBING THEM AND ALL OF THEIR BELIEFS. FILTER THE BELIEFS YOU ACCEPT AS TRUE AND NOT TRUE. ALLOW OTHERS TO BE AS THEY ARE. ALSO REMAIN TRUE TO YOUR OWN SELF. OBSERVE THEIR ENERGY AND AURA. BE OPEN MINDED. LISTEN TO UNDERSTAND. ONLY GIVE OPINIONS / ADVICE WHEN ASKED.

THE SUBCONSCIOUS MIND DOES NOT DISTINGUISH BETWEEN THE THINGS YOU CONSCIOUSLY DESIRE OR DO NOT DESIRE. IT JUST ACCEPTS EVERYTHING, AND SUPPORTS THOSE THINGS. IT IS NOT GOING TO ARGUE WITH WHAT YOU FEED TO IT. IT DOES NOT HOLD BIAS TO WHAT YOU THINK AND FEEL, IT SIMPLY SUPPORTS EVERYTHING YOU THINK AND FEEL. IT IS NOT 'OUT TO GET YOU' OR 'GOING TO SAVE YOU'. IT IS NEITHER A HERO OR A VILLAIN. IT HAS NO FILTER FOR DEFINING WHAT IS BENEFITTING YOU OR HINDERING YOU. THAT IS WHY IT IS IMPORTANT TO THINK AND FEEL ON THE FREQUENCY OF WHAT YOU DO DESIRE, NOT ON THE FEAR / WORRY OF WHAT YOU DO NOT DESIRE. IT LOVES TO SUPPORT YOU, AND DOES SO IN EVERY MOMENT. SEE YOUR THOUGHTS AND FEELINGS AS SEEDS YOU ARE PLACING IN IT. IT LOVES TO SUPPORT YOU, AND DOES SO THROUGH ACCEPTING EVERY SEED YOU PLACE IN IT AS TRUTH. THESE TRUTHS THEN SURFACE WITHIN EACH INDIVIDUAL'S CONSCIOUS ACTIONS AND REACTIONS TO LIFE. THIS IS WHY EMPOWERING AFFIRMATIONS AND QUESTIONS ARE SO POTENT IN TRAINING THE SUBCONSCIOUS MIND TO SUPPORT YOUR OWN DESIRED LIFE DESIGN.

IS THERE ANYTHING YOU WOULD DO / COULD DO IN LIFE THAT WOULD ALIGN YOU WITH YOUR MOST AUTHENTIC VERSION OF YOU IF YOU HAD DIFFERENT BELIEFS SUPPORTING YOU?

SUBCONSCIOUS LIMITING BELIEFS ARE THE BELIEFS YOU HAVE ABSORBED OR CREATED THROUGHOUT YOUR LIFETIME THAT LIMIT YOU FROM ACHIEVING YOUR PERSONAL DEFINITION OF SUCCESS. IT IS VERY IMPORTANT THAT YOU ARE GENTLE WITH YOURSELF WHEN UNCOVERING AND RELEASING EACH OF YOUR SUBCONSCIOUS LIMITING BELIEFS. YOUR SUBCONSCIOUS LIMITING BELIEFS ARE THE PATTERNS AND THE OVERALL STORY YOU LIVE BY DAY TO DAY WITHIN YOUR MIND, AND THEY EXTERNALIZE INTO YOUR WAKING REALITY. THEY HAVE [AND CONTINUE TO] SHAPE YOUR REALITY AS YOU KNOW IT BECAUSE THEY ARE THE SOURCE OF YOUR PERCEPTIONS, BELIEFS, REACTIONS AND IDEAS. OVERALL, THEY DETERMINE HOW YOU INTERACT WITH ANYONE OR ANYTHING IN LIFE.

EACH HUMAN BEING HAS A SUBCONSCIOUS MIND
AND THE MAJORITY OF THAT SUBCONSCIOUS MIND
TAKES FORM IN THE EARLY YEARS OF LIFE [YEARS 0-7].
DURING THIS TIME THE SUBCONSCIOUS MIND ABSORBS
ALL INFORMATION, TEACHINGS, SOCIETAL NORMS
AND SOCIETAL CONDITIONING AS TRUTH.

THE SOURCES OF THIS INFORMATION VARY WITHIN EACH INDIVIDUAL,
BUT THE MOST COMMON SOURCES ARE:
PARENTS, THE PEOPLE WHO RAISED YOU, THE PEOPLE WHO INFLUENCED YOU,
PAST EXPERIENCES, AND WHICHEVER CULTURE/SOCIETY/RELIGION YOU ARE BORN INTO.
AND RECOGNIZE THAT ALL OF THE SOURCES ALSO HAVE SUBCONSCIOUS MINDS,
THOSE SUBCONSCIOUS MINDS HAVE ALSO BEEN SHAPED BY OTHERS WHO CAME BEFORE
THEM, IT IS NOT THEIR FAULT FOR TEACHING YOU THE LIMITING BELIEFS.

IF YOU HAVE CHILDREN: BE MINDFUL AND AWARE OF WHAT YOU ARE PLACING AS TRUTH
WITHIN THEIR SUBCONSCIOUS MINDS, BLESS THEM EARLY ON WITH EMPOWERING BELIEFS.

'BY THE TIME A PERSON HAS REACHED THE AGE OF 35 THEY HAVE
A MEMORIZED SET OF BEHAVIORS, EMOTIONAL REACTIONS, AND THOUGHT PATTERNS THAT
HAVE BECOME 95% OF THEIR IDENTITY . THE GREATEST HABIT TO BREAK HAS THEN BECOME
BREAKING THE HABIT OF BEING ONESELF. BY REPEATING THE SAME ROUTINES DAY AFTER
DAY, WE BEGIN TO HARD WIRE OUR BRAIN INTO VERY SPECIFIC PATTERNS THAT REFLECT
OUR EXTERNAL WORLD, SO TO EFFECT CHANGE WE HAVE TO THINK BEYOND
THE ENVIRONMENT AND CONDITIONS IN OUR LIFE.'
- DR. JOE DISPENZA
[HOW TO CREATE CHANGE AND A NEW REALITY FOR ONESELF.
COMBINING THE FIELDS OF QUANTUM PHYSICS, NEUROSCIENCE, BIOLOGY, AND GENETICS.]

EACH INDIVIDUAL HAS BETWEEN 50,000 - 70,000 THOUGHTS PER DAY, AND APPROXIMATELY 98% OF THESE THOUGHTS ARE EXACTLY THE SAME AS THE DAY BEFORE. THIS PERCENTAGE IS LESS IF WE HAVE A LIFE CHANGE OR A MAJOR EVENT OCCUR, BUT ON AN AVERAGE DAY TO DAY BASIS THIS PERCENTAGE IS VERY ACCURATE. PAST AND PRESENT CIRCUMSTANCES IN OUR LIFE EVER-INCREASINGLY DEFINE THE PATTERNS OF OUR LIFE. PERSONAL LIFE PATTERNS STRONGLY INFLUENCE OUR PERSONAL SUBCONSCIOUS BELIEFS. CONSCIOUS THERAPY CAN VERY EASILY CONTINUE ON FOR A VERY LONG TIME, EVEN AN ENTIRE LIFETIME, BECAUSE THE SUBCONSCIOUS MIND IS SO MUCH MORE POWERFUL THAN THE CONSCIOUS MIND. 95% OF OUR PATTERNS, ACTIONS, THOUGHTS, FEELINGS, BELIEFS, ETC. COME FROM THE SUBCONSCIOUS, WHILE THE REMAINING 5% COME FROM OUR CONSCIOUS MIND. WE LIKE TO 'CONSCIOUSLY THINK' WE ARE IN CONTROL, BUT IN REALITY OUR CONSCIOUS MIND IS ONLY DETERMINING A VERY SMALL PERCENTAGE OF OUR LIFE. IT IS ACTING AND REACTING AS RESULT OF WHAT IS WITHIN OUR SUBCONSCIOUS MIND. HOWEVER, THAT DOES NOT MEAN OUR CONSCIOUS THINKING IS INSIGNIFICANT. OUR CONSCIOUS PRESENCE IN EACH MOMENT WE ARE EXPERIENCING IS BOTH CRUCIAL AND IMPORTANT BECAUSE THIS ALLOWS US TO MONITOR THE THOUGHTS, EMOTIONS AND FEELINGS WE EXPERIENCING IN THAT MOMENT. THUS, WE ARE ABLE TO CONSCIOUSLY RECOGNIZE WHAT OUR SUBCONSCIOUS MIND IS RELEASING TO US, AND WHAT WE ARE FEEDING TO IT THROUGHOUT OUR THOUGHTS / SPOKEN WORDS AND FEELINGS. WE ARE THEN ABLE TO CONSCIOUSLY DISREGARD THE THOUGHTS AND BELIEFS THAT DO NOT SERVE OUR DESIRED LIFE DESIGN, AND EMBODY THOSE THAT DO SERVE OUR DESIRED LIFE DESIGN. OVER TIME WE BECOME A NATURAL AT CONSCIOUSLY RECOGNIZING THE SUBCONSCIOUS PATTERNS THAT ARE PRESENT WITHIN OUR OWN LIFE. THE MORE CONSCIOUSLY AWARE WE BECOME THE MORE WE TRAIN OUR SUBCONSCIOUS SYSTEM TO OPERATE THROUGH EMPOWERING THOUGHTS, EMOTIONS, FEELINGS AND BELIEFS AS OUR TRUTH. OVER TIME THE POWERFUL SUBCONSCIOUS WILL BE OPERATING IN FULL SUPPORT OF OUR DESIRED LIFE DESIGN. THE 95% AND THE 5% WILL BE WORKING TOGETHER SO THAT WE ARE 100% SUPPORTIVE OF LIVING THE LIFE DESIGN WE PERSONALLY DESIRE. THIS IS WHY IT IS SO INCREDIBLY CRUCIAL TO UNCOVER AND UNDERSTAND WHAT OUR SUBCONSCIOUS MIND BELIEVES. ALSO RECOGNIZE THAT MEMORIES FROM PAST EVENTS AND CIRCUMSTANCES ARE STORED WITHIN THE CELLS OF YOUR BODY AND FEEL ABSOLUTELY REAL TO YOUR SUBCONSCIOUS, AS IF THESE EVENTS AND CIRCUMSTANCES ARE HAPPENING TO YOU NOW, NOT IN THE PAST. THIS IS BECAUSE THEY HAVE BEEN STORED AT A CELLULAR LEVEL, WITHIN THE CELLULAR SUBCONSCIOUS MEMORY. STUDIES PROVE THAT EMOTIONAL PAIN IS JUST AS REAL AS PHYSICAL PAIN, THE EMOTIONAL PAIN YOU HAVE FELT IS VERY REAL. UNCOVERING THE BELIEFS AND FEELINGS THAT ARE RESIDING WITHIN THE SUBCONSCIOUS ALLOWS YOU TO ACCEPT THEIR PRESENCE AND PURPOSE, AND THEN RELEASE THEM. YOU ARE THEN ABLE TO FILL YOUR SUBCONSCIOUS SYSTEM WITH EMPOWERING BELIEFS THAT DO SUPPORT THE LIFE DESIGN YOU PERSONALLY DESIRE TO LIVE. YOU ARE ABLE TO TRAIN YOUR SUBCONSCIOUS MIND THAT THE LIFE YOU DESIRE IS ABSOLUTELY TRUE AND HAPPENING TO YOU RIGHT NOW. AT A CELLULAR LEVEL THESE FEELINGS GENERATE THE FREQUENCIES OF YOUR DESIRES FULFILLED, AND AS STATED ABOVE THE SUBCONSCIOUS BELIEVES THIS IS HAPPENING TO YOU NOW BECAUSE ON THIS CELLULAR LEVEL YOU ARE TRULY EXPERIENCING THE THOUGHTS AND FEELINGS OF IT AS REAL RIGHT NOW. YOU THEN BEGIN TO SEE YOUR EXTERNAL REALITY CHANGE IN RESPONSE TO YOUR NEWLY EMBODIED INTERNAL FREQUENCIES. [AKA THE MANIFESTATION OF YOUR DESIRES OCCURS]

YOU ARE AN ETERNAL BEING AND DESERVE TO HAVE A SUBCONSCIOUS MIND FILLED WITH NOTHING BUT EMPOWERING BELIEFS! THE FOLLOWING PAGES SERVE AS A GUIDE FOR DISCOVERING YOUR OWN SUBCONSCIOUS LIMITING BELIEFS, AND HOW TO TRANSFORM THEM INTO SUBCONSCIOUS EMPOWERING BELIEFS!

YOU ARE PURE LOVE AT YOUR CORE, AN INFINITE BEING THAT HAS BEEN COVERED IN SKIN AND GIFTED THIS HUMAN LIFETIME, TO DREAM AND CREATE A BLISSFUL AND FULFILLING LIFE BEYOND YOUR WILDEST DREAMS. YOU ARE A MIRACLE IN THE FLESH, DO NOT EVER FEEL THAT YOU ARE ANYTHING LESS.

CREATING SUBCONSCIOUS EMPOWERING BELIEFS

FIRST, RECOGNIZE THAT [MOST LIKELY]
YOU ARE NOT CONSCIOUSLY AWARE OF ALL YOUR SUBCONSCIOUS LIMITING BELIEFS.
THEY ARE DEEP INSIDE YOU AND MUST BE EXTRACTED OUT BY **YOU**
THROUGH THE FOLLOWING PROCESS.
ALSO RECOGNIZE: **THIS IS A PROCESS** AND ADDITIONAL THINGS MAY CONTINUE TO SURFACE AT
LATER TIMES. OUR SUBCONSCIOUS [MORE OFTEN THAN NOT] RELEASES INFORMATION TO US
WHEN WE ARE LEAST EXPECTING, THAT IS HOW IT OPERATES. SETTING THE INTENT TO UNVEIL
THE INFORMATION CONTAINED IN OUR SUBCONSCIOUS IS THE FIRST STEP, BUT WE MUST BE PATIENT
IN AWAITING THE ANSWERS WE SEEK. GIVE YOURSELF TIME TO RELAX YOUR CONSCIOUS MIND.
GO INTO NATURE AND CONNECT, MEDITATE ON THE INFINITE NATURE OF YOUR SOUL.
BE GENTLE WITH YOURSELF, BE GRATEFUL FOR THIS LIFE EXPERIENCE AND THE LESSONS CONTAINED
WITHIN. EACH HUMAN LIFETIME IS A SOUL EVOLVING EXPERIENCE.

FOCUS ON WORKING WITH ONE AREA AT A TIME.
KNOW THAT YOU DO NOT NEED TO 'PERFECT' YOUR SUBCONSCIOUS IN ORDER TO MANIFEST YOUR
DESIRES. YOU DO NOT HAVE TO REMOVE ALL OF YOUR LIMITING BELIEFS BEFORE YOU CAN MANIFEST
YOUR DESIRES. EVOLVE YOUR MIND AS YOU ACTIVELY MANIFEST. EVOLVING AND CONSCIOUSLY
MANIFESTING GO HAND IN HAND, AS THEY BOTH REQUIRE A DEEP HARNESSING OF
YOUR PERSONAL INTERNAL POWER, EVER-INCREASINGLY IN EACH PRESENT MOMENT.
YOU WOULD END UP SPENDING A REALLY LONG TIME AND A LOT OF ENERGY ATTEMPTING GET TO
THE BOTTOM OF ALL YOUR LIMITING BELIEFS, WHILE STILL FEELING LIKE THERE'S NO END IN SIGHT.
THIS IS BECAUSE WHAT YOU FOCUS ON EXPANDS. SO, WHILE IT IS IMPORTANT TO FULLY
ACKNOWLEDGE THEM INITIALLY, AND THEN TRANSFORM THEM WHILE PARTAKING IN THIS EXERCISE,
DO NOT BECOME OBSESSED WITH THEM. THIS PRACTICE IS ABOUT RELEASING THEM AND EMBEDDING
EMPOWERING BELIEFS WITHIN YOUR SUBCONSCIOUS MIND TO REPLACE THEM, NOT OBSESSING OVER
THE LIMITING BELIEFS. BE MINDFUL OF THIS. IF YOU SINCERELY FEEL THE NEED TO PARTAKE IN
THIS PRACTICE AGAIN AT A LATER TIME, BY ALL MEANS ALLOW YOURSELF TO DO SO.
THIS PROCESS ALLOWS YOU TO EXPOSE THEM, ACCEPT THEM AND RELEASE THEM.
THEN, SHIFT YOUR FOCUS ENTIRELY ON EMBODYING EMPOWERING BELIEFS.
I HAVE PROVIDED VARIOUS WAYS TO DO SO ON THE FOLLOWING PAGES.

[REFER TO THE MIND & MANIFESTATION WARM UP PAGE]
CLOSE YOUR EYES FOR A FEW MINUTES,
CONNECT WITH YOUR HEARTBEAT, BREATH AND INNER POWER.

SET THE INTENTION TO EXTRACT YOUR INNERMOST SUBCONSCIOUS BELIEFS.

AREAS OF LIFE TO CONSIDER: HEALTH, WEALTH, LOVE, RELATIONSHIPS, MONEY, CAREER,
ADVENTURE, GROWTH, CREATIVITY, ENVIRONMENT. THESE ARE JUST A FEW OF THE MAIN
CATEGORIES, BUT THIS CAN BE APPLIED TO ANY AREA OF LIFE YOU CAN THINK OF.

JOURNAL:
WHAT ARE MY LIMITING BELIEFS IN REGARDS TO ___.
WRITE DOWN ANYTHING AND EVERYTHING THAT COMES TO MIND.
THINK DEEPLY INTO THE PATTERNS OF YOUR LIFE, ESPECIALLY AGES 0-7.
WHERE DO YOU FEEL THESE BELIEFS? [IN, ON AND AROUND YOUR BEING]
JOURNAL WITHOUT JUDGEMENT OR NEED FOR PERFECTION,
WRITE ALL YOUR INNERMOST BELIEFS DOWN.
QUESTION YOURSELF:
ARE MY BELIEFS THE RESULT OF EXTERNAL PROGRAMMING?
OR ARE THEY TRULY MY OWN HEARTFELT BELIEFS,
THAT RESONATE WITH THE CORE OF MY SOUL AND BEING?
OR A COMBINATION OF BOTH?
CONTINUE TO QUESTION EVERY SINGLE THING.
GO DEEP INTO YOUR SOUL
AND ASK YOURSELF
EVERYTHING.
PUT YOUR JOURNAL AWAY WHEN YOU HAVE FINISHED,
IF ANYTHING ARISES LATER ON TAKE OUT YOUR JOURNAL AND WRITE THEM DOWN.

YOUR PATTERNS ARE NOT NECESSARILY 'YOUR FAULT'
BUT THEY ARE ENTIRELY YOUR RESPONSIBILITY.

ONE EXAMPLE:
IF YOU HAVE ALWAYS HAD PARTNERS THAT TREAT YOU SIMILARLY: LOOK BACK INTO YOUR CHILDHOOD. CAN YOU MAKE DIRECT CORRELATIONS WITH HOW YOU WERE TREATED AS A CHILD AND WHAT YOU FIND / HAVE FOUND EXACTABLE TO BE TREATED IN YOUR RELATIONSHIP(S)? OR EVEN IN YOUR FRIENDSHIPS? OR WORKPLACES? THIS MAY INCLUDE BUT IS NOT LIMITED TO: CONTROL / EMOTIONAL CONTROL / INTELLECTUAL CONTROL / PHYSICAL CONTROL / BEING TOLD WHAT TO DO, JUST STRAIT UP BEING DISRESPECTED, BEING TOLD WHAT TO BELIEVE, BEING TOLD WHAT IS RIGHT, BELIEVING YOU ONLY DESERVE ____ AND NOT ____ BECAUSE YOU JUST ARE NOT GOOD ENOUGH FOR THAT, OR WERE NOT BORN INTO THAT, OR ARE NOT SMART ENOUGH FOR THAT, OR BEAUTIFUL ENOUGH FOR THAT. ANY REASONING LIKE THIS. OR MAYBE YOUR PATTERNS ARE AROUND FINANCIAL LACK, OR ANY OTHER TYPES OF LACK OF FULFILLMENT / SATISFACTION. OR THEY MAY EVEN BE SO SUBTLE THAT YOU DO NOT CONSCIOUSLY RECOGNIZE THEIR EXISTENCE. ASK YOUR INTUITION AND/OR YOUR DIVINE LIFE SOURCE TO GUIDE YOU INTO RECOGNIZING WHAT PATTERNS YOU HAVE IN YOUR LIFE AND WHERE YOUR PATTERNS OF THINKING, DOING AND LIVING COME FROM. ALSO RECOGNIZE THE POSITIVE PATTERNS YOU HAVE. TAKE THE TIME TO RECOGNIZE ALL THE PATTERNS. ALL. OF. THEM. BE RAW, OPEN, HONEST AND NON JUDGMENTAL WITH YOURSELF. OWN YOUR SHADOW SIDE. OWN YOUR DARKNESS, WOUNDS AND BAD HABITS. EVERY SINGLE REOCCURRING PATTERN. WHATEVER IT IS THEY PERTAIN TO. DO SO, SO THAT YOU CAN DEFINE WHICH PATTERNS YOU WANT TO KEEP, WHICH PATTERNS YOU WANT TO RELEASE AND ALSO WHICH NEW PATTERNS YOU WOULD LIKE TO EMPOWER YOURSELF WITH MOVING FORWARD. YOUR SHADOW SIDE AND PATTERNS ARE NOT 'OUT TO GET YOU'. ACTUALLY, THEY ARE THE EXACT OPPOSITE OF THAT, THEY ARE HOLDING A BEAUTIFUL MEANING FOR YOU. THEY ARE WAITING FOR YOU TO RIP OFF THE REOCCURRING SCAB, TO FINALLY LET LIGHT AND LOVE FLOOD INTO THEM. TO HEAL AT LAST, SO THEY MAY BE ACCEPTED AND TRANSFORMED. DEFINE ALL THE PATTERNS YOU DO DESIRE TO HAVE IN LIFE. EMBODY THEM AS ALREADY YOURS. BELIEVE YOU DESERVE AND THE UNIVERSE WILL SERVE. ALWAYS BE GENTLE WITH YOURSELF AS YOUR WORK THROUGH THE PRACTICES AND PROCESSES, BECAUSE THEY ARE JUST THAT: PRACTICES AND PROCESSES. THEY TAKE TIME TO GROW INTO. ENJOY BEING WHERE YOU ARE, AND ENJOY EVOLVING TO WHERE YOU DESIRE TO BE. ONE DAY YOU WILL BE LIVING WITHIN YOUR DESIRED LIFE DESIGN AND YOU WILL BE GLAD THAT YOU DID ENJOY ALL PIECES OF THE PROCESS, FOR TRULY ENJOYING ENTIRE JOURNEY ALLOWS YOU TO APPRECIATE THE REWARD SO MUCH MORE. JUST FOR TODAY SAVOR EACH MOMENT ~ THAT IS HOW YOU WILL GET A TASTE OF INFINITY.

IF YOUR LIMITING BELIEFS HAVE BEEN ESTABLISHED FIRMLY FROM PAST EXPERIENCE
[I WILL USE THE EXAMPLE OF PAST RELATIONSHIPS, BUT THIS CAN APPLY TO ANYTHING]
ASSESS WHETHER YOU ARE:
STRONGLY FOCUSED ON WHAT YOU DO NOT WANT IN ___ SITUATION / AREA OF YOUR LIFE,
OR IF YOU ARE FOCUSED ON WHAT YOU DO IN FACT WANT IN ___ SITUATION / AREA OF YOUR LIFE.
THESE TYPES OF SUBCONSCIOUS BELIEFS CAN EASILY REMAIN DORMANT AS WE FEEL THAT WE ARE SIMPLY DEFINING WHAT WE 'DO NOT WANT TO EXPERIENCE AGAIN',
BUT TRUTHFULLY WE MUST LET GO OF OBSESSING OVER THE THINGS / TRAITS WE DO NOT WANT,
AND RECOGNIZE WHAT WE ARE IN FACT DESIRING TO HAVE IN PLACE OF WHAT WE DO NOT WANT.
WHAT WE FOCUS ON EXPANDS, ENERGY GOES WHERE ATTENTION FLOWS.
THEREFORE, WE ALWAYS WANT TO DIRECT OUR EMPOWERING BELIEFS
TO SUPPORT WHAT WE DO WANT. NOT STRESSING / WORRYING ABOUT WHAT WE DO NOT WANT.
SO, [CONTINUING WITH THE RELATIONSHIP EXAMPLE] WE MUST ESTABLISH THE EMPOWERING SUBCONSCIOUS BELIEF THAT OUR PERFECTLY ALIGNED RELATIONSHIP DOES EXIST WITH A PERSON WHO EMBODIES THE TRAITS WE DO DESIRE. WE RELEASE THE SUBCONSCIOUS LIMITING BELIEFS THAT CAUSE US TO STRESS OVER WHETHER THIS PERSON EMBODIES THE TRAITS WE HAVE REPEATEDLY SEEN WITHIN OUR PAST RELATIONSHIPS AND DO NOT DESIRE TO HAVE IN ANY PRESENT / FUTURE ONES.

ONCE YOU FEEL THAT YOUR SIGNIFICANT LIMITING BELIEFS AND PATTERNS
ARE LISTED WITHIN YOUR JOURNAL:

~ BEGIN INFUSING YOUR SUBCONSCIOUS BELIEF SYSTEM WITH EMPOWERING BELIEFS ~
WRITE DOWN THE OPPOSITE OF EACH LIMITING BELIEF YOU HAVE IDENTIFIED,
AND / OR MODIFY EACH BELIEF INTO THE EXACT BELIEF [MINDSET] YOU WOULD BE IN
WHILE LIVING YOUR DESIRED LIFE DESIGN.

IF YOU FEEL YOURSELF BEGINNING TO SAY 'YA BUT ___' OR 'I CANNOT ____ BECAUSE ___'
RECOGNIZE THAT THESE ARE IN FACT YOUR SUBCONSCIOUS LIMITING BELIEFS SURFACING,
AND THEY MUST BE TRANSFORMED AS THEY SURFACE. MOVE BEYOND YOUR COMFORT ZONES,
OR YOU WILL FOREVER REMAIN WHERE YOU ARE. IT IS YOUR CHOICE, YOUR FREE WILL TO DECIDE.

YOU ONLY PERCEIVE ____ IS IMPOSSIBLE BECAUSE YOUR BELIEFS TELL YOU SO. RESTRUCTURE THOSE
BELIEFS TO WORK FOR YOU, SO THAT YOU CAN KNOW AND FEEL THAT ____ IS ENTIRELY POSSIBLE.

THIS WILL SEEM SO UNNATURAL AND STRANGE
SINCE THESE EMPOWERING SUBCONSCIOUS BELIEFS ARE DEFYING ALL
THE LIMITING BELIEFS THAT HAVE BEEN SO DEEPLY ENGRAINED WITHIN YOU AS TRUTH.
BUT DEEP DOWN THE EMPOWERING BELIEFS REALLY DO **FEEL** PLEASURABLE TO YOU PERSONALLY.
YOU REALLY DO DESIRE FOR THEM TO BE YOUR TRUTH THAT YOU LIVE YOUR ENTIRE LIFE BY.

THE AWKWARD FEELINGS AND THE URGE TO REJECT THESE NEWFOUND BELIEFS MEANS THAT MEANS
THE PROCESS IS WORKING! ONCE YOU HAVE YOUR LIST OF EMPOWERING BELIEFS WRITE EACH OF
THEM INTO A PRESENT TENSE STATEMENT. WRITE THESE STATEMENTS IN A PLACE WHERE YOU CAN
EASILY REFLECT ON THEM, AND DO SO OFTEN. THE MORE YOU DO SO THE MORE **NATURAL** THEY WILL
BEGIN TO **FEEL** AND THE MORE YOUR SUBCONSCIOUS MIND WILL BEGIN TO ACCEPT THEM AS **TRUTH**,
TO SUPPORT YOUR PERSONAL DESIRES AND DESIRED LIFE DESIGN. MAKE SURE YOU PRACTICE BOTH
THINKING / SPEAKING AND **FEELING** THEM AS YOUR TRUTH. A GREAT TIME TO REFLECT ON THESE
PRESENT TENSE STATEMENTS IS IN THE MORNING **WHILE YOU ARE JUST WAKING UP FROM YOUR SLEEP**
AND **RIGHT BEFORE YOU GO TO BED**. RIGHT BEFORE BED YOU ARE ABOUT TO SINK INTO YOUR
SUBCONSCIOUS MIND WHERE YOU WILL BE **MARINATING** FOR THE NEXT 8 HOURS [GIVE OR TAKE]. THE
STATE OF MIND YOU ARE IN 5-10 MINUTES BEFORE FALLING ASLEEP [AND ALL THE WAY INTO FALLING
ASLEEP] SETS THE TONE FOR THE VIBRATIONAL FREQUENCY IN WHICH YOU WILL DREAM-- THE
VIBRATIONAL FREQUENCY YOU ARE TRAINING YOUR SUBCONSCIOUS MIND TO ACCEPT AS
TRUTH. THUS, YOUR SUBCONSCIOUS WILL SUPPORT THE MANIFESTATION OF THIS VIBRATION WITHIN
YOUR WAKING LIFE. **WHAT EXACTLY DO YOU WANT YOUR SUBCONSCIOUS MIND TO HELP YOU
MANIFEST WITHIN YOUR LIFE?** DURING YOUR WAKING HOURS START TAKING THE INSPIRED ACTION
STEPS TOWARDS YOUR DESIRES - DO THE THINGS THAT TRULY PROPEL YOU OUT OF YOUR COMFORT
ZONES. THE REASON THESE THINGS SCARE YOU IS BECAUSE YOUR LIMITING BELIEF SYSTEM IS
SCREAMING: NO THAT IS AGAINST WHAT YOU HAVE ALWAYS ACCEPTED AND LIVED BY AS TRUE! STOP!
PLEASE, JUST STAY WHERE WE ARE SAFE AND COMFORTABLE, STAY WITH THE COMFORTABLE
THOUGHTS AND FEELINGS WE ARE USED TO. AND YOU ARE ACTIVELY TRANSFORMING YOUR LIMITING
BELIEFS INTO EMPOWERING BELIEFS BY TAKING ACTION TO SUPPORT YOUR NEWFOUND EMPOWERING
BELIEFS! YOU ARE NOW CHASING DOWN THE THINGS THAT SCARE YOU THE MOST, TAMING THEM AND
TRANSFORMING THEM TO WORK WITH YOU AND FOR YOU! IT IS WHAT YOU DO NOT DO THAT WILL
LATER ON BOTHER YOU. DO NOT LET THE FEAR OF TAKING ACTION TOWARDS YOUR DESIRED LIFE
DESIGN PARALYZE YOU. THE PAIN OF REGRET FOR NOT TAKING THE ACTION WILL FAR OUTWEIGH THE
FEAR YOU FEEL IN ANY GIVEN MOMENT TOWARDS TAKING THAT STEP OF INSPIRED ACTION.

AS STATED BEFORE, DO NOT GET CAUGHT UP IN DIGGING TO THE BOTTOM OF SUBCONSCIOUS
LIMITING BELIEFS, YOU WILL COME TO FIND THERE IS NO 'BOTTOM'. THIS IS BECAUSE WHAT YOU
FOCUS ON EXPANDS. DO NOT EXPAND THEM, STOP THEM IN THEIR TRACKS.
RECOGNIZE THEIR EXISTENCE AND LET THEM GO. DIRECT YOUR FOCUS ONTO THE EMPOWERING
BELIEFS YOU ARE REPLACING THEM WITH. BEGIN BY REPLACING ANY LIMITING BELIEFS THAT ARISE
WITH PURE SOURCE ENERGY, OR VISUALIZE A VIOLET FLAME DISSIPATING THEM.
HIGHER VIBRATIONS ALWAYS DISSOLVE ANY LOWER VIBRATIONS

YOU MUST BELIEVE YOU DESERVE ___ BEFORE YOU CAN MANIFEST IT.

KNOW THAT WHAT YOU DESIRE ALSO DESIRES YOU.

THE THINGS DEEP WITHIN YOUR HEART ARE NOT RANDOM, THEY ARE YOUR CALLING.

WHEN BUILDING EMPOWERING SUBCONSCIOUS BELIEFS
TO SUPPORT YOUR DESIRED LIFE DESIGN IT IS CRUCIAL TO RISE ABOVE THE FEAR OF REJECTION.

MANTRA:
I CANNOT BE REJECTED BECAUSE I VALUE MY OWN OPINION ABOUT MYSELF AND MY LIFE ABOVE
ANYONE ELSE'S OPINION(S) ABOUT MYSELF AND MY LIFE. I LOVE MYSELF.
I BELIEVE I AM WORTHY OF ALL I DESIRE.

OTHER PEOPLES' OPINIONS / ACTIONS / REACTIONS ARE A MIRROR OF THEIR OWN INNER SELF.
DO NOT TAKE THEIR OPINIONS / ACTIONS / BEHAVIORS PERSONALLY.
ALLOW OTHERS TO BE.
JUST OBSERVE, DO NOT ABSORB.
IF ANYONE IS EVER RUDE OR DISRESPECTFUL SIMPLY REPLY 'THANK-YOU FOR YOUR OPINION'
DO NOT TAKE IT PERSONALLY, IT IS A REFLECTION OF THEIR INNER VOICE.
SIMPLY, LEAVE IT AT THAT AND REMOVE YOURSELF FROM THE SITUATION.

TOOLS FOR EMPOWERING YOUR SUBCONSCIOUS:

REFLECT ON THE I AM AFFIRMATIONS / REPHRASING QUESTIONS PAGE.

**DESIGNATE A SPECIFIC WORD OR PHRASE
TO STOP LIMITING BELIEFS, NEGATIVE THOUGHTS AND OLD PATTERNS IN THEIR TRACKS.
WHEN YOU ARE EXPERIENCING LIMITING BELIEFS OR FEEL THEM COMING ON
SAY THIS WORD TO YOURSELF TO REMIND YOUR SUBCONSCIOUS MIND
TO HEAL THIS AREA THROUGH DISSIPATING ANY LOWER VIBRATIONS WITH
PURE SOURCE ENERGY, LOVE, AND EMPOWERING BELIEFS.**

FOR EXAMPLE: 'VIOLET FLAME'
IF YOU CHOOSE TO USE THE WORDS 'VIOLET FLAME'
THIS CAN ALSO SERVE AS A REMINDER THAT YOU ARE ENCOMPASSED IN THE HIGH VIBRATIONAL
ENERGY OF THE VIOLET FLAME, WHICH IS DISSIPATING ANY LOWER VIBRATIONS INSTANTLY,
WHILE RAISING YOUR PERSONAL VIBRATION BACK INTO ITS PUREST STATE.

Forgiveness sets me free as I let go, rise up and harmonize with my desires so they may effortlessly flow into my life.

Hand write a list on a sheet of paper.

List every single thing within your life that needs to be forgiven.

This may include situations, circumstances or other people.

Most importantly think about

the forgiveness you need to send to your own self.

For example, this may include forgiveness of your past actions,

negative self-talk or financial debt.

You can **feel** the pain, the regret, the guilt, the shame,

the hate, the regret, the anger, the fear, all the negative feelings

that these things bring when thinking of them.

List them all.

Finances can be especially difficult to forgive,

but you must be grateful for the things and experiences

which you have enjoyed through your past spending.

In order to effortlessly attract more abundance into your life

it is crucial to spend money cheerfully and gratefully from this moment on.

In regards to forgiving others:

Make sure that you are not caught up in mental fantasies of revenge / wishing negativity / failure on another. Ever. Period. The thinking state of revenge places you in a low-vibrational frequency and will not impact the other. Your own thoughts, emotions, feelings and overall vibrational frequency will only ever return to impact you. The vibrations you embody will be matched as events and circumstances manifested within your life. This is an example of your innate power of manifestation working in a self-sabotaging, destructive way. Your power of manifestation cannot be turned off. Choose to recognize this fact and harness it. Discipline yourself in only thinking on and feeling the vibrations you do wish to manifest within your own life. This also means that another cannot wish negativity or revenge on you. Any person focused on the egotistical feelings of revenge will only attract that vibration into their own life. Forgive others to set yourself free from any dense energy cords / vibrations. This act of forgiveness is not for them. You do not need an apology from them, this does not mean you are deeming their behaviors acceptable, and you do not need to tell them you are forgiving them. It is an internal act of forgiveness for your personal freedom. This is for your highest good. Forgive them and then remove them from your life / keep them out of your life / keep your boundaries with them very strong and aligned with your highest good.

After listing every single thing you can think of,
give thanks for the lessons or insight that each has given you, and for the clarity
you have gained on how you desire this specific area of your life to be.
This will be more difficult for certain things than others,
but that is all the more reason why it is important to do this exercise.
Guilt and shame are the lowest vibrational frequencies. They must be let go of in
order to vibrate higher and manifest your desired life design. Send love and
forgiveness to each item on your list as you work through crossing them all off.
PHYSICALLY cross them off. In doing so you are showing your mind that you are now
creating space within your mind and your energy frequency
for the universe to move in and fulfill your desired manifestations.
Shred and burn this list [safely] when you are finished with the exercise.

♥

'Forgive yourself first. Release the need to replay a negative situation over and over
again in your mind. Don't become a hostage to your past by always reviewing and
reliving your mistakes. Don't remind yourself of what should have, could have or
would have been. Release it and let it go. Move on.' -- Les Brown

You must let go of thinking about what was and what is
and only focus on what you desire.
You would not go watch the same crappy movie over and over and over,
so why would you do this with your own life?
Apply the self discipline to let go of what was and what is and
focus your attention, intention, energy, and feeling state on what you do desire.

**It feels amazing to let go, be free, rise up and
harmonize with my desires so they may effortlessly flow into my life.**

♥

Do your best to stop apologizing for things that do not require an apology.
INSTEAD, REPHRASE AND GIVE THANKS.

'Lately I've been replacing my "I'm sorry"s with "thank you"s,
like instead of "sorry I'm late" I'll say "thanks for waiting for me",
or instead of "sorry for being such a mess"
I'll say "thank you for loving me and caring about me unconditionally"
and it's not only shifted the way I think and feel about myself
but also improved my relationships with others
who now get to receive my gratitude instead of my negativity.' -- Unknown

CORE VALUES & BOUNDARIES

WE MUST RESPECT EACH OTHER'S JOURNEY,

AS WE PERSONALLY DESIRE TO BE RESPECTED FOR WHO WE ARE.

TAKE THE TIME TO DEFINE YOUR PERSONAL CORE VALUES AND BOUNDARIES.

PHYSICALLY WRITE THEM DOWN.

DOING SO ALLOWS YOU TO STAY ALIGNED THROUGHOUT YOUR ENTIRE LIFE JOURNEY.

HAVING BOUNDARIES SUPPORTS AND PROTECTS YOUR ENERGY.

WHAT DO YOU VALUE IN LIFE?

WHAT ARE YOUR COMFORTABLE WITH?

WHAT ARE YOU NOT COMFORTABLE WITH?

DO YOU FIND YOURSELF DRAINED OF ENERGY OFTEN? OR ARE YOU FULL OF ENERGY?

DOES YOUR BODY FEEL TENSE? ARE YOU CALM AND RELAXED?

DO YOU SAY NO WHEN YOU WANT TO?

ANSWERING THESE QUESTIONS ALLOWS YOU TO DETERMINE THE STRENGTH OF YOUR

BOUNDARIES AND WHERE THEY NEED TO BE STRENGTHENED WITHIN YOUR LIFE.

COMMUNICATE YOUR BOUNDARIES CLEARLY TO YOURSELF AND TO OTHERS.

DECIDE AHEAD OF TIME WHAT ACTION WILL YOU TAKE IF BOUNDARIES ARE NOT RESPECTED

[THE CONSEQUENCES], AND TAKE THESE ACTIONS IF YOUR BOUNDARIES LIMITS ARE

OVERSTEPPED. IF YOU DO NOT ABIDE BY YOUR BOUNDARIES THEY ARE NOT SERVING THEIR

PURPOSE. IF YOU DO NOT TAKE THEM SERIOUSLY NEITHER WILL ANYONE ELSE.

KEEPING A WRITTEN COPY OF PERSONAL BELIEFS AND BOUNDARIES IS A WONDERFUL TOOL,

ALLOWING YOU TO CONSISTENTLY BE IN ALIGNMENT WITH YOUR DESIRED LIFE DESIGN.

CREATING BOUNDARIES MAY NOT ALWAYS BE EASY BUT IT IS NECESSARY,

AND OVER TIME YOU WILL REALIZE HOW VERY EMPOWERING IT IS.

IF YOU ALREADY HAVE A WRITTEN COPY:

REFLECT ON THEM, AND EDIT THEM AS YOU DESIRE. ALWAYS ABIDE BY THEM.

YOU DECIDE THEM — SO YOU SHOULD ALWAYS DESIRE TO ABIDE BY THEM.

REMEMBER THIS:

THE ONLY PEOPLE WHO WILL EVER BE UPSET BY YOU SETTING BOUNDARIES ARE

THE ONES THAT BENEFITTED FROM YOU HAVING NONE.

'LOVE YOURSELF ENOUGH TO SET BOUNDARIES. YOUR TIME AND ENERGY ARE PRECIOUS. YOU GET TO CHOOSE HOW YOU USE IT. YOU TEACH PEOPLE HOW TO TREAT YOU BY DECIDING WHAT YOU WILL AND WON'T ACCEPT.'
- ANNA TAYLOR

'YOUR PERSONAL BOUNDARIES PROTECT THE INNER CORE OF YOUR IDENTITY AND YOUR RIGHT TO CHOICES.' - GERARD MANLEY HOPKINS

'WHEN WE FAIL TO SET BOUNDARIES WE HOLD OTHER PEOPLE ACCOUNTABLE, WE FEEL USED AND MISTREATED.' - BRENE BROWN

'Lack of Planning on Your Part, Does Not Constitute an Emergency on My Part' -UNKNOWN

'GIVERS NEED TO SET LIMITS BECAUSE TAKERS RARELY DO.' - RACHEL WOLCHIN

"SETTING BOUNDARIES IS A WAY OF CARING FOR MYSELF, IT DOESN'T MAKE ME MEAN, SELFISH, OR UNCARING [JUST] BECAUSE I DON'T DO THINGS YOUR WAY, I CARE ABOUT ME, TOO.' - CHRISTINE MORGAN

'BOUNDARIES DEFINE US. THEY DEFINE WHAT IS ME AND WHAT IS NOT ME. A BOUNDARY SHOWS ME WHERE I END AND WHERE SOMEONE ELSE BEGINS, LEADING ME TO A SENSE OF OWNERSHIP. KNOWING WHAT I AM TO OWN AND TAKE RESPONSIBILITY FOR GIVES ME FREEDOM. - HENRY CLOUD

PROTECTIVE HERBS:
BASIL, WHITE SAGE, ROSEMARY, EUCALYPTUS, LAVENDER, SANDALWOOD, FENNEL, CLOVE, OREGANO.
THERE ARE MANY OTHER HERBS THAT CAN BE UTILIZED FOR PROTECTION, THESE ARE SIMPLY A FEW OF THE MOST COMMON.

PROTECTIVE HEALING CRYSTALS:
HEALING CRYSTALS CAN ALSO SUPPORT US IN KEEPING OUR BOUNDARIES STRONG.
YOU CAN DO YOUR OWN RESEARCH ON WHICH HEALING CRYSTALS ARE BEST UTILIZED FOR PROTECTION [MIND, BODY AND SOUL]. THERE ARE MANY GREAT OPTIONS AVAILABLE, AND THAT IS PRECISELY WHY I WILL LEAVE THE RESEARCH TO YOU, BECAUSE ULTIMATELY YOU WILL FIND THE RIGHT ONE(S) FOR YOU PERSONALLY WHEN YOU TRUST YOUR INTUITION AND GO WITH WHAT **FEELS** RIGHT FOR YOU. FOR DAILY JEWELRY WEAR / HEALING CRYSTALS YOU DESIRE TO CARRY WITH YOU IT IS BEST TO STAY AWAY FROM HEALING CRYSTALS THAT IGNITE YOUR THIRD EYE AND INTUITION. THIS IS BECAUSE THEY WILL MAKE YOU EXTREMELY SENSITIVE TO YOUR ENVIRONMENT(S) AND ALL OF THE ENERGIES AROUND YOU. THEY ALSO EASILY ABSORB THE ENERGIES OF THE ENVIRONMENTS THEY ARE WITHIN, RESULTING IN YOU CARRYING THOSE ENERGIES INTO YOUR PERSONAL SPACE / SACRED SPACE WITH YOU, AND THEN WONDERING WHY YOU STILL FEEL THE ENERGIES OF THESE ENVIRONMENTS SO STRONGLY WHEN YOU ARE FAR FROM THEM. CONSIDER RESERVING THE USE OF HEALING CRYSTALS THAT FALL INTO THESE CATEGORIES FOR YOUR SACRED SPACES AND SACRED PRACTICES, MEDITATIONS, AND OTHER ENVIRONMENTS / TIMES LIKE THESE.

There is power in clean & tidy

Be the authentic you,

Gradually [or all at once]

Let go of everything that is not

Part of / supporting

The most authentic version of you.

Take exceptional care of
Yourself
&
Your belongings.
Show the universe you are
Grateful
&
Deserving
Of your desires.

Opt for less, in better quality.

Over more, in poor quality.

Expensive does not always equate to quality.

Should you find yourself overwhelmed by the amount of belongings to care for
Do downsize.

Ask yourself:
Do I see myself still having all of this stuff
When I am living within my desired life design?
This simple question allows you to define what is meaningful and what is not.
Get rid of excess stuff, you'll be surprised how good it makes you feel.
This is because the more stuff you accumulate and own, the more stuff owns you.
Letting go shows you know there is an abundance of everything you will ever desire.

Detachment is not that you should own nothing,
But that nothing should own you.
- Ali Ibn Abi Talib

GIVE!

GIVE AWAY EVERYTHING THAT DOES NOT BRING YOU PURE JOY.
HOLD IT AND FEEL WHAT IT BRINGS TO YOU.

CHOOSE TO SURROUND YOURSELF WITH THE THINGS YOU TRULY LOVE,
DISCARD THE REST.
[APPLY THIS TO ANY ENVIRONMENT, SACRED SPACE,
HOME SPACE, MIND SPACE, FOOD .. FRIENDSHIPS/ RELATIONSHIPS.]

GIVE THANKS TO EACH THING YOU LET GO OF.
RESPECT THAT AT ONE MOMENT IT DID BRING YOU JOY, EVEN IF THAT WAS ONLY
IN THE MOMENT WHEN YOU PURCHASED IT AND NEVER USED IT.
RELEASE.
ALLOW FOR SPACE TO BE CREATED IN YOUR LIFE FOR MIRACLES TO MANIFEST
SIMPLY BY LETTING GO.

**BE GENTLE WITH YOURSELF,
YOU ARE DOING YOUR BEST IN EACH MOMENT.**

THE SPACES AROUND YOU EITHER SUPPORT OR LIMIT YOUR VIBRATIONAL FREQUENCY.
EVERY SINGLE THING IS ENERGY AND HAS ITS OWN UNIQUE FREQUENCY.
RESEARCH FENG SHUI.
THE ART OF FENG SHUI USES ENERGY FORCES
TO HARMONIZE INDIVIDUALS WITH THEIR SURROUNDING ENVIRONMENT
AND CREATE OPTIMAL ENERGY FLOW WITHIN THE CHOSEN ENVIRONMENT.

SACRED SPACE BY DENISE LINN IS A SPECTACULAR BOOK
FOR CLEARING AND ENHANCING THE ENERGY OF YOUR HOME.

'YOU ARE THE AVERAGE OF THE 5 PEOPLE YOU SPEND THE MOST TIME WITH'
RECOGNIZE THAT IN THIS PRESENT DAY AND AGE
YOU HAVE THE POWER TO DEFINE THESE 5 PEOPLE BY NON-PHYSICAL MEANS.
FOR EXAMPLE: PODCASTS, YOUTUBE, AUDIBLE, BOOKS, SOCIAL MEDIA .. ETC
THEY ARE THE 5 PEOPLE YOU RESONATE WITH THE MOST,
THE PEOPLE WHOSE ENERGY YOU DESIRE TO FILL YOUR MIND AND YOUR TIME WITH.

WATCH THIS SHORT & INSPIRING TED TALK ON YOUTUBE:
THE MAGIC OF NOT GIVING A F*** | SARAH KNIGHT | TEDxCoconutGrove

DETOX YOUR SOCIAL MEDIA.
YES, THIS IS ACTUALLY VERY IMPORTANT TO DO.
PAUSE FOR A MOMENT AND TRULY CONSIDER HOW SIGNIFICANT SOCIAL MEDIA, TEXTING, ETC.
IS WITHIN THE LIVES OF MOST PEOPLE NOWADAYS. OUR WORLD IS EVOLVING RAPIDLY,
DO NOT GIVE AWAY YOUR REAL LIFE EXPERIENCE TO ELECTRONIC DEVICES.
LIVE THIS LIFE YOU HAVE BEEN GIFTED.
YOU DO NOT NEED TO GIVE THEM UP ENTIRELY, BUT DO DETOX YOUR ELECTRONIC DEVICE(S).
AND BE MINDFUL OF HOW MUCH OF YOUR LIFE IS BEING DEDICATED TO THEM.
WHAT CONTENT IT IS THAT YOU ARE EXPOSING YOUR MIND TO?
WHEN YOU ARE AT THE END OF YOUR LIFE AND LOOKING BACK .. WILL YOU BE HAPPY YOU SPENT
____ HOURS / MINUTES PER DAY ONLINE / ON YOUR ELECTRONIC DEVICE(S)?
IS THE CONTENT YOU ARE CONSUMING IGNITING THOUGHTS OF LIKING, OR DISLIKING?
HOW IS IT IMPACTING YOUR MOOD? BOTH SHORT TERM AND LONG TERM.
ANYTHING THAT INFLUENCES YOUR THOUGHTS AND FEELINGS DIRECTLY IMPACTS
THE MANIFESTATIONS YOU RECEIVE WITHIN YOUR LIFE.
WHAT ELSE COULD YOU SPEND THIS AMOUNT OF TIME DOING THAT WOULD LEAVE YOU FEELING
ABSOLUTELY FULFILLED AND HAPPY IN THESE MOMENTS AND
ALSO WHEN LOOKING BACK ONE DAY?
MEDITATE ON THIS OFTEN, AND ADJUST ACCORDINGLY. .

SIGNS / SYNCHRONICITIES / SYMBOLISM

We often encounter beautiful signs, synchronicities and symbols
that remind us we are in fact aligned with our desired life design
and desired manifestations. These signs and synchronicities
may provide us with insight, inspiration or guidance.
The way you personally choose to interpret signs, synchronicities and symbolism
is entirely up to you,
there is no right or wrong way.

Here is my own personal perception:
when experiencing a sign or synchronicity within life
become fully present. disregard any distractions for the moment.
do not try to capture the sign or synchronicity.
allow yourself to focus solely on the sign / synchronicity / symbol.
immerse yourself in the moment, and ask yourself:
what significance does this sign / synchronicity / symbol hold
for me right now? what symbolism does this hold for me personally?
Trust your intuition entirely in these moments. wait until the sign / synchronicity /
symbol has passed completely before noting it on paper or in your phone. do not over
analyze the sign / synchronicity / symbol. wait until later in the day, or another day
entirely to revisit the notes you have taken in regards to this sign / synchronicity /
symbol. when you revisit the notes, do so from an intuitive perspective. does anything
else stand out to you? what has this sign / synchronicity / symbolism always meant to
you personally? how does this resonate with your life right now / your desired life
design? Do not immediately turn to what another person / group of others has
interpreted this sign / synchronicity / symbolism to mean. You may desire to research
others' opinions, but wait until you have asked your own intuition first. the intuitive
insights you uncover in regards to signs / synchronicities / symbolism within your life
will always be far more significant than what others' have personally / collectively
assigned to these signs / synchronicities / symbolism.

Do your best to keep these things personal,
you will begin to see more of them when you do.
and in doing so, you will also begin to recognize
your intuitive insights growing stronger as well.

Don't 'look' for signs / synchronicities / symbols
simply be present in each moment,
so that you are aware of them when they appear for you.

THE POWER OF BELIEVING

Do you truly believe you will receive your desires?
Do you believe your intentions are powerful?
Do you fully believe in your internal power?
Starting small in manifestation
is not because you cannot manifest larger.
It is about what you believe.
If you simply cannot envision and FEEL your desires as already your reality
then start with the things you can envision as your reality,
and work your way up from there.
Utilize the long term blueprint - breakdown big desires into a series of steps.
Recognize your power to manifest is entirely within what you are
right now able to shift into fully envisioning and FEELING as already your truth.
You have your entire lifetime to manifest, that is a blessing.
Be excited to receive a constant flow of blessings as you continue to evolve and grow.
Do not be afraid or discouraged to start small.
~ Where you are beginning is perfect ~
Be excited as you constantly grow, ever-increasingly harnessing your internal power.

♥

You will always receive proof of what you believe.
Recognize this truth and you will gain control of your entire life.
This is our free will as human beings.
We have the choice to believe that we can obtain our best life
with little to no resistance in the process,
or [as many humans have been previously conditioned to believe]
we can decide that obtaining our own best life is nearly impossible,
there will always be obstacles and years of hard work and little to no fun in the
process, and / or any other limiting beliefs will also ALWAYS be proven correct.

This is universal law:
For whatever predominant combination of thoughts and feelings
you do embody within your being you will always receive events and circumstances
that are the perfect, harmonious match to those predominant thoughts and feelings.
Each person always receives events and circumstances into their physical reality
that provide them with the exact feeling state they have been embodying.
Thoughts and Feelings of lack, fear and doubt equal
more events and circumstances manifested to feel lack, fear and doubt.
Thoughts and Feelings of peace and satisfaction equal
more events and circumstances to feel peace and satisfaction.
This is true for any predominant combination of thoughts and feelings
and their harmonious physical manifestation.
That is why the practice of ever-increasingly embodying the combination of thoughts
and feelings as if your desires have already manifested attracts them into your life.
This is universal law. We are always emitting a frequency [our feeling state we are
embodying - often ignited by thought] and this frequency is always being matched.
Our near future will contain events and circumstances which are perfectly aligned
with our predominately embodied vibrational frequencies.

IF YOU ARE EMBODYING THE THOUGHTS AND FEELINGS THAT LIFE HAS TO BE HARD AND THAT THE CONCEPT OF YOUR MIND AND FEELING STATE CREATING YOUR REALITY IS BS .. WELL, YOUR PHYSICAL [EXTERNAL] REALITY IS GOING TO REFLECT YOUR [INTERNAL] STATE OF BELIEVING, THINKING AND FEELING. THUS, PROVIDING YOU WITH PROOF THAT YOU ARE IN FACT CORRECT. THIS IS BECAUSE YOU ARE PREDOMINANTLY EMITTING THAT FREQUENCY, THEREFORE YOUR EXTERNAL MANIFESTATIONS ARE IN PERFECT HARMONY WITH YOUR INTERNAL FREQUENCY EMBODIED. YOU CANNOT HIDE OR DISGUISE YOUR FREQUENCY. THE ORGANIZING INTELLIGENCE THAT EMANATES THROUGHOUT EVERY SINGLE FIBER OF YOU AND EVERYTHING ELSE IN THE UNIVERSE CANNOT BE FOOLED BY ANYONE OR ANYTHING. IN EACH MOMENT YOUR FREQUENCY IS READ PERFECTLY, WITHOUT QUESTION OR ERROR. YOUR PREDOMINANT FREQUENCY WILL ALWAYS BE MATCHED WITH MANIFESTATIONS INTO YOUR PHYSICAL REALITY ON THAT FREQUENCY. YOU ARE IN FACT MANIFESTING PROOF OF EVERYTHING YOU BELIEVE AND FEEL ALL THE TIME, JUST LOOK AROUND YOU AND YOU CAN SEE THE REFLECTION OF WHERE YOU ARE AT INTERNALLY. IS THERE ANYTHING YOU DESIRE TO CHANGE? ALL YOU MUST DO IS APPLY THE SELF DISCIPLINE AND EVER-INCREASINGLY SHIFT YOUR BELIEFS, THOUGHTS AND FEELING STATES. DEDICATE YOURSELF TO SHIFTING YOUR THOUGHTS, EMOTIONS AND FEELING STATE IN EACH MOMENT, SO THAT THEY BECOME EVER-INCREASINGLY HARMONIOUS WITH THE BELIEF THAT YOU CAN OBTAIN A TRULY FULFILLING LIFE WITH LITTLE TO NO RESISTANCE. IT IS NOT 'I WISH FOR ___ AND NOW I SHALL WAIT TO RECEIVE ___ WITHOUT EMBODYING THE THOUGHTS, EMOTIONS AND FEELINGS THAT ALIGN WITH THAT OR TAKING ANY INSPIRED ACTION TOWARDS THAT.' NO. TRUE MANIFESTATION IS NOT A SURFACE LEVEL PRACTICE. YOU MUST EVER-INCREASINGLY EMBODY THE THOUGHTS AND FEELING STATES OF HAVING YOUR DESIRE COMPLETELY FULFILLED, WHILE ALSO TAKING INSPIRED ACTION IN ALIGNMENT WITH YOUR DESIRE [MORE ON INSPIRED ACTION LATER]. YOUR FEELING STATE YOU EMBODY IN EACH MOMENT IS YOUR INTENTION YOU ARE SENDING OUT. YOU MUST ALIGN YOUR FEELING STATE WITH THE EXACT FEELING STATE THAT YOUR DESIRES FULFILLMENT WILL BRING ONCE IT IS ALREADY HERE, AND EVER-INCREASINGLY MAINTAIN THAT FREQUENCY OF SATISFACTION. THOUGHTS AND WORDS MATTER BECAUSE THEY IGNITE FEELING STATES. HOWEVER, IF WE ARE BLANDLY THINKING / SPEAKING / WRITING WORDS AND NOT IGNITING OUR FEELING STATE AND INTENT SO THAT IT IS IN HARMONIOUS SUPPORT OF THEM THEY WILL NOT HOLD THE AMOUNT OF POWER THAT THEY ARE CAPABLE OF HOLDING. WE ARE ABLE TO REAP THE MOST OUT OF THOUGHTS AND WORDS [FOR EXAMPLE: AFFIRMATIONS] WHEN OUR FEELING STATE AND INTENT ARE IN PERFECT HARMONY WITH THEM. IT IS THE INTENT THAT RESIDES BENEATH THE WORDS THAT GIVES THEM POWER. THE DIVINE IS RESPECTFUL OF YOUR INTENT AND FEELING STATE YOU DECIDE TO EMBODY AND EMIT, SO IT ALWAYS PROVIDES YOU WILL AN EXACT MATCH. YOU DON'T HAVE TO HOPE IT WILL, IT ALWAYS WILL. IT IS YOUR FREE WILL TO DECIDE IF YOU DESIRE TO BECOME CONSCIOUS OF THE BELIEFS, THOUGHTS AND FEELING STATES YOU EMBODY. YOU WILL ALWAYS RECEIVE PHYSICALLY MANIFESTED PROOF THAT YOU ARE IN FACT CORRECT.

CHOOSE CONSCIOUSLY. AWAKEN AND THRIVE.

WHILE EVOLVING ALONG THE JOURNEY OF HARNESSING YOUR INNATE CREATIVE POWERS IT IS CRUCIAL TO RECOGNIZE THAT YOUR THOUGHTS, SPOKEN WORDS AND FEELING STATE MUST ALL BE IN HARMONY WITH EACH OTHER.

IF YOU ARE THINKING / SPEAKING AFFIRMATIONS AND OTHER WORDS THAT SUPPORT YOUR DESIRES BUT YOUR FEELING STATE DOES NOT MATCH [OR YOU ARE ALSO THINKING / SPEAKING DOUBT] YOUR DESIRES WILL NOT MANIFEST BECAUSE YOU ARE NOT HOLDING ABSOLUTE FAITH AND MAINTAINING THE VIBRATION THAT IS ALIGNED WITH THEIR MANIFESTED FORM. YOUR THOUGHTS INFLUENCE YOUR FEELING STATES, AND YOUR PREDOMINANT FEELING STATES DETERMINE WHAT WILL MANIFEST INTO YOUR LIFE. UNIVERSAL LAW SIMPLY IS ALWAYS WORKING, PERFECTLY. IT DOES NOT CARE IF YOU BELIEVE IN IT OR NOT. IT IS NOT EXCLUSIVE TO ANY SPECIFIC CULTURE OR RELIGIOUS GROUP. IT APPLIES TO EVERY SINGLE HUMAN BEING ON PLANET EARTH. THIS IS HOW OUR EXISTENCE WORKS. THIS IS HOW WE ARE ABLE TO CONSCIOUSLY CREATE, THROUGH GAINING CONTROL OVER OUR PRESENT FEELING STATES IN EACH MOMENT WE ARE HARNESSING OUR FUTURE LIFE EVENTS AND CIRCUMSTANCES. THIS IS A MOMENT BY MOMENT PRACTICE, IT IS ALWAYS AT WORK. YOU CAN HARNESS YOUR PREDOMINANT VIBRATION THROUGH CONSCIOUSLY HARNESSING EACH PRESENT MOMENT. LIFE IS NOT HAPPENING TO US, IT IS RESPONDING TO US THROUGH PROVIDING US WITH A LIFE THAT MATCHES OUR PREDOMINANT FEELING STATES. AFFIRMATIONS, VISION BOARDS, MANTRAS, VISUALIZATION, MEDIATION AND MANY OTHER PRACTICES LIKE THESE ARE WONDERFUL BECAUSE THEY ALLOW US TO IGNITE THE THOUGHTS AND FEELING STATES AS IF OUR DESIRES ARE ALREADY OURS. THUS, IN PRACTICING AND EVER-INCREASINGLY MASTERING THE FEELING STATES WE WISH TO RECEIVE WE WILL INEVITABLY BEGIN TO RECEIVE EVENTS AND CIRCUMSTANCES THAT MATCH THESE FEELING STATES PERFECTLY. WE DO NEED TO TAKE INSPIRED ACTION AND NOT JUST SIT AROUND AND FEEL ALL THE TIME, BUT OUR EMBODIED FEELING STATES IN COMBINATION WITH INSPIRED ACTION WILL ALWAYS BRING ABOUT THE MANIFESTATION OF OUR DESIRES. ACTION WITHOUT EMBODYING THE FEELING STATES [AS IF OUR DESIRE HAS MANIFESTED] KEEPS US IN LACK WHILE TAKING ACTION [WHAT MANY PEOPLE SPEND THEIR ENTIRE LIFE DOING]. IT IS THE COMBINATION OF BOTH THAT WORKS MIRACLES. IT IS CRUCIAL TO REALIZE THAT AFFIRMATIONS, VISION BOARDS AND ALL THINGS ALIKE ONLY DO GOOD IF THEY IGNITE THE THOUGHTS AND FEELING STATES AS IF THESE THINGS ARE ALREADY YOURS. IF YOU ARE SPEAKING / WRITING / THINKING WORDS THAT ARE ALIGNED WITH YOUR DESIRES FULFILLED BUT FEELING LACK / OUT OF ALIGNMENT WITH ALREADY HAVING THIS DESIRE THEN YOU ARE NOT EMITTING THE FREQUENCY OF ALREADY HAVING. THUS, YOU WILL RECEIVE EVENTS AND CIRCUMSTANCES THAT PROVE YOU DO NOT HAVE THIS DESIRE, BECAUSE THAT IS THE FREQUENCY YOU ARE EMITTING.

Since Thoughts / spoken words / beliefs often do ignite feeling states that are truly harmonious with them, but not always, it is not only important but crucial to **observe your feeling state in each moment and be honest with yourself**: am I feeling in alignment with already having my desire? Am I feeling the peace and satisfaction I will feel once my desire has already manifested as my reality? As humans we often believe we can hide our feelings deep within and no one will know. And this is true: more often than not other humans cannot read our innermost feelings, so we grow accustomed to thinking we can hide them within and disguise them with unaligned words. But, our life source / the universe / God / the divine [whichever you prefer to refer to this power as] always reads our feeling state, not our words / thoughts alone. We cannot hide or disguise our innermost feelings from the power that is supplying us with the events and circumstances that match our energetic vibrational frequencies [feeling states] embodied. This power allows us the free will to embody the feeling state we desire, to consciously manifest the life we desire. It comes down to whether or not we choose to acknowledge this fact and consciously harness this internal power to manifest our desires. It is not going to 'save us from ourself' if we are embodying low vibrational feeling states or feeling states unaligned with our desires. It respects our free will and always provides us with manifestations that are in perfect harmony with the feeling states we predominantly embody. This is precisely why harnessing and ever-increasingly mastering our feeling state in each present moment is crucial in creating the life design we do desire. The reason why you may have previously not been aware that you are always manifesting [before beginning this journey of conscious manifesting] is because you have always embodied the familiar feeling states that are reactions to your external life circumstances. Therefore, you have been emitting the feeling states that have provided you with more of what is already around you, more of what is familiar to you. Thus, it has appeared and felt as if life is just happening to you, rather than responding to you. Once you begin to truly harness your thoughts and feeling states in each moment you will begin to see profound results in your external life. At which point you will recognize that you do contain immense power within you to create the life design you personally desire. **You are immensely powerful, Goddess.**

MANIFESTATION & FREE WILL

YOU CAN AMPLIFY ANOTHER'S DESIRED MANIFESTATION
BY ALSO DESIRING THE SAME THING FOR THEM, BECAUSE THEY WANT IT FIRST,
AND YOU ARE ADDING MORE ENERGY IN SUPPORT OF THEIR DESIRE. OTHERS CAN AMPLIFY YOUR
DESIRED MANIFESTATION IF THEY PUT ENERGY TOWARDS WANTING THE SAME FOR YOU, TOO.

THIS IS VERY IMPORTANT TO KNOW, AND APPLY THROUGHOUT OUR CREATIVE JOURNEY OF LIFE:
THE ONLY WAY ANYONE CAN IMPACT YOU INTO MANIFESTING SOMETHING YOU DO NOT WANT
IS IF THEY CONVINCE YOU THIS THING YOU DO NOT WANT IS COMING TO YOU AND YOU BELIEVE IT.
THEN YOU ARE PUTTING YOUR THOUGHTS, EMOTIONS AND FEELINGS IN ALIGNMENT WITH
MANIFESTING THIS THING THAT YOU DO NOT WANT. BE MINDFUL OF THIS.
ESPECIALLY WHEN SOMEONE TRIES TO INTRODUCE NEGATIVITY OR CHAOS INTO YOUR MIND AND
LIFE. IF YOU CHOOSE TO BELIEVE THE FEAR THEY ARE FEEDING YOU THEN YOU WILL BECOME IN
ALIGNMENT WITH RECEIVING THAT BECAUSE YOUR ENERGETIC FREQUENCY IS ALIGNED WITH THAT,
AND THEY WILL ALSO BE PUTTING ENERGY TOWARDS IT SO THERE IS A VERY POWERFUL SURGE OF
ENERGY BEING PUT TOWARDS THIS THING THAT YOU DO NOT ACTUALLY WANT TO MANIFEST.
CHOOSE TO SIMPLY RESPOND 'THANK-YOU' AND DISREGARD WHAT THIS PERSON IS INTRODUCING.
[YOU DO NOT HAVE TO TELL THEM YOU DO NOT BELIEVE THEM, LET IT BE WATER OFF A DUCKS BACK]

RECOGNIZE THAT ANY PERSON ATTEMPTING TO INTRODUCE NEGATIVE / LOW VIBRATIONAL
THOUGHTS, EMOTIONS AND FEELINGS [EVEN IF IT IS DIRECTED TOWARDS YOU / YOUR LIFE]
WILL ALWAYS RECEIVE A MANIFESTED MATCH INTO THEIR OWN LIFE [AS EVENTS / CIRCUMSTANCES
THAT ARE HARMONIOUS WITH THE FEELING STATE THEY ARE EMITTING]. THEY ARE ONLY EVER
IMPACTING THEIR OWN FUTURE LIFE EVENTS AND CIRCUMSTANCES, NOT YOURS. NO ONE OUTSIDE
OF YOU CAN MANIFEST ANYTHING [GOOD OR BAD] FOR YOU. THEY CAN ONLY ATTEMPT TO
INFLUENCE YOU INTO ALIGNING YOUR FEELING STATE WITH THIS THING. THEIR FEELING STATE WILL
ALWAYS IMPACT THEM, YOUR FEELING STATE WILL ALWAYS IMPACT YOU. YOU HAVE THE FREE WILL
TO EMBODY THE FEELINGS YOU DO DESIRE TO RECEIVE. OTHER PEOPLE ARE ALWAYS GOING TO
RECEIVE THE FEELINGS THEY EMBODY, THIS IS UNIVERSAL LAW. YOU DO NOT NEED TO EXPLAIN THIS
TO THEM EITHER. THEY PROBABLY WON'T UNDERSTAND, SO JUST LET IT BE, AND
EMBODY HIGHER VIBRATIONAL FREQUENCIES [FEELING STATES].

IF WHAT THEY HAVE SAID TO YOU IS LINGERING IN YOUR MIND:
SIMPLY WRITE DOWN THE OPPOSITE OF WHAT THEY INTRODUCED, SOMETHING FAITH BASED THAT
WILL HAVE A MASSIVELY POSITIVE IMPACT ON YOU AND YOUR LIFE. OR CHOOSE TO DISREGARD THE
TOPIC ALTOGETHER, AND FOCUS ON THE DESIRES YOU PERSONALLY WANT TO MANIFEST WITHIN
YOUR OWN LIFE. PREDOMINATELY EMBODY THE THOUGHTS, EMOTIONS AND FEELINGS THAT YOUR
DESIRES FULFILLMENT WILL BRING, AND YOU SHALL MANIFEST EXACTLY THAT.

I ALSO RECOMMEND DOING AN ENERGETIC CORD CUTTING RITUAL IN REGARDS TO ANYONE
INTRODUCING NEGATIVITY OR FEAR, AND ALSO IN REGARDS TO THE IDEAS THEY HAVE ATTEMPTED
TO INTRODUCE. KEEP YOUR VIBRATION AND YOUR WILL STRONG, PEACEFUL AND FOCUSED, YOU
WILL BE VIBRATING FAR TOO HIGH FOR ANY LOWER VIBRATIONS TO EVER REACH OR IMPACT YOU.

EVEN IF WE DESIRE TO MANIFEST SOMETHING GOOD FOR SOMEONE ELSE
WE ARE UNABLE TO HELP THEM MANIFEST THIS IF THEY DO NOT ALSO HAVE THEIR THOUGHTS,
EMOTIONS AND FEELINGS IN ALIGNMENT WITH THIS THING. REALIZE THAT YOU ARE UNABLE HELP
SOMEONE WHO WANTS TO BE STUCK IN AN OLD STORY. ANY GIVEN PERSON HAS TO DESIRE CHANGES
IN THEIR LIFE BEFORE YOU ARE ABLE TO SUPPORT THEIR CHANGES. WE ARE ALWAYS THE GREATEST
INFLUENCE FOR WHAT WE MANIFEST IN OUR OWN LIFE, OTHER PEOPLE ARE THEIR OWN GREATEST
INFLUENCE FOR WHAT THEY MANIFEST IN THEIR OWN LIFE.

IT IS ALSO CRUCIAL TO UNDERSTAND THAT YOU CANNOT MANIFEST BAD THINGS UPON OTHERS, OR
A GROUP OF OTHERS. IF YOU DO EVER ATTEMPT TO DO SO THAT WHICH YOU ARE ATTEMPTING TO
MANIFEST UPON ANOTHER WILL RETURN INTO YOUR LIFE,
TEN FOLD OR LARGER.

IF YOU ARE ANGERED TOWARDS ANOTHER, OR HAVE BEEN TRULY WRONGED BY ANOTHER,
OR FEEL NEGATIVELY TOWARDS ANOTHER FOR WHATEVER REASON ..
CHOOSE TO SEND THE VIBRATIONS OF PURE LOVE IN THEIR DIRECTION WHENEVER THEY ARISE
WITHIN YOUR MIND OR REALITY. YOU DO NOT HAVE TO INTERACT WITH THIS PERSON AT ALL.
YOU CAN CUT THEM OUT OF YOUR LIFE IN A PEACEFUL, HIGH VIBRATIONAL MANNER.
THE IMPORTANT CONCEPT IS TO RECOGNIZE THAT WHAT YOU FEEL
IS COMING BACK INTO YOUR LIFE AS EVENTS AND CIRCUMSTANCES WITHIN YOUR OWN LIFE.
EVEN IF YOU ARE THE ONE ATTEMPTING TO CONVINCE ANOTHER TO FEEL NEGATIVELY,
ATTEMPTING TO MANIPULATE ANOTHER INTO ATTRACTING NEGATIVITY,
THAT IS A NEGATIVE INTENTION EMBODIED WITHIN YOU. THEREFORE, YOUR NEGATIVE INTENT
TOWARDS THEM WILL INSTEAD RETURN INTO YOUR LIFE AS EVENTS AND CIRCUMSTANCES
ON THAT LOW VIBRATIONAL FREQUENCY. YOUR INTENTIONS TOWARDS ANOTHER
WILL ALWAYS IMPACT YOU MORE THAN IT WILL EVER IMPACT THE OTHER. NO MATTER WHAT.
KEEP YOUR INTENTIONS PURE AND FOCUSED ON YOUR OWN SELF.

IT WILL FEEL VERY STRANGE [AT FIRST] TO RADIATE FEELINGS OF COMPASSION,
ON THE HIGH VIBRATIONAL FREQUENCY OF LOVE INSTEAD OF NEGATIVITY, TO ANY PERSON OR
GROUP OF PEOPLE WHO HAVE WRONGED YOU OR TREATED YOU BADLY.
HOWEVER, JUST REMIND YOURSELF THAT THESE FEELINGS YOU ARE EMBODYING AND RADIATING ARE
FOR YOU AND YOUR LIFE. DO NOT ALLOW ANY PERSON OR GROUP OF PEOPLE TO CAUSE YOU TO
EMBODY LOW VIBRATIONAL FEELING STATES JUST BECAUSE OF THEIR CHOICE(S) / ACTIONS.
THEIR CHOICES / ACTIONS HOLD NO POWER OVER YOU, WHEN YOU DO NOT ALLOW THEM TO.
THEY WILL ONLY EVER END UP IMPACTING THEM.
REST IN KNOWING THIS.

FREE YOURSELF FROM FEELING AND RECEIVING LOWER VIBRATIONS, DO NOT SEEK 'REVENGE'. SEEK TO MANIFEST A HIGH VIBRATIONAL LIFE BEYOND YOUR WILDEST DREAMS. ONLY EVER FOCUS ON THE THINGS AND FEELINGS YOU DO WANT TO RECEIVE MORE OF IN THIS LIFETIME. THIS CONCEPT REMAINS TRUE EVEN IF THESE FEELINGS ARE SUBCONSCIOUS ONES, SMALL ONES, OR IN THE FORM OF GOSSIP. BE AWARE OF YOUR FEELING STATE TOWARDS / ABOUT OTHERS. ALWAYS. IF THE THINGS BEING THOUGHT / SAID WOULDN'T BE SAID TO THE FACE OF THIS PERSON, OR IF YOU WOULD NOT WANT THESE THINGS SAID ABOUT YOURSELF .. THEN WHY ARE THEY BEING THOUGHT / SAID AT ALL? IT IS BEST TO FOCUS ONLY ON YOURSELF AND EMBODYING THE FEELING STATE OF THE LIFE DESIGN YOU DO DESIRE.

IMAGINE FOR A FEW MOMENTS: YOU ARE ALREADY LIVING THE LIFE OF YOUR ULTIMATE DESIRES. ARE YOU REALLY WAISTING ANY ENERGY OR TIME THINKING OR SPEAKING LOW VIBRATIONALLY ABOUT OTHERS?? NO! YOU ARE TOO BUSY FEELING AMAZING AND ENJOYING YOUR LIFE TO BE CONCERNED WITH ANYONE ELSE! ESPECIALLY ANYONE LIVING IN LOW VIBRATIONS. IF YOU ARE ALWAYS THINKING OF / SPEAKING OF OTHERS, DO RECOGNIZE YOU ARE DOING THIS, AND BEGIN TO SWITCH YOUR THOUGHTS / TOPICS TO ONES OF HIGHER VIBRATIONS, SUCH AS PRODUCTIVE AND CREATIVE IDEAS, SOLUTIONS TO ANY 'PROBLEMS'. FEEL GENUINE GRATITUDE FOR THE JOYS WITHIN YOUR LIFE RIGHT NOW, AS WELL AS FOR THE ONES YOU DESIRE TO EXPERIENCE IN YOUR LIFE. PRACTICE WEEDING YOUR THOUGHTS / CONVERSATION TOPICS EVER-INCREASINGLY, UNTIL YOU NO LONGER THINK OF / SPEAK OF OTHERS OR LOW VIBRATIONAL TOPICS AT ALL. THEN CONTINUE TO FOCUS ON YOURSELF AND EMBODYING THE FEELINGS OF WHAT YOU DO DESIRE IN LIFE. ONLY. YOU WILL MASTER THIS. IT SIMPLY TAKES A LITTLE EFFORT AND PRACTICE.

DENISE LINN'S BOOK 'ENERGY STRANDS' IS AN OUTSTANDING BOOK WHICH EXPLAINS THE ABOVE CONCEPTS IN DEPTH AS WELL AS HOW YOU CAN FREE YOURSELF FROM THE LOWER VIBRATIONS OF OTHERS AND PAST EVENTS OR KARMA. EVEN IF YOU DON'T HAVE LOWER VIBRATIONAL PEOPLE OR CIRCUMSTANCES IN YOUR LIFE, HER BOOK WILL STILL BENEFIT YOUR LIFE JOURNEY MORE THAN I CAN EXPRESS WITH WORDS, DO READ IT!

RECOGNIZE, BECAUSE EACH INDIVIDUAL HAS FREE WILL, YOU CANNOT MANIFEST FOR SPECIFIC PEOPLE TO TREAT YOU DIFFERENTLY / RESPECT YOU / TREAT YOU A SPECIFIC WAY. YOU CAN TREAT PEOPLE AS YOU DESIRE TO BE TREATED, AND THIS MAY ALTER HOW THEY TREAT YOU. BUT, ULTIMATELY, HOW THEY TREAT YOU IS ENTIRELY THEIR OWN FREE WILL. YOU CAN MANIFEST PEOPLE WHO WILL TREAT YOU IN THE SPECIFIC WAYS YOU DO DESIRE TO BE TREATED, BUT NOT FOR SPECIFIC PEOPLE TO TREAT YOU A SPECIFIC WAY. THE DIFFERENCE IS YOU ARE SETTING THE INTENTION FOR AN UNSPECIFIED PERSON TO COME INTO YOUR LIFE THAT WILL IN FACT TREAT YOU THIS SPECIFICALLY DESIRED WAY, RATHER THAN ATTEMPTING TO HAVE A SPECIFIC PERSON TREAT YOU THIS SPECIFIC WAY. THERE ARE PEOPLE WHO WILL NATURALLY DESIRE TO TREAT YOU AS YOU DEEPLY DESIRE TO BE TREATED, BUT YOU CANNOT PUT THESE CHARACTERISTICS AND TRAITS UPON ANYONE WHO HAS NO DESIRE TO EMBODY THEM. THIS DOES NOT MEAN ANYONE IS 'RIGHT' OR 'WRONG', IT IS SIMPLY PREFERENCE. DIVERSITY IS WONDERFUL, IT ALLOWS EACH INDIVIDUAL TO BE AS THEY PLEASE AND TO MANIFEST OTHERS WHO DO EMBODY THE TRAITS THEY PERSONALLY DESIRE WITHIN OTHERS IN THEIR LIFE. YOUR EXPECTATIONS OF PEOPLE DO HAVE A DEGREE OF INFLUENCE ON THEIR BEHAVIOR AND ABILITY TO BE THE BEST VERSION OF THEIR OWN SELF, SO DO CHOOSE TO ENVISION AND BELIEVE IN THEIR ABILITY TO BE THE BEST VERSION OF THEIR SELF. BUT ALSO KNOW THAT ULTIMATELY YOU CANNOT CHANGE ANOTHER AGAINST THEIR FREE WILL TO BE AS THEY PLEASE. IN CHOOSING TO ENVISION THE BEST AND MOST ABUNDANT VERSION OF EVERY PERSON WITHIN YOUR REALITY YOU WILL ATTRACT THIS WITHIN YOUR OWN SELF, AND IMPACT THE QUALITY OF PEOPLE YOU ATTRACT INTO YOUR LIFE, AS WELL AS POSITIVELY INFLUENCE EACH INDIVIDUAL WHO IS ALREADY WITHIN YOUR REALITY. KEEP YOUR BOUNDARIES AND THE POWER OF YOUR PROTECTIVE BARRIERS ALIGNED. BUT DO NOT DO SO IN A WAY THAT YOUR MINDSET IS ALWAYS MEDITATING ON THE WORST CASE SCENARIOS AND WORST TRAITS / PROBLEMS YOU SEE IN PEOPLE. BE AWARE AND ALERT, DO NOT ALLOW ANYONE AT ALL TO OVERSTEP YOUR BOUNDARIES. EVER. BUT, DO KEEP YOUR OWN MINDSET PURE BY ENVISIONING THE BEST IN EVERYONE. THIS WILL ELEVATE YOUR VIBRATIONAL FREQUENCY AND FUTURE ATTRACTIONS SO MUCH. THIS DOES NOT MEAN THAT YOU SHOULD HOLD ONTO UNHEALTHY RELATIONSHIPS, OR KEEP PEOPLE IN YOUR LIFE WHO DO NOT RESPECT YOUR BOUNDARIES. IT SIMPLY MEANS YOU ARE CHOOSING TO NOT OBSESS OVER, OR GIVE ANY ENERGY TO WORST CASE SCENARIOS, AND / OR LOW VIBRATIONAL PEOPLE. ALLOW OTHERS TO DO AND BE AS THEY PLEASE. WE CANNOT CHANGE OTHERS, JUST AS OTHERS CANNOT CHANGE US. EVEN IF OTHERS WANT US TO CHANGE THEM, OR WE WANT EXTERNAL PEOPLE TO CHANGE US, PERSONAL CHANGE SIMPLY DOES NOT WORK THAT WAY. CHANGE IS AN INTERNAL CHOICE, A PERSONAL DECISION. EACH INDIVIDUAL MUST EMBODY THE DESIRE AND SELF-DISCIPLINE TO CHANGE. IF SOMEONE IS NOT READY TO CHANGE [STUCK IN OLD PATTERNS, OLD STORIES, VICTIM PERSPECTIVE / MENTALITY] NO ONE OUTSIDE OF THEM CAN CHANGE THAT. CIRCUMSTANCE AFTER CIRCUMSTANCE WILL REVEAL THEIR PATTERNS TO THEM, AND OTHERS CAN INTRODUCE NEW PERSPECTIVES. HOWEVER, THEY MUST BE THE ONE TO DECIDE THEY DESIRE TO CHANGE ANY PATTERNS, AND APPLY THE SELF DISCIPLINE TO CHANGE THEIR INTERIOR STATE. RECOGNIZE: IF ANY OTHER OR GROUP OF OTHERS HAS TREATED YOU LESS THAN HOW YOU DESERVE TO BE TREATED IT IS NOT A DEFICIENCY ON YOUR PART. THIS IS ENTIRELY A REFLECTION OF THEIR OWN INABILITY TO TREAT ANOTHER WITH RESPECT. THIS HAS NOTHING TO DO WITH YOUR WORTH. YOUR INTERNAL DIALOGUE, YOUR INTERNAL MINDSET AND YOUR ENERGY VIBRATION IS WHO / WHAT IS GOING TO POSITIVELY BENEFIT THE MOST FROM ENVISIONING THE BEST VERSION OF EACH PERSON IN YOUR REALITY. INFINITELY BLESS YOUR FUTURE THROUGH SHIFTING YOUR INTERNAL PERSPECTIVES. ULTIMATELY IT IS NOT ABOUT ANYONE ELSE, IT IS ABOUT YOUR ABILITY TO HARNESS YOUR OWN VIBRATIONAL FREQUENCY. WE ARE ABLE TO SEE POSITIVE / NEGATIVE ASPECTS WITHIN ANYONE AND ANYTHING. IT COMES DOWN TO THE INTERNAL PERCEPTION WE ARE HOLDING IN ANY GIVEN MOMENT. CHOOSE TO ENVISION THE BEST VERSION OF EVERY PERSON IN YOUR REALITY. THIS IS NOT JUSTIFYING THEIR BEHAVIOR OR WAYS. IT IS FOR THE BENEFIT OF YOUR OWN MINDSET, WELLBEING AND OVERALL FREQUENCY YOU ARE EMITTING. DO NOT ALLOW YOUR FREQUENCY TO BE LOWERED BECAUSE OF ANYONE ELSE. YOUR FREQUENCY EQUALS YOUR MANIFESTED LIFE EVENTS AND CIRCUMSTANCES.

EXAMINE:

ARE YOU BEING A PERSON WHO IS ALWAYS TYING TO 'GET THINGS' OUT OF PEOPLE AND SITUATIONS?

IF YOU ARE DOING THIS THEN YOU ARE OPERATING ON A FREQUENCY OF LACK, BECAUSE CLEARLY

YOU DO NOT HAVE ENOUGH AND ARE NOT SATISFIED IF YOU ARE ALWAYS TRYING TO GET THINGS

OUT OF PEOPLE AND SITUATIONS THAT ARISE IN YOUR LIFE. INSTEAD OF DOING THIS, SHIFT YOUR

PERSPECTIVE AND THINK OF WHAT QUALITY AND WORTH YOU ARE CAPABLE OF BRINGING INTO

EACH OF YOUR LIFE SITUATIONS. IT WILL BENEFIT YOU. THIS IS NOT FOR OTHER PEOPLE. ALTHOUGH,

OTHERS WILL BENEFIT AS RESULT. YOU DO NOT NEED TO GIVE PHYSICAL THINGS TO BRING QUALITY

TO OTHERS OR SITUATIONS. YOU DO NOT NEED TO BURN YOURSELF OUT EXPENDING ALL YOUR

ENERGY AND ATTENTION EITHER. OPERATE FROM A PLACE OF KNOWING YOUR SELF WORTH AND

THE QUALITY YOU AS AN INDIVIDUAL BRING TO THIS LIFE JOURNEY OF YOURS AND THE

COLLECTIVE, ALL THE WHILE REMAINING HUMBLE. PROVIDE TRUE QUALITY WHENEVER YOU CAN,

ALL THE TIME IF YOU CAN. YOU DO NOT HAVE TO GO OUT OF YOUR WAY TO DO SO, JUST DO SO

WHEN LIFE PROMPTS YOU TO OR WHEN YOUR INTUITION NUDGES YOU TO. STOP RUNNING

YOURSELF DRY IN THE ACCUMULATION GAME. DO NOT 'NEED' ANYTHING. STOP OPERATING ON THE

FREQUENCY OF LACK AND PARADOXICALLY SO MUCH MORE WILL COME TO YOU, AND IT WILL BE OF

MUCH HIGHER QUALITY, NO MATTER WHAT IT IS. WHEN YOU OPERATE ON THE FREQUENCY

OF PEACE, GRATITUDE AND SATISFACTION MORE THINGS TO FEEL PEACEFUL, GRATEFUL AND

SATISFIED ABOUT WILL IN FACT BE ATTRACTED TO YOU. BE SATISFIED. KNOW YOU ARE THE CREATOR

OF YOUR REALITY AND YOU ARE THE ONLY ONE WHO CAN BRING YOUR DESIRES TO YOU.

CONSCIOUSLY EMBODYING THE FREQUENCY OF SATISFACTION [YOUR DESIRES ALREADY FULFILLED]

+ TAKING INSPIRED ACTION IN THE DIRECTION OF YOUR DESIRES + UNWAVERING FAITH = YOUR

DESIRED LIFE DESIGN MANIFESTED BEFORE YOUR EYES. APPLY THE SELF DISCIPLINE TO TURN

INWARDS AND RELY SOLELY ON YOURSELF AND THE DIVINE TO FULFILL YOU WITH THE FEELINGS OF

PURE SATISFACTION. ANYONE ELSE'S SUPPORT IS EXTRA, AND DO BE GRATEFUL FOR IT. BUT, DO NOT

CONSTANTLY SEEK FROM OTHERS, WHETHER THAT BE PHYSICAL ITEMS, ENERGY, ATTENTION, LOVE ,

OR ANYTHING ELSE.

IS YOUR POWER OF MANIFESTATION BEING MANIPULATED?

DO NOT GIVE YOUR POWER OF MANIFESTATION AWAY TO THE THINGS YOU ARE AGAINST,
DO NOT SPEND ALL OF YOUR POWER FOCUSING ON PROBLEMS. DO NOT EXPEND ALL OF YOUR TIME,
ENERGY AND POWER TOWARDS WHAT YOU DO NOT WANT TO SEE MORE OF.
PUT YOUR TIME, THOUGHTS, FEELINGS AND ENERGY TOWARDS THE THINGS THAT YOU FIND
BEAUTIFUL AND EMPOWERING. THE THINGS YOU DO WANT TO SEE MORE OF,
THE THINGS THAT WILL MAKE THE WORLD A MORE PEACEFUL AND HARMONIOUS PLACE.
THIS IS AN IMPORTANT CONCEPT THAT DESERVES FOCUS, AS IT IS VERY PREVALENT WITHIN
OUR LIVES TODAY. IF YOU ARE ALWAYS FIGHTING AGAINST SOMETHING THEN YOU ARE
PUTTING YOUR OWN POWER OF MANIFESTATION TOWARDS WHAT YOU DO NOT DESIRE TO SEE MORE
OF. THIS IMMENSE FOCUS GIVES MORE POWER TO WHATEVER IT IS THAT YOU DO NOT LIKE / DO NOT
APPROVE OF. ENERGY GOES WHERE ATTENTION FLOWS, AND THIS IS NO EXCEPTION. PUT YOUR
ENERGY TOWARDS WHAT YOU DO DESIRE TO SEE EXPAND, NOT THE OPPOSITE. THIS IS NOT TO SAY
THAT WE SHOULD JUST TURN OUR HEADS TO THE WORLD, OR ANY PROBLEMS THAT ARISE, BUT WE CAN
MONITOR HOW MUCH OF OUR OWN ATTENTION, ENERGY AND FEELINGS ARE BEING PLACED
TOWARDS THE THINGS WE DO NOT LIKE / DO NOT APPROVE OF. WE CANNOT CONTROL THE WORLD
AROUND US, BUT WE CAN CONTROL HOW WE REACT TO IT. WHEN YOU CONSCIOUSLY ELEVATE YOUR
VIBRATIONAL FREQUENCY, TO CONSCIOUSLY HARNESS YOUR MANIFESTING POWER, YOU WILL
OBSERVE THAT YOUR PERSPECTIVES TOWARD ALL OTHER THINGS GRADUALLY BEGIN TO CHANGE AS
WELL. THINK ABOUT IT LIKE THIS: WHEN YOU ARE IN A HIGH VIBRATIONAL STATE OF BEING [HAVING A
GREAT DAY] ANY LOW VIBRATIONAL OCCURRENCES DO NOT BOTHER YOU AS MUCH AS THEY MIGHT
HAVE IF YOU WERE IN A LOW VIBRATIONAL STATE [HAVING A BAD DAY]. THE VIBRATIONAL
FREQUENCY YOU ARE IN [IN ANY GIVEN MOMENT] WILL IMPACT HOW YOU PERCEIVE AND FEEL
TOWARDS ANYTHING THAT MAY ARISE. ALSO, THE ENERGY OF EACH ATMOSPHERE OR SITUATION IS
DETERMINED BY OUR EMOTIONAL ENERGY WE ARE EACH RADIATING. WHEN A GROUP OF PEOPLE ARE
ALL EMBODYING SIMILAR VIBRATIONAL FREQUENCIES THE ENERGY WILL BE VERY INTENSE, AND THERE
IS IMMENSE AMOUNTS OF POWER BEING GIVEN TO THE FOCAL POINT. BE CONSCIOUS OF THIS
CONCEPT. A LOT OF INFORMATION IS INTELLIGENTLY CURATED WITH THE GOAL OF GRABBING YOU
BY YOUR ADRENALINE, CORTISOL AND NOREPINEPHRINE. THESE ARE YOUR FIGHT OR FLIGHT
HORMONES THAT DIRECTLY IMPACT YOUR THOUGHTS, EMOTIONS AND YOUR FEELING STATES. THUS,
YOU ARE ALLOWING YOUR INNATE POWERS OF MANIFESTATION TO BE CONTROLLED BY THESE
EXTERNAL SOURCES, WHICH ARE REALLY GOOD AT KEEPING YOU ADDICTED TO THE MINDSET OF
WHAT YOU DO NOT LIKE OR DO NOT WANT. LOW VIBRATIONAL EMOTIONS [SUCH AS JUDGEMENT] ARE
AN ADDICTIVE STATE OF THINKING AND FEELING. THE MORE WE JUDGE EVERYTHING OUTSIDE OF US
THE MORE WE BEGIN TO JUDGE OUR OWN SELF AND PLACE UPON OURSELF LIMITING BELIEFS THAT
HINDER OUR ABILITY TO CREATE THE LIFE DESIGN WE SO DEEPLY DESIRE TO LIVE WITHIN.

IN EACH MOMENT REMIND YOURSELF THAT YOUR THOUGHTS AND FEELINGS ARE BEING MAGNETIZED BACK INTO YOUR LIFE BY THE ENTIRE UNIVERSE. EVENTS AND CIRCUMSTANCES ON THE SAME LEVEL OF FREQUENCY WILL INEVITABLY MANIFEST, BOTH IN YOUR OWN LIFE AND WITHIN THE COLLECTIVE. THIS SIMPLY IS UNIVERSAL LAW, AND IT IS ALWAYS WORKING. IF THE TOPIC OF CONVERSATION IS NOT SOMETHING YOU WISH TO SEE MANIFEST, OR IT SIMPLY DOES NOT FEEL GOOD, THAT IS A PERFECT SIGN THAT YOU SHOULD ALLOW LITTLE TO NO TIME OR ENERGY TO BE SPENT ON IT.

QUESTIONS TO ASK YOURSELF:

IS THIS SOURCE DRAWING ATTENTION TOWARDS A PEACEFUL SOLUTION?

OR A SOLUTION AT ALL? OR ONLY FOCUSING ON THE PROBLEM?

IF WHAT IS BEING TALKED ABOUT IS CONJURING NEGATIVE EMOTIONS:

IT IS A SIGN THAT IT IS SOMETHING YOU DO NOT WANT. DO NOT GIVE YOUR ATTENTION, ENERGY AND VIBRATIONAL FREQUENCY [YOUR POWER OF MANIFESTATION] TO WHAT YOU DO NOT WANT.

QUESTION WHETHER ANY GIVEN PERSON / SOURCE OF INFORMATION

HAS A BIAS IN REGARDS TO THE TOPIC.

DO THEY CARE ABOUT / FAVOR THE TOPIC? OR ARE THEY AGAINST / DISLIKE THIS TOPIC?

DO THEY DESIRE TO HAVE YOU RETURN TO THEM FOR MORE INFORMATION?

DO THEY MAKE MONEY OFF YOUR ATTENTION?

OBSERVE, DO NOT CONSTANTLY ABSORB OR REACT.

THIS APPLIES TO ANYTHING AND EVERYTHING, NOT JUST WIDESPREAD TOPICS.

IT CAN ALSO APPLY TO YOUR DAILY CONVERSATIONS WITH PEOPLE. QUESTION EVERYTHING. LISTEN TO UNDERSTAND, BUT BE SKEPTICAL. FEEL INTO THE TRUE INTENT BEHIND THE WORDS. YOU ARE NOT REQUIRED TO GIVE EVERYTHING YOUR ATTENTION AND ENERGY. IT IS NOT UNCARING OR WRONG TO DISREGARD CERTAIN THINGS AND CONSCIOUSLY FILL YOUR MIND WITH OTHER [PEACEFUL / LOVING] THINGS. WE SIMPLY ARE NOT GOING TO RUN OUT OF THINGS THAT 'BOTHER US'. WE CAN FIND GOOD OR BAD TO FOCUS ON WITHIN ANY PERSON, THING OR SITUATION. THEREFORE, WE MUST CONSCIOUSLY DECIDE TO SHIFT OUR PERSPECTIVE WHEN THESE BOTHERSOME THINGS ARISE AND EITHER SEE THEM IN A NEW LIGHT, FOCUS ON FINDING AND APPLYING THE HIGH VIBRATIONAL, PEACEFUL SOLUTION OR DISREGARD THEM ALTOGETHER. CHOOSE TO TAKE CONTROL OF YOUR ATTENTION AND ENERGY FLOW, DIRECT IT TOWARDS WHAT YOU DESIRE TO SEE MORE OF. ENERGY TRULY DOES GO WHERE ATTENTION FLOWS. EVEN IF THE ATTENTION IS IN THE FORM OF DISLIKING OR DISAPPROVAL, IT IS STILL ENERGY THAT IS BEING PUT TOWARDS THIS THING. BREAK THE HABIT OF ALLOWING YOUR PERSONAL ENERGY FREQUENCY TO BE EASILY MANIPULATED BY EXTERNAL SOURCES. THIS IS APPLICABLE TO ANYONE OR ANY GROUP OF PEOPLE. WE OFTENTIMES THINK AND FEEL THAT IN ORDER TO DEFEAT SOMETHING WE ARE AGAINST WE MUST FIGHT AGAINST IT, AND THIS IS UNDERSTANDABLE BECAUSE THIS IS WHAT MOST PEOPLE HAVE BEEN CONDITIONED TO BELIEVE OVER THE COURSE OF THEIR LIFETIME. HOWEVER, THE TRUTH IS THAT THE ONLY WAY TO DISSIPATE SOMETHING LOW VIBRATIONAL IS TO EMBODY HIGHER VIBRATIONAL FREQUENCIES THAN THIS THING. WE CAN DO SO THROUGH FIRST SHIFTING OUR PERSPECTIVE, AND AS RESULT CONSCIOUSLY EMBODYING THE VIBRATIONAL FREQUENCY OF A/THE PEACEFUL SOLUTION. PEACEFUL DOES NOT EQUATE TO WEAKNESS. THE ABILITY TO EMBODY PEACE IS STRENGTH. PEACE IS ONE OF THE HIGHEST VIBRATIONAL FREQUENCIES. EMBODYING PEACE WITHIN ANY CIRCUMSTANCE WILL DISSIPATE ANY LOWER VIBRATIONS. PEACE IS STRENGTH. IF THIS SEEMS BIZARRE IT IS ONLY BECAUSE YOUR SUBCONSCIOUS MIND HAS BEEN CONDITIONED TO BELIEVE OTHERWISE. FIGHTING AGAINST SOMETHING WITH FEAR, ANGER OR ANY OTHER LOW VIBRATIONAL FREQUENCY IN ORDER TO DEFEAT IT ONLY FUELS THE FIRE AND GIVES MORE POWER TO THIS THING. HIGHER VIBRATIONS ALWAYS DISSIPATE LOWER VIBRATIONS, THIS IS ALWAYS TRUE. ONE PERSON EMBODYING HIGH VIBRATIONAL FREQUENCIES DISSIPATES THE LOWER VIBRATIONAL FREQUENCIES OF TENS OF THOUSANDS, IF NOT HUNDREDS OF THOUSANDS. KNOW THIS AND CHOOSE TO EMBODY THE HIGH VIBRATIONAL FREQUENCIES OF THE PEACEFUL SOLUTION(S). YOU WILL IMPACT YOUR OWN LIFE AND THE COLLECTIVE IN A VERY POWERFUL WAY. THERE IS IMMENSE POWER IN YOUR CALM.

ASSESS:

THE MAJORITY OF THE TIME ARE YOU BEING REACTIVE? OR CREATIVE?
CONSCIOUSLY MONITOR THIS AND DIRECT THE MAJORITY OF YOUR ENERGY AND POWER
INTO WHAT YOU DO DESIRE TO SEE MORE OF.
WHAT ARE THE SOLUTIONS / POTENTIAL SOLUTIONS
TO THE PROBLEMS THAT ARE BEING FOCUSED ON? SOLUTIONS THAT ARE
FOR THE HIGHEST GOOD OF ALL SOULS, NOT JUST FOR EGOTISTICAL / OPINIONATED DESIRES.
CONSCIOUSLY DECIDING TO NOT PUT YOUR ENERGY TOWARDS WHAT YOU DO NOT LIKE DOES NOT
MEAN THAT YOU DO NOT CARE, OR THAT YOU ARE DEEMING ANYTHING AS ACCEPTABLE. RECOGNIZE
THAT YOU ARE RISING UP BY DIRECTING THE POWER OF YOUR VIBRATIONAL FREQUENCY [THOUGHTS
AND FEELING STATES] INTO WHAT YOU DO IN FACT DESIRE TO SEE MANIFEST. ADAPT THE HABIT OF
ASKING YOURSELF: WHAT IS THE HIGH VIBRATIONAL, PEACEFUL SOLUTION THAT WILL DISSIPATE THE
LOW VIBRATIONS OF THE PROBLEM? EMBODYING PEACE, GRATITUDE AND THE FEELINGS OF
SATISFACTION PRODUCE MANIFESTATIONS THAT PROVIDE MORE OF THESE FEELINGS. EMBODYING LOW
EMOTIONS SUCH AS ANGER, JUDGEMENT, RAGE, ETC. PRODUCE MANIFESTATIONS THAT PROVIDE MORE
OF THESE FEELINGS. IT IS BEST TO NOT SEEK OUT OR EXPOSE YOURSELF TO NEGATIVITY ON PURPOSE, BUT
IF YOU ARE EXPOSED TO NEGATIVITY: THIS ALONE ISN'T GOING TO CAUSE NEGATIVITY TO MANIFEST
WITHIN YOUR LIFE. DO NOT SPEND TIME OR ENERGY WORRYING ABOUT THAT. WORRYING ABOUT IT
DOING SO IS WHAT WILL IGNITE LASTING LOW VIBRATIONAL FREQUENCIES. FOCUS ON
ACKNOWLEDGING THE NEGATIVITY IS NEGATIVE, AND THEN SHIFT YOUR PERSPECTIVE INTO A
SOLUTION MINDSET. OR, IF THE TOPIC IS NOT SOMETHING YOU PERSONALLY DESIRE TO FIND A
PEACEFUL SOLUTION FOR, DISREGARD THE TOPIC ALTOGETHER. FIND A WAY TO SHIFT YOUR
PERSPECTIVE AND/OR FOCUS ON AN ENTIRELY DIFFERENT TOPIC [SUCH AS YOUR DESIRED LIFE DESIGN]
THAT WILL LIFT YOUR VIBRATION INTO PURE LOVE, PEACE AND ABSOLUTE FAITH. DO SO AS SOON AS
YOU ARE ABLE. THERE IS NOTHING WRONG WITH STANDING UP FOR WHAT YOU BELIEVE IS RIGHT, BUT
CONSCIOUSLY DO SO BY PLACING YOUR ENERGY AND ATTENTION ON EMBODYING THE HIGH
VIBRATIONAL THOUGHTS AND FEELINGS THAT ARE ALIGNED WITTH THE/A PEACEFUL SOLUTION. KNOW
THAT THE INVISIBLE CONSCIOUSNESS EMBEDDED WITHIN THE ENTIRE UNIVERSE IS IN FACT
RESPONDING TO YOUR VIBRATIONAL FREQUENCY IN EACH MOMENT. HAVE FAITH IN THE
INCOMPREHENSIBLE POWER OF THIS ORGANIZED INTELLIGENCE. THE HIGH VIBRATIONAL FREQUENCIES
OF PEACE AND LOVE RESONATE STRONGLY WITH PURE SOURCE ENERGY, AND ARE MUCH MORE
POWERFUL THAN ANY LOW VIBRATIONAL PERSON OR GROUP OF PEOPLE. CONSCIOUSLY EMBODY THE
FREQUENCIES YOU DESIRE TO SEE MANIFEST. BE HUMBLE ENOUGH TO KNOW THAT THE LIMITS OF THE
HUMAN MIND AND PHYSICAL EYES DO IN FACT RESTRICT THE CAPACITY TO KNOW AND PERCEIVE
EVERYTHING THERE IS. THERE ARE REALMS UNSEEN BY THE PHYSICAL EYES, AND AN INVISIBLE FORCE
THAT IS MATCHING THE VIBRATIONAL FREQUENCIES WE EMBODY THROUGH PROVIDING EVENTS AND
CIRCUMSTANCES HARMONIOUS WITH THOSE FREQUENCIES EMITTED. WE EACH HAVE THE FREE WILL TO
CREATIVELY EMOBDY THE FREQUENCIES WE DESIRE TO MANIFEST MORE OF. ENJOY THAT FACT. FALL IN
LOVE WITH IT. BE OPEN MINDED TO NEW PERSPECTIVES. CONSCIOUSLY CHOOSE TO FOCUS YOUR
ATTENTION AND FEELING STATES ON THINGS YOU DESIRE. FOCUS ON WHAT YOU CAN DO FOR THE
HIGHEST GOOD FOR ALL SOULS. THE MORE ATTENTION LOW VIBRATIONS RECEIVE THE MORE THEY
EXPAND, THAT IS UNIVERSAL LAW. WE DO NOT GET TO DECIDE THAT IT IS NOT. IT JUST IS. UNIVERSAL,
UNBREAKABLE LAW. UNDERSTAND THAT AND BE CONSCIOUS, AWAKEN, TAKE YOUR POWER BACK AND
CONSCIOUSLY CREATE THE LIFE DESIGN YOU DESIRE. ELEVATE YOUR VIBRATIONAL FREQUENCY AND
YOU WILL POSITIVELY IMPACT THE ENTIRE COLLECTIVE.

IF YOU HAVE LOW VIBRATIONAL PEOPLE IN YOUR LIFE THAT YOU SIMPLY CANNOT AVOID

[FOR WHATEVER REASON] CHOOSE TO:

1. RECOGNIZE THAT THEY ARE NEGATIVE / LIVING IN A LOW VIBRATIONAL FREQUENCY

2. ACCEPT THAT YOU CANNOT CHANGE ANOTHER
[IT IS THEIR FREE WILL TO LIVE WITHIN A LOW VIBRATIONAL FREQUENCY]

3. DECIDE [BY MEANS OF YOUR OWN FREE WILL] THAT YOU DESIRE TO LIVE ON A VIBRATIONAL FREQUENCY THAT IS IN HARMONY WITH YOUR DESIRED LIFE DESIGN.

4. HAVE SOMETHING [SUCH AS A WORD OR PHRASE] YOU CAN EASILY RECALL THAT REMINDS YOU TO TUNE INTO YOUR BREATH AND RAISE YOUR OWN FREQUENCY WHILE SHIELDING YOURSELF FROM / DISREGARDING ANY LOW VIBRATIONAL FREQUENCIES.

IF THEY ARE SPEAKING DIRECTLY TO YOU SIMPLY KEEP IT AS SHORT AND SIMPLE AS YOU CAN, WHILE YOU FOCUS ON YOUR OWN FEELING STATE.

WHEN AROUND LOW VIBRATIONAL SOURCES YOU CAN BEGIN TO THINK AND FEEL ON THE GENUINE GRATITUDE YOU FEEL FOR YOUR DESIRES FULFILLED. BEGIN THANKING YOUR ANGELS AND GUIDES FOR ALWAYS PROTECTING YOU, YOUR AURA AND YOUR FREQUENCY. COMPREHEND THE BIG PICTURE ~ WE ARE ALL SPIRIT HAVING A HUMAN EXPERIENCE ~ THE THINGS WE EXPERIENCE WHILE ON OUR JOURNEY HERE ARE FOR THE GROWTH OF OUR SOUL. SURROUND YOURSELF WITH THE ENERGY OF UNCONDITIONAL LOVE AND ALLOW IT TO RADIATE OUT TO LOW VIBRATIONAL PEOPLE, THEY NEED IT THE MOST.

WHEN WE ARE IN A HEIGHTENED INTERNAL STATE WE ARE MORE REACTIVE. INTERNAL PEACE AND BALANCE ALLOWS FOR CLARITY AND CALM. LOW VIBRATIONAL PEOPLE AND GROUPS WANT YOU TO REACT, THAT IS THEIR GOAL. IT GIVES THEM A SENSE OF POWER, BECAUSE THEY ARE IN FACT TAKING YOUR POWER AWAY FROM YOU. CALM IS A SUPERPOWER. HIGHER FREQUENCIES WILL ALWAYS DISSOLVE ANY LOWER FREQUENCIES. CONSCIOUSLY CHOOSE TO EMBODY PEACE AND CALM ~ STAY IN YOUR POWER.

KNOW YOU ARE ALWAYS DIVINELY GUIDED AND PROTECTED.
BE CONFIDENT AND HOLD FAITH IN THIS FACT.
YOU ARE STRONGEST WHEN YOU DO NOT NEED TO EXTERNALIZE EVERYTHING TO OTHERS. CULTIVATE EVERYTHING FROM WITHIN, KEEP IT PERSONAL AND PRIVATE. NO LOWER VIBRATIONS CAN HAVE A SAY OR OPINION IF THEY DO NOT KNOW ABOUT IT IN THE FIRST PLACE. EMPOWER YOURSELF AND DO NOT EVER FEEL THE NEED TO PROVE YOURSELF TO ANYONE LIVING WITHIN A LOWER VIBRATION. THIS IS WHEN CALM TRULY IS POWER, THIS IS WHEN SILENCE IS POWER. THIS IS WHEN YOU MUST TURN INWARD AND FEEL INTO THE DEPTHS OF YOUR POWER. YOU ARE SUCH A STRONG AND POWERFUL BEING.

NOTE: IT IS NOT GOOD TO FOCUS ON OTHERS' INTENTIONS. STAY CENTERED AND BALANCED WITHIN YOUR OWN INTENTIONS RATHER THAN WONDERING OR WORRYING ABOUT WHAT ANYONE ELSE THINKS OR INTENDS. EACH INDIVIDUAL'S THOUGHTS, SPOKEN WORDS, DEEPEST INTENTIONS, DEEDS AND FEELING STATES EMBODIED WILL MANIFEST BACK INTO THEIR OWN LIFE AS EVENTS AND CIRCUMSTANCES ON THAT SAME EXACT FREQUENCY. EACH PERSON'S FREQUENCY IS THEIR OWN RESPONSIBILITY, EACH PERSON'S FREQUENCY WILL ONLY EVER DIRECTLY IMPACT THEIR OWN LIFE ON THE DEEPEST LEVELS. MOST OF THE TIME WE DO NOT NEED TO FOCUS ON INVOKING PROTECTION, BECAUSE WHEN WE ARE VIBRATING AT OUR HIGHEST WE ARE SIMPLY UNABLE TO BE IMPACTED BY ANY LOWER VIBRATIONS OR NEGATIVE INTENTIONS OF OTHERS. HOWEVER, SOMETIMES [ESPECIALLY WHEN WE ARE FEELINGS LOW ON ENERGY FOR ANY REASON] WE DO BENEFIT FROM INVOKING PROTECTION. IN DOING SO WE ARE ABLE TO BANISH NEGATIVE INTENTIONS, NEGATIVE ENERGIES, AND ANY PSYCHIC ATTACK, SENDING THESE ENERGIES BACK TO THEIR SOURCE.

BELOW IS A POWERFUL MANTRA WHICH WILL BANISH NEGATIVE INTENTIONS, ENERGY OR PSYCHIC ATTACK, AND DRAW IN PROTECTION, LOVING GUIDANCE AND INSPIRATION FROM YOUR HIGHEST VIBRATIONAL ANGELS, SPIRIT GUIDES, HIGHER SELF AND THE DIVINE. YOU WILL THEN BE ABLE TO PROGRESS IN THE DIRECTION OF YOUR DESIRED LIFE DESIGN WITHOUT RESISTANCE, AND WITH THE FULL EMBODIMENT OF HEALING, INSPIRATIONAL, LOVING ENERGY.

ANY NEGATIVE INTENTIONS, ENERGIES, ACTIONS, WORDS OR THOUGHTS

DIRECTED TOWARDS ME OR ABOUT ME

NEVER REACH ME OR IMPACT ME,

AT ALL.

THESE INTENTIONS, THESE ENERGIES, THESE ACTIONS, THESE WORDS, THESE THOUGHTS

ALWAYS RETURN DIRECTLY TO THEIR ORIGIN,

ONLY EVER IMPACTING THEIR ORIGIN.

MY HIGHEST VIBRATIONAL ANGELS AND SPIRIT GUIDES

ARE ALWAYS SHIELDING, GUIDING AND PROTECTING ME.

BLESSINGS ARE ALWAYS IN CONSTANT FLOW TO ME.

I AM EVER-SO-GRATEFUL AND BLESSED.

I AM VIBRANT, I AM RADIATING PURE LOVE

AND MANIFESTING THE LIFE OF MY CHOOSING

WITH POWERFUL INTENT.

EMOTIONAL WELL-BEING IS NOT AN OPTION, IT IS A PRIORITY.
IT MUST BE TOP PRIORITY, ALWAYS.
YOUR EMOTIONAL WELL-BEING IS THE FOUNDATION ON WHICH YOU ARE SETTING
YOUR INTENTIONS FROM AND TRULY OPERATING FROM,
WITHIN ALL ASPECTS OF LIFE.
EMOTIONAL WELL-BEING CANNOT BE COVERED UP, PUSHED DOWN OR DISCARDED.
YOUR EMOTIONAL WELL-BEING MUST BE RAWLY AND OPENLY ASSESSED, BY YOU.
UNDERSTAND, ACCEPT, RELEASE, HEAL, RESTORE BALANCE, HARMONIZE, BLOSSOM.

AS STATED EARLIER: WE CANNOT FORCE OTHERS TO CHANGE OR DO INNER WORK.
IT IS ENTIRELY A PERSONAL CHOICE AND SHOULD BE DONE ONLY WITH ONESELF,
NEVER FOR ANYONE ELSE OR WITH ANYONE ELSE. INNER WORK IS MEANT TO BE
PRIVATE SO THAT IT IS RAW, PURE AND TRUE. ATTEMPTING TO PERSUADE ANOTHER
TO DO INNER WORK IS LIKELY TO ONLY PUSH THEM FURTHER AWAY FORM THE
IDEA, THEIR JOURNEY WILL LEAD THEM INTO DOING INNER WORK WHEN THE
TIMING IS RIGHT. IF ANOTHER ASKS FOR SUPPORT, BY ALL MEANS LOVE THEM
UNCONDITIONALLY AND SUPPORT THEM. SHOW THEM YOU BELIEVE IN THEM AND
SHOW THEM THE TOOLS THEY CAN USE TO GUIDE THEM INWARD, IN THE RIGHT
DIRECTION. BUT MAKE SURE THEY RECOGNIZE THEIR PROGRESS IS ENTIRELY
RELIANT ON THEIR OWN SELF-DISCIPLINE AND DESIRE TO CHANGE. WE SIMPLY
CANNOT CHANGE ANOTHER BECAUSE WE CANNOT THINK AND FEEL FOR THEM.
THEY HAVE FREE WILL AND THEY ARE THE CREATOR OF THEIR OWN REALITY.
TELLING ANOTHER WE CAN CHANGE THEM WILL ONLY LEAD TO DISAPPOINTMENT
AND EVEN ANGER. THIS IS ALSO LIKELY TO LEAD OURSELF INTO LOWER
FREQUENCIES AS RESULT. IF SOMEONE TRULY DESIRES TO PARTAKE IN INNER WORK
TO CHANGE THEIR LIFE, THEY WILL RECOGNIZE THIS ON THEIR OWN AND EMBODY
THE SELF DISCIPLE TO DO SO. FORCING THIS ON ANOTHER IS NEVER
RECOMMENDED AS THIS IS LIKELY TO PUSH THEM AWAY FROM PARTAKING IN INNER
WORK FOR A LONG PERIOD OF TIME. SIMPLY, BE A GUIDE WHEN ASKED. DO NOT
ATTEMPT TO INTRODUCE THE CONCEPT WITHOUT BEING ASKED. IT IS ALSO NOT
WISE TO ATTEMPT TO HELP ANOTHER WORK THROUGH THEIR INNER WORK, IT IS A
VERY DEEP AND PERSONAL PRACTICE. NO MATTER HOW WELL WE BELIEVE WE KNOW
SOMEONE WE WILL NEVER KNOW THEM LIKE THEY KNOW THEIR OWN SELF, AND
LIKEWISE NO ONE WILL EVER TRULY KNOW AND UNDERSTAND OURSELF LIKE WE
KNOW OURSELF. THAT IS PRECISELY WHY THIS SHOULD BE KEPT EXCLUSIVE AND
PERSONAL. IF THIS IS ATTEMPTED FOR YOU BY ANOTHER, OR BY YOU FOR ANOTHER,
THE RESULTS WILL NOT BE NEAR AS FULFILLING AND CAN LEAD ONE TO
DISREGARDING THE POTENCY OF TRUE INNER WORK ALTOGETHER.
SO, FOCUS ON YOURSELF ONLY. ALLOW OTHERS TO BE, JUST OBSERVE THEM
WITHOUT JUDGEMENT, DON'T ABSORB THEM, THEY ARE IN THEIR OWN JOURNEY.
YOU ARE ON YOUR OWN JOURNEY. WE ARE EACH ON OUR OWN JOURNEY.

DO NOT EVER BE ASHAMED OF HOW YOU ARE TRULY FEELING,
GIVE YOURSELF PERMISSION TO RAWLY FEEL INTO THE DEPTHS OF EMOTIONS.
CHOOSE TO UNDERSTAND THEM, RATHER THAN PRETENDING THEY DO NOT EXIST
OR COVERING THEM UNTIL THEY FADE AWAY .. ONLY TO RETURN AGAIN
AT A LATER TIME, OFTEN MUCH MORE INTENSE.
'WHAT YOU RESIST NOT ONLY PERSISTS, BUT WILL GROW IN SIZE.' - CARL JUNG
FEELING INTO EMOTIONS ALLOWS YOU TO UNDERSTAND THEM, ACCEPT THEM
AND RELEASE THEM. THEN, YOU ARE ABLE TO RESTORE INTERNAL BALANCE
WHICH SERVES AS FERTILE SOIL FOR THE SEEDS OF YOUR INTENTIONS.
ALLOWING YOUR SEEDS TO SPROUT AND BLOSSOM.
EMOTIONAL WELL-BEING IS ALWAYS TOP PRIORITY.
ALLOWING YOURSELF TO ACCEPT EVERYTHING THAT YOU EMOTIONALLY FEEL
IS IN FACT A POSITIVE INTENTION EMBODIED.
WE ARE SPIRIT HAVING A HUMAN EXPERIENCE. OUR HUMAN BODY IS NOT IMMORTAL, BUT
OUR SOUL IS. WHEN WE CONSCIOUSLY SHIFT PERSPECTIVES WE ARE THEN ABLE TO STOP
TAKING EVERYTHING THAT HAS HAPPENED / IS HAPPENING IN OUR LIFE JOURNEY SO
PERSONALLY. WITH THIS [BIG PICTURE] PERSPECTIVE WE ARE ALSO ABLE TO KNOW THAT
WHEN LOVED ONES TRANSCEND THEIR HUMAN LIFETIME THEY TRULY ARE NOT GONE.
THIS LIFE WE ARE LIVING IS A DREAM-LIKE EXPERIENCE, A SPECK, WITHIN OUR SOUL'S
ETERNAL EXISTENCE. THIS HUMAN EXPERIENCE IS EXACTLY THAT - AN EXPERIENCE.
HUMAN EMOTIONS ARE A PART OF THE EXPERIENCE. THE PAIN, THE BLISS AND
EVERYTHING IN-BETWEEN. TO LIVE OUR OWN MOST FULFILLING EXPERIENCE WE MUST
NOT FEAR, ATTEMPT TO ESCAPE OR COVER-UP OUR EMOTIONS. EMBRACE EACH EMOTION,
FEEL INTO THEM. IMMERSE YOURSELF INTO THE DEPTHS OF THEM WITH THE INTENTION
OF UNDERSTANDING THEIR ENTIRETY, SO THAT YOU CAN RELEASE THEM ONCE YOU HAVE
FULLY EXPERIENCED AND UNDERSTOOD THE DEEPER MESSAGE WITHIN THEM. WHEN YOU
DO THIS YOU CAN THEN FILL THE SPACE CREATED WITH PURE MAGICK AND GOLD.
GODDESS, YOU ARE AN ALCHEMIST. YOU ARE FULLY CAPABLE OF TURNING YOUR PAIN
AND YOUR WOUNDS INTO THE MOST BEAUTIFUL TREASURES. THIS MAGICK IS WHAT YOU
ARE AT YOUR VERY CORE. I DO NOT SAY THESE THINGS JUST TO SAY THEM. I KNOW THEY
ARE TRUTH. I HAVE COMPASSION FOR ALL YOU MAY HAVE EXPERIENCED / ARE
EXPERIENCING IN YOUR LIFETIME BECAUSE I HAVE FELT THE TRAUMA, THE HEARTBREAK,
THE PAIN OF LOSING LOVED ONES, THE DEPTHS OF LONELINESS IN THE DARKEST OF
NIGHTS, AND MORE. EVEN IF YOU DO NOT EXPERIENCE ANYTHING EXTREMELY
DEVASTATING IN YOUR LIFETIME THAT DOES NOT MEAN THAT YOU DO NOT KNOW WHAT
IT MEANS TO FEEL REAL EMOTIONAL PAIN AND OTHER EMOTIONAL STATES THAT ARE LESS
THAN BLISSFUL. ALL THESE EMOTIONS ARE VERY, VERY REAL AND IMPACT US ON A VERY
REAL LEVEL. I AM NOT IN ANY WAY, SHAPE OR FORM IMPLYING THAT THEY DO NOT OR
SHOULD NOT. BUT I ALSO KNOW, FROM EXPERIENCING THESE THINGS, WE EACH HOLD
IMMENSE POWER WITHIH TO ACCEPT, UNDERSTAND, RELEASE AND TRANSFORM .. TO
DESIGN OUR LIFE AND EVOLVE OUR SOUL. WE EACH HAVE THE CHOICE TO LET THIS
EXPERIENCE CONTROL WHERE OUR INTERNAL POWER IS EXERTED, OR HARNESS OUR
POWER TO RISE UP DESPITE ANY PAST OR PRESENT CIRCUMSTANCES / EXPERIENCES. IN
DOING SO WE CAN IN FACT MANIFEST THE LIFE DESIGN WE PERSONALLY DESIRE AND
DESERVE. YOU DO HAVE THE POWER WITHIN YOU TO HEAL, TO BE COMPLETE ENTIRELY
ON YOUR OWN, TO GROW, TO EVOLVE, TO LOVE MORE THAN EVER BEFORE, TO CREATE
WITH SOUL, TO FULLY LIVE WITHIN THE LIFE DESIGN YOU DESIRE. VALUE YOUR EMOTIONS,
ALL OF THEM. TEARS ARE JUST AS HEALING AS LAUGHTER IS. **HONOR YOUR TEARS,
GODDESS. TOXINS ARE RELEASED FROM THE BODY THROUGH TEARS.**

HIGHS AND LOWS ARE NATURAL. RELEASE THE NEED TO CONTROL. ALLOW YOURSELF TO BE. TAKING THE SMALLEST STEPS TOWARDS YOUR PERSONAL DREAMS IS PURE POWER. LOWS ALLOW TRUE TRANSFORMATION TO OCCUR. REMEMBER: YOU ARE HUMAN, SO AM I, SO ARE THEY. HUMANS EXPERIENCE EMOTION, THIS IS NOT A FAULT IN OUR COMPOSITION. THIS IS WHAT WE ALL EXPERIENCE IN OUR SOUL EVOLVING JOURNEY. WE AS HUMANS ARE NOT PERFECT, WE ARE AUTHENTICALLY GORGEOUS. DELVE INTO WHAT YOU FEEL. SEEK TO REVEAL YOUR AUTHENTICITY. WHEN YOU ARE EXPERIENCING A LOW FEEL INTO YOUR INNER MESSAGES, WHAT IS SO DEEPLY RESIDING BELOW THE EMOTIONS? ALLOW YOUR PERSPECTIVES TO SHIFT. NEW PERSPECTIVES ON REOCCURRING FEELINGS WILL FUEL YOUR GROWTH. FEELING LOW DOES NOT MEAN YOU ARE BELOW, IT MEANS YOU ARE WORTHY. YOU ARE [PARADOXICALLY] PERMANENTLY ELEVATING YOUR SOUL BY EXPERIENCING THIS LOW AND PERSISTING. YOU ARE WITHIN A POWERFUL PHASE OF GROWTH, IT IS A SIGN THAT YOU ARE IN FACT DIVINE. DON'T NUMB IT OUT, FEEL INTO THE DEPTHS OF IT. READ DARK POETRY IF IT RESONATES IN THIS MOMENT, OR LISTEN TO INSPIRATION IF THAT RESONATES IN THIS MOMENT. ONLY YOU KNOW WHAT YOU ARE SOULFULLY CRAVING IN THIS MOMENT. GO DEEP INTO THE INTENSITY OF YOUR PSYCHE, IN YOUR OWN DARKNESS YOU ARE SHINING BRIGHTER THAN A MILLION SUNS COMBINED. IN RECOGNIZING YOU FEEL LOW YOU CAN ACKNOWLEDGE AND DEFINE THAT WHICH MAKES YOU FEEL THE MOST ALIVE. DO NOT PUSH YOURSELF TO BE LIGHT WHEN YOU ARE FEELING HEAVY, BUT RATHER, DELVE INTO YOUR HEAVY FEELINGS, ALLOW THEM TO BE WELL INTENDED HEAVY FEELINGS. FEEL GOOD ABOUT YOUR DARKNESS AS WELL AS YOUR LIGHT AND THERE WILL NEVER BE NEGATIVITY IN YOUR DARKNESS OR IN YOUR LIGHT. YOU ARE SUCH A POWERFUL BEING, KEEP GOING. THE BEST IS YET TO COME. YOU ARE TRANSFORMING, YOU ARE GOD IN THE FLESH AND YOUR ESSENCE OF BEING ~ YOUR SPIRIT ~ WITHIN THIS HUMAN BODY IS PERFECT. HUMAN EXISTENCE IS NOT PERFECT. IT IS AUTHENTIC, AN IMPERFECT, EVER-CHANGING, SOUL-EVOLVING EXPERIENCE. YOU WILL RETURN TO YOUR PURE AND PERFECT SPIRIT NATURE SOON ENOUGH, EMBRACE THIS EVOLUTIONARY EXPERIENCE WHILE IT'S YOURS ~ WISH GRANTED ~ YOU CAN NOW DO ANYTHING YOU WANT, KNOW THAT.

THERE IS A DIFFERENCE BETWEEN HAVING A LOW VIBRATIONAL MINDSET AND BELIEF SYSTEM AND SIMPLY HAVING ONE [OR A FEW] LOW VIBRATIONAL DAYS. DO NOT STRESS OR WORRY THAT YOU WILL MANIFEST SOMETHING NEGATIVE IN TIMES LIKE THIS. WE ALL EXPERIENCE THESE MOMENTS OR DAYS FROM TIME TO TIME. WE ARE HUMAN, IT IS NATURAL. WHEN YOUR MINDSET AND FEELING STATES ARE PREDOMINATELY STRONG AND FOCUSED WITHIN THE VIBRATIONAL FREQUENCY OF WHAT YOU DO WANT THIS WILL DISSIPATE ANY LOWER EMOTIONAL STATES THAT MAY OCCASIONALLY APPEAR. HERE IS AN ANALOGY TO BETTER UNDERSTAND THIS CONCEPT: IF YOU HAVE AN EMPTY CUP AND YOU DESIRE TO FILL IT WITH PURE ORANGE JUICE BUT A LITTLE APPLE JUICE GETS MIXED IN WITH THE ORANGE JUICE YOU AREN'T REALLY GOING TO TASTE THE APPLE JUICE UNLESS YOU HAVE POURED IN A SIZABLE, CONCENTRATED AMOUNT OR CONTINUE TO FILL THE CUP WITH APPLE JUICE INSTEAD OF ORANGE JUICE. LIKEWISE, OUR PREDOMINATE THOUGHTS AND FEELINGS ARE WHAT MANIFEST INTO OUR LIFE, NOT THE SMALL DOSES OF THOUGHTS AND FEELINGS THAT ARE UNALIGNED WITH THE PREDOMINATE ONES. THIS IS EMPOWERING TO RECOGNIZE FOR TWO REASONS. I: WE ARE NOT GOING TO INSTANTLY MANIFEST 'BAD' THINGS IF WE ARE HAVING AN OFF MOMENT OR DAY. 2: WE MUST EMBODY THE FREQUENCY OF OUR DESIRES PREDOMINATELY IN ORDER TO SEE THEM MANIFEST WITHIN OUR LIFE. THINKING AND FEELING IN ALIGNMENT WITH THEIR FREQUENCY EVERY ONCE IN A WHILE, BUT FEELING LACK, ETC. THE REST OF THE TIME IS NOT GOING TO BRING THEM INTO OUR REALITY BECAUSE THIS IS NOT THE PREDOMINATE FREQUENCY WE ARE RESIDING IN. THE BUFFER OF TIME WITHIN MANIFESTATION, THE REASON WHY OUR MANIFESTATIONS TAKE A PERIOD OF TIME TO MANIFEST IS A BLESSING. IF EVERY THOUGHT AND FEELING OF EVERY PERSON ON EARTH INSTANTLY MANIFESTED WE WOULD BE LIVING IN CHOAS, BECAUSE INEVITABLY WE AS HUMANS ARE NOT PERFECT. FEELING INTO EMOTIONS AND THEIR MESSAGES DOES NOT IN ANY WAY NEED TO BE A LOW VIBRATIONAL EXPERIENCE. EMOTIONS HOLD MESSAGES FOR THE HIGHEST GOOD OF YOUR SOUL'S EVOLUTION. YOU CAN TRANSFORM ANY EMOTION INTO A HIGH VIBRATIONAL EXPERIENCE. EMOTIONS ARE INDICATORS FOR WHERE WE ARE AT WITHIN OUR JOURNEY. DO NOT USE THIS AS AN EXCUSE TO TREAT OTHERS OR YOURSELF POORLY. DELVING INTO YOUR EMOTIONS DOES NOT MEAN LACKING SELF CONTROL. YOUR UNDERLYING INTENTIONS ARE WHAT WILL ALWAYS BE REFLECTED BACK INTO YOUR LIFE, WE EACH RECEIVE EVENTS AND CIRCUMSTANCES INTO OUR LIFE THAT MATCH OUR INTENTIONS WE HAVE EMBODIED / ARE EMBODYING. THIS ALSO MEANS THAT IF YOU 'APPEAR / ACT' NICE BUT HAVE LOW VIBRATIONAL INTENTIONS THESE LOW VIBRATIONAL INTENTIONS WILL MANIFEST WITHIN YOUR OWN LIFE, NOT THE FALSE OUTWARD APPEARANCES / ACTIONS. BE AUTHENTIC WITH YOURSELF AND THE WORLD AROUND YOU. AS RESULT YOU WILL FIND YOURSELF LIVING WITHIN THE BEAUTY OF THOSE AUTHENTIC, AND PURE INTENTIONS MIRRORED BACK TO YOU. BEING FALSELY OPTIMISTIC WHEN WE EMOTIONALLY FEEL OTHERWISE IS ACTUALLY [DEEP WITHIN US] A BAD FEELING WE ARE EMBODYING, FEELING BAD ABOUT EMOTIONS IS ALSO A BAD FEELING EMBODIED, BUT BEING TRUTHFUL AND ASSESSING THE EMOTION FOR WHAT IT IS [EVEN IF IT NOT A FEEL GOOD EMOTION] IS AN ACT FUELED WITH POSITIVE INTENTION.

YOU DO NOT NEED TO TRY TO CHANGE YOUR EMOTIONS ALLOW YOURSELF TO BE. JUST BREATHE AND OBSERVE. ACCEPT AND ALLOW THE YOURSELF TO BE. PARADOXICALLY, THIS WILL LIKELY ALLOW YOU TO FEEL BETTER. BY ACKNOWLEDGING THE EMOTIONS EXISTENCE, RATHER THAN COATING OR BURYING, WE ARE EMBODYING A POSITIVE INTENTION. IN DOING SO WE ARE NOT SENDING OUT BAD FEELINGS THAT WE WILL RECEIVE BACK - THIS IS IMPORTANT TO RECOGNIZE. EMBODYING NEGATIVE INTENTIONS / FEAR BASED BELIEFS AND FEELINGS / ANGER / HATRED / ETC. IS WHAT IS TRULY LOW VIBRATIONAL AND THAT WILL GENERATE LOW VIBRATIONAL MANIFESTATIONS. INTEND TO BE IN A MINDSET OF PEACE AND FAITH, NOT DESPAIR AND FEAR. DELVE INTO EACH OF YOUR EMOTIONS WITH POSITIVE INTENTION, FOR THIS WILL ALLOW YOU TO UNCOVER THE MESSAGES THAT HOLD PROFOUND MEANING FOR YOUR SOUL'S EVOLUTION IN THIS HUMAN LIFETIME, AND YOU WILL IN FACT TRANSFORM THE EMOTIONS ONCE AND FOR ALL. EMOTIONS ARE NOT EVER LOW VIBE WHEN YOU CHOOSE TO APPROACH THEM WITH THE POSITIVE INTENTION TO UNDERSTAND THE DEEPER MEANING WITHIN THEM. THERE'S A STRONG DIFFERENCE BETWEEN EMBODYING A NEGATIVE MINDSET / BELIEF SYSTEM / INTENT AND OPENLY ACKNOWLEDGING WE FEEL AN EMOTION WITH THE POSITIVE INTENT TO UNCOVER ITS MEANING RATHER THAN COATING IT WITH FALSE 'HIGH EMOTION'. FEELING INTO OUR EMOTIONS IS AN ACT OF SELF LOVE THAT STEMS FROM POSITIVE INTENTION, REGARDLESS OF THE EMOTION. BURYING OR COATING THEM MAKES US FEEL HEAVY AND LESS THAN WORTHY. DELVE INTO THE EMOTIONS YOU EXPERIENCE, THEY ARE NOT A DEFINITION OF YOU, THEY ARE SIMPLY A MESSAGE FOR YOU, A TEMPORARY EXPERIENCE IF YOU ALLOW THE MESSAGE TO COME THROUGH TO YOU. RECOGNIZE THAT NO ONE OUTSIDE OF YOU CAN DEFINE THE MEANING OF YOUR EMOTIONS FOR YOU. TAKE OTHERS' OPINIONS OR INSIGHTS WITH A GRAIN OF SALT, FOR YOU MUST ULTIMATELY GO DEEP WITHIN YOUR OWN SELF IN ORDER TO UNDERSTAND EMOTIONS RAWLY FOR WHAT THEY ARE AND UNVIEL THE MESSAGE THEY HOLD. THEN, WHEN THE TIME FEELS RIGHT TO DO SO: RELEASE THEM, TRANSFORM THE ENERGY OF THEM. YOU HOLD IMMENSE POWER WITHIN YOU, BOTH IN YOUR DARKNESS AND IN YOUR LIGHT. OWN EVERY SINGLE OUNCE OF YOUR ENERGY. HARNESS IT, DO NOT ALLOW IT TO HARNESS YOU. THE ONES WHO SCREAM POSITIVE VIBES ONLY AT THE WORLD AND REJECT, COVER OR BURY EMOTIONS DO NOT UNDERSTAND THE IMMENSITY OF GODDESS POWER EXISTING WITHIN BOTH THE DARK AND THE LIGHT. GODDESS, YOU ARE AN ALCHEMIST, NOT A SINGLE EMOTION WITHIN YOU IS NEGATIVE WHEN YOU CHOOSE TO SEE IT WITH YOUR TRANSFORMATIVE GODDESS VISION. YOU ARE THE HEROINE OF YOUR STORY, KNOW AND FEEL HOW EMPOWERING THAT TRUTH IS. ALSO RECOGNIZE IT IS NOT YOUR JOB TO FIX ANOTHER AND YOU CANNOT HEAL ANYONE WHO WANTS TO BE SICK. YOU CAN SHOW ANOTHER A SHIFT IN PERSPECTIVE, AND LEAVE IT AT THAT, FOR THEM TO DO AS THEY PLEASE. EACH PERSON MUST PERSONALLY DESIRE TO GO WITHIN.

UNCOVERING THE MESSAGES IN EMOTIONS:

WHERE IS THIS STEMMING FROM?

WHAT BELIEF IS AT THE ROOT OF / CREATING THIS EMOTION?

WHERE EXACTLY DO I FEEL IT IN MY BODY?

WHEN DID I FIRST FEEL THIS EMOTION?

IS THIS EMOTION TIED TO ANYONE ELSE?

WHAT ARE THE EXACT EMOTIONS I AM EXPERIENCING?

WHAT WILL IT TAKE FOR ME TO FEEL BETTER?

THE DEEPER MESSAGE YOU UNCOVER IS LIKELY TO LEAVE YOU FEELING INSPIRED.

THE GOAL IS TO MOVE OUT OF CONFUSION AND OVERWHELM,

AND INTO A STATE OF CLARITY AND CONTROL.

DELVE INTO YOUR OWN SHADOWS AND DISCOVER,

ARE THERE ANY DEEPER FEELINGS AND VULNERABILITIES FROM THE PAST THAT ARE
ASSOCIATED WITH THE EMOTIONS YOU ARE FEELING? ASK YOURSELF: WHAT DEEPER
MESSAGE ARE THESE EMOTIONS TRYING TO BRING TO MY AWARENESS?

REFLECT ON THE SUBCONSCIOUS BELIEFS PAGES, FORGIVENESS PAGES, BOUNDARIES
PAGES, CLEAN AND TIDY PAGES, THE I AM AFFIRMATIONS PAGE AND ANY OTHER
PAGES YOU FEEL DRAWN TO WHILE WORKING THROUGH EMOTIONS.

THE ABILITY TO PLACE YOUR OWN PERCEPTIONS ASIDE
AND TO [WITHOUT JUDGEMENT] DO YOUR BEST TO VIEW THINGS FROM ANOTHER'S
PERSPECTIVE IS POWERFUL. THIS ALLOWS YOU TO NOT TAKE ANYTHING
PERSONALLY, OTHER PEOPLE'S WORDS AND ACTIONS ARE A REFLECTION OF THEIR
INNERMOST PERCEPTIONS AND BELIEFS. KNOWING THIS ALSO ALLOWS YOU TO
UNDERSTAND HOW YOUR OWN WORDS AND ACTIONS MAY BE MISUNDERSTOOD BY
ANOTHER. WE EACH HAVE UNIQUE PERCEPTIONS. BE MINDFUL OF YOUR WORDS
AND ACTIONS TOWARDS OTHERS, BE AS CLEAR AS YOU CAN SO THAT THE TRUE
MEANING WITHIN YOUR MESSAGE IS CONVEYED CORRECTLY,
WITHOUT MISUNDERSTANDING.

YOU CAN'T ALWAYS CONTROL WHAT HAPPENS,
BUT YOU CAN CONTROL HOW YOU REACT TO WHAT HAPPENS.

WRITE A LETTER

TO YOUR HIGHER SELF / THE DIVINE / YOUR HIGHEST VIBRATIONAL ANGELS AND GUIDES [WHICHEVER YOU PREFER OR A COMBINATION] ALLOW EVERYTHING YOU ARE FEELING TO BE POURED OUT INTO THIS LETTER. THEN, SEAL IT UP AND PUT IT AWAY. IN A DAY OR SO, OPEN THE LETTER AS IF A STRANGER HAS SENT THIS LETTER TO YOU. VIEW IT FROM THE PERSPECTIVE AS IF IT IS ANOTHER PERSON SPEAKING TO YOU, ASKING FOR YOUR INTUITIVE INSIGHT IN REGARDS TO THE CONTENTS OF THE LETTER. DO NOT LET YOUR ANALYTICAL MIND CHIRP IN, WRITE A RESPONSE TO THIS LETTER FROM YOUR INTUITION. WRITE THE RESPONSE AS IF YOU ARE RESPONDING TO THE STRANGER .. NOT YOURSELF. SHIFT PERSPECTIVES AS MUCH AS YOU CAN AND LOOK FOR SYMBOLISM OR PATTERNS THAT STAND OUT TO YOU WITHIN THE ORIGINAL LETTER. DON'T OVER THINK THIS, SIMPLY WRITE THE RESPONSE FROM A PLACE OF INTUITION.

THEN, SEAL UP THE RESPONSE AND PUT IT AWAY.

IN A DAY OR SO, OPEN THE RESPONSE AND RECEIVE THE GUIDANCE AS THOUGH YOUR OWN PERSONAL GUARDIAN ANGEL HAS DELIVERED THIS LETTER TO YOU. WHAT SYMBOLISM DO YOU FIND WITHIN THIS RESPONSE LETTER? REMEMBER: THE SYMBOLISM OF ANY GIVEN THING MAY HAVE UNIVERSAL MEANINGS, BUT MORE IMPORTANTLY WE MUST ASSESS WHAT SYMBOLISM THIS HOLDS UNIQUE TO OUR OWN SELF AND OUR OWN LIFE. WHAT ___ MEANS TO ONE PERSON OR GROUP OF PEOPLE MAY HAVE AN ENTIRELY DIFFERENT MEANING FOR YOU.

THIS IS APPLICABLE WITHIN WAKING LIFE AS WELL AS WITHIN OUR NIGHTLY DREAMS. FOR DREAMS, WRITE DOWN YOUR DREAMS AS SOON AS YOU AWAKEN. DO NOT ATTEMPT TO DEFINE THE DEEPER MEANING RIGHT THEN. COME BACK TO YOUR JOURNALING OF THE DREAM LATER THAT DAY. WHAT SIGNIFICANCE DOES THIS DREAM HOLD FOR YOU? DO YOU NOTICE ANY PATTERNS IN YOUR DREAMS? WHAT SIGNIFICANCE DOES YOUR INTUITION TELL YOU THESE PATTERNS HOLD?

TO RELEASE EMOTIONS:

GO LAY ON MOTHER EARTH AND VISUALIZE YOURSELF RELEASING EVERYTHING INTO HER. SHE WILL TRANSFORM THE ENERGY YOU RELEASE INTO HER AND FILL YOU WITH PEACE AND CLARITY. IT HAS BEEN SCIENTIFICALLY PROVEN THAT WHEN OUR BARE SKIN IS IN CONTACT WITH THE EARTH WE ABSORB ELECTRONS. THIS IS SIGNIFICANT BECAUSE THESE ELECTRONS ARE NATURE'S PURE AND POWERFUL ANTIOXIDANTS. THEY NEUTRALIZE FREE RADICALS [FREE RADICALS LEAD TO INFLAMMATION / DISEASE]. WHEN YOU ARE EXPERIENCING STRONG EMOTIONS GO INTO NATURE, WALK BAREFOOT OR LAY ON THE GROUND AND WATCH THE CLOUDS GO BY AS YOU RELEASE EVERYTHING INTO HER AND ABSORB THE HEALING ELECTRONS. WATCH THE CLOUDS AND CONTEMPLATE YOUR PLACE IN THIS VAST UNIVERSE. KNOW YOU ARE INFINITELY GUIDED, SUPPORTED AND PROTECTED. ALL YOU MUST DO IS TUNE INTO YOUR PURE AND PERFECT SPIRIT NATURE, KNOW THAT YOU ARE A PART OF SOMETHING MUCH BIGGER THAN YOU CAN EVEN BEGIN TO COMPREHEND WITH YOUR LIMITED HUMAN MIND. DO NOT RESIST CHANGE OR HOLD ON TO THINGS, AS CHANGE IS INEVITABLY A PART OF THIS HUMAN LIFETIME. WHEN WE BEGIN TO SET INTENTIONS FOR THE LIFE WE DO DESIRE WE MUST ALSO NOT BE SHOCKED THAT THINGS WILL CHANGE AND OUR LIFE WILL BEGIN TO PURGE ITSELF OF THE THINGS / PEOPLE / SITUATIONS THAT ARE NOT ALIGNED WITH / SERVING OUR DESIRED LIFE DESIGN. THE ENTIRE UNIVERSE IS CONSPIRING ON YOUR BEHALF, TO BRING YOU WHAT YOU HAVE ASKED FOR. WHEN YOU CHOOSE TO TUNE INWARDS AND LISTEN TO YOUR INTUITION, YOUR DIVINE INNER GUIDANCE, YOU WILL RECEIVE PROFOUND MESSAGES AND INSIGHTS THAT WILL LEAD YOU INTO YOUR DESIRED LIFE DESIGN. YOU HAVE ASKED WITH INTENTION, YOUR DIVINE LIFE SOURCE IS GUIDING YOU INTO WHAT YOU HAVE INTENDED. KNOW THAT, TRUST THAT, FULLY EMBODY AND BELIEVE THAT. ALL YOU ARE GOING THROUGH IS LEADING YOU INTO THE LIFE DESIGN YOU HAVE INTENDED YOU DESIRE TO THRIVE WITHIN. DON'T DOUBT THE UNSEEN, AS THE UNSEEN IS FAR MORE POWERFUL THAN WHAT YOUR HUMAN VISION IS PERCEIVING. THIS IS ALSO WHY IT IS VERY IMPORTANT TO INTEND THAT YOUR INTENTIONS ARE SET FOR THE HIGHEST GOOD OF ALL SOULS, AND WILL COME IN THE MOST PEACEFUL AND LOVING WAY.

I NOW VIEW ANY REJECTION OR PERCEIVED LOSS AS A REDIRECTION FROM MY SOURCE TO VIBRATE EVEN HIGHER AND DREAM EVEN BIGGER. THERE TRULY ARE NO LOSSES, ONLY WINS AND ONLY LESSONS.

IF YOU ARE DISTRESSED BY ANYTHING EXTERNAL, THE PAIN IS NOT DUE TO THE THING ITSELF, BUT TO YOUR ESTIMATE OF IT; AND THIS YOU HAVE THE POWER TO REVOKE AT ANY MOMENT. -MARCUS AURELIUS

EMPATHS

Assess:
Is this emotion my own?
Or is it stemming from someone else's emotions they are experiencing?

Recognize other people's emotions are messengers for them, not you. You are not responsible for uncovering the messages other people's emotions have for them. Turn them inward. Envision yourself as a straw, not a sponge. By this I mean: be fully present and listen to understand, not just to respond, but do not absorb the emotions as your own. Visualize yourself allowing them to flow through a strong, bright white cord, down into Mother Earth. The emotions are transformed into unconditional love as they travel through this cord.
You can also do a cord cutting meditation.

A key to understanding the differences between the following:

Pity: i acknowledge your suffering.

Sympathy: I care about your suffering.

Empathy: I feel your suffering.

Compassion: I want to relieve your suffering.

It is okay to acknowledge, care, feel and desire to relieve another's suffering, but remember to love yourself first. Putting your self first is not selfish, it is an act of self love, and it is very important. Especially for empaths. You are able to help others more when you are not absorbing, but observing, within a strong and healthy vibrational state of your own.

'The biggest mistake you can make in life is believing that you cannot control your emotions. You may believe that you cannot change how you feel, but that belief is why you are a slave to your emotions. So many people who call themselves empaths are really just emotionally unstable, and rather than stabilize their volatile emotions, they define themselves as empaths and wear their sentimentality like a badge of honor. But the true empath can feel everyone's feelings without attaching to them or reacting to them emotionally. A true empath can feel their own feelings to their fullest depths without being drowned by them, or without identifying with them. The next time you feel a difficult emotion, do not simply surrender to it. Instead, give the emotion your full attention: wherever you feel the difficult emotion in your body, flood that area with attention and awareness and watch as the emotion gradually transforms or disappears. By consistently working in this manner, you can become non-reactive to your emotions. Feelings may still come in waves and they may still be intense, but you will be riding a boat of calm observation rather than drowning in the sea. The true empath never says, 'I am sad,' but simply, 'I feel sadness.' Understand the difference and free yourself from the tyranny of your emotions.' - Shaman Nabeel Redwood

THE EMOTIONS YOU EXPERIENCE AS RESULT OF YOUR OWN PERSONAL LIFE
ARE NOT THE SAME ABSORBING OTHERS' NEGATIVITY, ETC.
UNCOVERING THE DEEPER MEANING WITHIN YOUR PERSONAL EMOTIONS IS A POSITIVE
INTENTION EMBODIED. FOCUSING ON OTHERS' NEGATIVITY ONLY ALLOWS YOUR POWER
OF MANIFESTATION TO BE MANIPULATED. BE ABLE TO DETERMINE THE DIFFERENCE.
[SEE PAGES 58-60]

JUDGEMENT IS ADDICTIVE,
THE JUDGEMENT WE FEEL IS A REFLECTION OF OUR OWN INNER SELF,
WHEN WE RECOGNIZE WE ARE JUDGING OTHERS WE MUST ASSESS WITHIN OUR OWN SELF
WHY WE ARE DOING SO. IS IT BECAUSE OF DEEPLY ROOTED INSECURITIES?
SO THAT WE HAVE REASON TO FEEL GOOD ABOUT OURSELF?
ARE WE JUDGMENTAL TOWARDS EVERYTHING ALL THE TIME,
ESPECIALLY OUR OWN SELF?
IS THE JUDGEMENT WE ARE MAKING ACTUALLY TRUE ABOUT OUR OWN SELF?
TAKE THE TIME TO FEEL INTO WHY.

IF JUDGEMENT IS STEMMING FROM JEALOUSY THEN ASK YOURSELF TRUTHFULLY:
WHAT IS IT THAT I SO DEEPLY DESIRE THAT THIS PERSON HAS / EMBODIES?
GO DEEP WITHIN. JUDGMENT AND JEALOUSLY ALWAYS HOLD MESSAGES FOR US,
WE MUST INTEND TO UNCOVER THE MESSAGES AND THEN LET GO OF THEM,
FOR THEY BLOCK US FROM MANIFESTING THE LIFE DESIGN WE DESIRE.

FEELING THE LACK OF SOMETHING EQUALS PAIN.
ASESS:
ARE YOU REALLY LACKING ANYTHING?
OR ARE YOU JUDGING YOUR LIFE IN COMPARISON TO
SOMETHING OR SOMEONE ELSE? IF SO, YOUR PAIN STEMS FROM COMPARISON,
AND NOT BEING TRUE TO YOU AND YOUR SOUL.

COMPARISON IS THE THIEF OF JOY.
- THEODORE ROOSEVELT

DO NOT FOCUS ON MANIFESTING SOMETHING THAT IS SOMEONE ELSE'S.
YOU CAN FOCUS ON SOMETHING SIMILAR TO WHAT THEY HAVE,
BUT NEVER THE EXACT THING THAT BELONGS TO ANOTHER.

I FEEL ___ EMOTION BECAUSE I WANT / NEED [X].
SO, HOW WOULD IT FEEL IF YOU ALREADY HAD [X]?
REALLY FEEL INTO THIS. CLOSE YOUR EYES AND VISUALIZE YOU HAVE [X].
DOES HAVING [X] TRULY FULFILL YOU?
HAS YOUR PAIN / EMOTION DISSIPATED?
IF YES, THEN CONTINUE TO FEEL AS IF YOU ALREADY HAVE [X],
AND YOU SHALL MANIFEST THE FULFILLMENT OF [X].
IF NO, CONSIDER WHAT WILL TRULY FULFILL YOU.
MAYBE SOMETHING DIFFERENT?
OR SOMETHING THAT OFFERS A TRULY DEEPER LEVEL OF FULFILLMENT.
REFLECT ON THE 'POWER IN CLEAN AND TIDY' PAGES,
MOST OFTEN WE DO NOT 'NEED' ANYTHING TO FEEL BETTER,
BUT RATHER, THE OPPOSITE.

IF YOUR JUDGEMENT IS STEMMING FROM ANGER / DISAPPROVAL TOWARDS ANOTHER / OTHERS WHO HAVE BEHAVED / ARE BEHAVING IN A WAY THAT YOU PERCEIVE AS WRONG FROM YOUR PERSPECTIVE AND BELIEF SYSTEM, RECOGNIZE THAT YOU ARE NOT IN CONTROL OF OTHERS' BEHAVIORS AND THEIR BEHAVIORS ARE A REFLECTION OF THEIR PERSPECTIVES AND INNERMOST BELIEFS. THIS DOES NOT MEAN YOU ARE DEEMING THEIR BEHAVIORS AS ACCEPTABLE, BUT SIMPLY YOU ARE NO LONGER ALLOWING THEIR BEHAVIORS TO MANIPULATE YOUR POWER OF MANIFESTATION [YOUR FEELING STATE], AS STATED PREVIOUSLY. IF YOU TRULY FEEL THE DESIRE TO COMBAT THINGS THAT GO AGAINST YOUR BELIEFS, GO ABOUT IT EMBODYING THE POSITIVE INTENTION OF PROVIDING A PEACEFUL SOLUTION THAT WILL BENEFIT THE HIGHEST GOOD OF ALL. ENERGY GOES WHERE ATTENTION FLOWS. DO NOT FOCUS ON THE PROBLEMS AND JUDGING THEIR SOURCE(S), THIS GENERATES NEGATIVE FEELING STATES WITHIN YOUR OWN BEING. THE RESULT OF THESE NEGATIVE FEELING STATES WILL MANIFEST BACK INTO YOUR LIFE AS EVENTS AND CIRCUMSTANCES THAT MAKE YOU FEEL THESE SAME LEVELS OF JUDGMENT AND ALL OTHER NEGATIVE FEELINGS EMBODIED. THE SUBCONSCIOUS MIND AND THE UNIVERSE DO NOT DISCRIMINATE BETWEEN I DO NOT WANT [X] AND I DO WANT [X]. THEY SEE A PERSON EMBRACING [X] WITH ALL THEIR ATTENTION, THOUGHTS, EMOTIONS AND FEELINGS AND THINK 'OKAY, YOU REALLY WANT MORE [X]'. WHEN IN FACT YOU DO NOT WANT MORE OF THIS THING. THE MOST EMPOWERING THING YOU CAN DO TO MAKE A CHANGE AND MAKE A POSITIVE AND LASTING IMPACT IS TO FOCUS ON THE IDEAL SOLUTION, BE A POSITIVE EXAMPLE, PAVE THE WAY IN SHOWING OTHERS THE WAY TO THE SOLUTION THAT WILL BENEFIT THE HIGHEST GOOD OF ALL. FOCUSING ALL ATTENTION, THOUGHTS, EMOTIONS, FEELINGS AND ENERGY TOWARDS A POSITIVE SOLUTION WILL RESULT IN YOUR SUBCONSCIOUS MIND AND THE ENTIRE UNIVERSE SUPPORTING THIS POSITIVE SOLUTION. MEANING, YOU WILL RECEIVE EVER-INCREASING IDEAS AND INSPIRATIONS FOR THE SOLUTION THAT WILL BENEFIT THE HIGHEST GOOD OF ALL, AND YOU WILL CONTINUOUSLY SEE IMPROVEMENT BECAUSE WHAT YOU FOCUS ON EXPANDS. THE UNIVERSE WILL DELIVER MORE AND MORE EVENTS AND CIRCUMSTANCES THAT MATCH THE POSITIVE SOLUTION YOU ARE FOCUSED UPON.

COMPASSION ALLOWS BEAUTIFUL PERSPECTIVE SHIFTS TO OCCUR.
KNOW THAT THE WAY OTHERS TREAT YOU IS THE WAY THEY TREAT THEIR OWN SELF. THE WAY THAT YOU TREAT OTHERS IS THE WAY THAT YOU TREAT YOURSELF.
DO YOUR BEST TO NOT TAKE ANYTHING OTHERS' DO PERSONALLY.
ALSO RECOGNIZE THAT THE WAY YOU TREAT OTHERS
IS A DIRECT REFLECTION OF HOW YOU TREAT YOURSELF INTERNALLY.
DO YOU LIKE HOW YOU ARE TREATING YOURSELF?

EXPERIENCING EMOTIONS WITH THE POSITIVE INTENTION OF UNDERSTANDING THEIR DEEPER MEANING IS VERY BENEFICIAL, BUT WE SHOULD ALSO MONITOR HOW LONG WE ARE EXPERIENCING THE EMOTION(S) FOR THE EMOTION EXPERIENCED ONLY BECOMES HARMFUL WHEN YOU FIND YOURSELF EXPERIENCING A BAD FEELING FOR A LONG TIME. AS YOU MAINTAIN THIS STATE LONG ENOUGH IT BECOMES A MOOD. AS YOU HOLD THE MOOD LONG ENOUGH, IT BECOMES A TEMPERAMENT. AS YOU SUSTAIN THE TEMPERAMENT IT'S BECOMES PART OF YOUR PERSONALITY. DR. JOE DISPENZA STATES IT BEST: 'YOUR PERSONALITY CREATES YOUR OUR PERSONAL REALITY. YOUR PERSONALITY IS MADE UP OF WHAT YOU THINK, FEEL, AND DO. ONLY ABOUT 5% OF WHAT YOU THINK, FEEL, OR DO IN A DAY IS ACTUALLY CONSCIOUS AND THE REST IS ON AUTO-PILOT.'

THIS AUTO PILOT MODE IS YOUR SUBCONSCIOUS, WHICH IS WHY BUILDING SUBCONSCIOUS EMPOWERING BELIEFS AND REFLECTING ON THESE EMPOWERING BELIEFS EACH DAY IS SO POTENT IN RETRAINING THE SUBCONSCIOUS TO DISREGARD THE OLD AND ACCEPT THE NEW. THUS, WE ARE RECREATING OUR PERSONAL REALITY, DOING SO IS CRUCIAL AND BENEFICIAL AS YOUR PREDOMINANT THOUGHTS, SPOKEN WORDS, DEEPEST INTENTIONS AND FEELING STATES EMBODIED ARE YOUR KARMA THAT WILL MANIFEST BACK INTO YOUR LIFE AS EVENTS AND CIRCUMSTANCES ON THE SAME FREQUENCY. YOU CAN IN ANY MOMENT CHANGE YOUR KARMIC PATH BY CHANGING YOUR VIBRATIONAL FREQUENCY AND PREDOMINANTLY MAINTAINING THE NEW FREQUENCY.

IT IS CRUCIAL TO UNCOVER AND SINK OUR TEETH ALL THE WAY INTO THE DEPTHS OF TRUTH THAT EXIST WITHIN THE MESSAGES OF OUR EMOTIONS, BOTH TEMPORARY AND REOCCURRING, BUT IT IS ALSO JUST AS CRUCIAL TO LET GO OF OUR OLD STORY AND PROGRESS FORWARD WITH A NEW STORY. WE MUST NOT STAY IN THE PROCESS OF UNCOVERING MESSAGES BENEATH OUR EMOTIONS, STIRRING THE POT JUST TO SEE IF ANYTHING ELSE ARISES, FOR THIS WILL LEAD INTO SEVERE SELF PITY, CONFUSION AND A STRONGER ASSOCIATION WITH THE OLD STORY. OLD STORYLINES AND NARRATIVES WE TELL OURSELVES AND OTHERS ABOUT OUR LIVES UP TO THIS POINT IN TIME ARE VERY ADDICTIVE. THIS IS BECAUSE OVER TIME THEY HAVE ESTABLISHED STRONG, WELL ROOTED PATTERNS WITHIN OUR LIFE THAT REFLECT THE STORY WE ARE TELLING, AND SO WE BECOME EVEN MORE DEEPLY ENGRAINED IN TELLING THIS STORY AS OUR TRUTH. WHETHER WE RECOGNIZE IT OR NOT EVERY ONE OF US IS VERY CAPABLE OF BECOMING ADDICTED TO THE LOW VIBRATIONAL STATES THE OLD STORY WE ARE TELLING IGNITES BECAUSE THEY FEEL FAMILIAR AND COMFORTABLE TO US. WE OFTEN RECEIVE ATTENTION AND COMPASSION FROM OTHERS WHEN TELLING THIS STORY, WHICH SUBCONSCIOUSLY FUELS US TO DO SO AGAIN AND AGAIN. A LARGE MAJORITY OF THE TIME WE DO NOT CONSCIOUSLY RECOGNIZE THE ONLY REASON THIS STORY IS OUR STORY IS BECAUSE WE CONTINUE TO INFUSE IT WITH ATTENTION AND ENERGY THROUGH OUR THOUGHTS, EMOTIONS AND FEELINGS.

OUR SUBCONSCIOUS MIND ACCEPTS WHAT WE PREDOMINATELY THINK AND FEEL AND FUELS OUR CONSCIOUS THINKING WITH BELIEFS AND THOUGHTS THAT REINFORCE OUR STORY WE ARE TELLING AS CORRECT. AND THE UNIVERSE IS RESPONDING TO THE VIBRATIONAL FREQUENCY WE EMIT THROUGH SENDING US MORE EVENTS AND CIRCUMSTANCES THAT MATCH HOW WE FEEL, SO WE ARE RECEIVING EVEN MORE PROOF THAT OUR STORY IS TRUE AND WILL CONTINUE TO THRIVE AS WE TELL IT, EVEN IF IT IS A LOW VIBRATIONAL STORY THAT WE 'DISLIKE' OR DO NOT ENJOY. DO FEEL INTO THE DEPTHS, ACCEPT AND EMBRACE THE ENTIRETY OF WHAT HAS BROUGHT YOU TO WHERE YOU ARE TODAY, BUT STAYING IN THIS PLACE TOO LONG CAN REINFORCE NEGATIVE PATTERNS / FAMILIAR FEELINGS THAT DO NOT SERVE OUR HIGHEST GOOD AND DESIRED LIFE DESIGN. ONCE EXTRACTED, USE THE MESSAGES TO TRANSFORM SUBCONSCIOUS BELIEFS AND OLD PATTERNS STORIES.

HARNESS THE CONCEPT OF DEATH IN THE MOST BEAUTIFUL, ENLIVENING AND EMPOWERING WAYS. MANY HUMANS HAVE BEEN CONDITIONED TO BELIEVE THE PHYSICAL DEATH WE EACH INEVITABLY WILL EXPERIENCE IS 'THE ULTIMATE END' AND SUBCONSCIOUSLY THIS IS A MAJOR REASON MANY ALSO RESIST ALLOWING THE DEATH OF PATTERNS, BELIEFS AND STORIES THAT DO NOT SERVE THEIR OWN HIGHEST GOOD, AS WELL AS ALL OTHER INEVITABLE CHANGES THAT TAKE PLACE WHILE ON THIS HUMAN EXPERIENCE. WE ARE ALL INFINITE BEINGS, DEATH IS NOT THE ULTIMATE END. IT IS THE RELEASE OF WHAT NO LONGER SERVES OUR HIGHEST GOOD SO THAT WE MAY EXPAND BACK INTO PURE SOURCE ENERGY. DEATH ALLOWS EXPANSION AND NEW GROWTH, AND AS RESULT THIS EVOLVES OUR SOUL FOR THE ENTIRETY OF OUR SOUL'S EXISTENCE. OBSERVE NATURE AND YOU WILL SEE FIRSTHAND HOW NATURAL, BEAUTIFUL AND EMPOWERING THIS CONCEPT OF DEATH [RELEASING/TRANSFORMATION] TRULY IS. NOTHING EVER TRULY DIES IN THE WAY WE HAVE BEEN TAUGHT. DEATH IS TRANSFORMATION, ENERGY CANNOT BE CREATED OR DESTROYED. IN RELEASING AND ALLOWING OLD THE PATTERNS AND STORYLINES TO DIE WE ARE IN FACT EMBRACING THE PUREST AND MOST POTENT FORMS OF ALCHEMY WE HOLD WITHIN US. AS WE DO SO WE ARE FULLY SUPPORTED BY THE ENTIRE UNIVERSE THAT SURROUNDS US AND THRIVES WITHIN US.

IF YOU REALIZE THAT ALL THINGS CHANGE,
THERE IS NOTHING YOU WILL TRY TO HOLD ON TO.
IF YOU ARE NOT AFRAID OF DYING,
THERE IS NOTHING YOU CANNOT ACHIEVE.
- LAO TZU

ON A PIECE OF PAPER WRITE DOWN YOUR STORY, YOUR PATTERNS, YOUR LOW VIBRATIONAL BELIEFS ABOUT YOURSELF AND YOUR LIFE. THEN, SHRED THIS PAPER INTO PIECES AND THEN BURN THE PIECES IN A FIRESAFE BOWL [SAFELY]. THIS SHOWS YOUR MIND AND THE UNIVERSE THAT YOU ARE LETTING GO, FOREVER. WHILE DOING THIS RITUAL BREATHE IN DEEPLY ~ PAUSE AND TENSE YOUR ENTIRE BODY AS YOU FEEL THE LIMITING BELIEFS, OLD PATTERNS AND ALL OLD ENERGY ~ THEN EXHALE FULLY AND ENVISION THESE THINGS BEING FULLY RELEASED FROM YOUR BEING. INHALE DEEPLY AND FILL THESE SPACES WITH THE PUREST FORMS OF SOURCE ENERGY AND LIGHT [ALSO SEE PAGE 100]. THIS IS INTERIOR ALCHEMY AT ITS FINEST, YOUR INNER GODDESS POWER THRIVING. IT DOES NOT MATTER WHETHER YOU CHOOSE TO ENVISION THIS RELEASE IN THE PROCESS STATED ABOVE, OR OCCURRING ENTIRELY WITHIN YOUR OWN BEING. ULTIMATELY IT IS THE SAME THING, SINCE ALL IS ONE. BUT, MOST PEOPLE WILL FIND THAT IT IS EASIER FOR THEIR MIND TO RELEASE FULLY THROUGH ENVISIONING OLD ENERGY PATTERNS 'PHYSICALLY' LEAVING THEIR BEING, AND BRINGING IN PURIFIED ENERGY FROM THE DIVINE. IF YOU RESONATE WITH OTHERWISE AND THAT IS MORE POTENT FOR YOU, BY ALL MEANS DO THAT WHICH RESONATES WITH YOU. THE IMPORTANT THING TO RECOGNIZE IS THAT WE ARE ONE WITH THE POWER THAT EXISTS 'OUTSIDE' OF US. WE ARE THIS POWER, THERE TRULY IS NO 'IN HERE' AND 'OUT THERE'. BUT, OUR HUMAN MIND AND PHYSICAL VISION IS LIMITED, SO WE OFTENTIMES CANNOT EASILY COMPREHEND THAT. WHICH IS WHY ALLOWING OUR PHYSICAL EYES TO SEE THE OLD BE TRANSFORMED INTO FLAMES WHILE ALSO VISUALIZING AND BREATHING THE REMAINING ENERGIES OUT OF OUR BEING TO ALLOW FOR HIGHER FREQUENCIES TO FILL OUR BEING IS SO POTENT. WE HAVE THE FREE WILL TO UNCONSCIOUSLY LIVE THROUGH REACTING, WHICH OFTEN LEADS TO LOW FREQUENCIES EMBODIED. OR WE CAN CHOOSE TO CONSCIOUSLY EMBODY HIGH FREQUENCIES. WE ARE THE WHOLE UNIVERSE, THE UNIVERSES, WE ARE NOT SEPARATE FROM SOURCE — THAT'S THE ILLUSION CREATED BY THE EGO THAT IS OFTENTIMES BELIEVED. WE ARE EACH DIVINE ENERGY EXPRESSED IN HUMAN FORM, WE ARE ONE. RELEASING OLD STORYLINES AND NARRATIVE WE TELL OURSELVES AND OTHERS ABOUT OUR LIFE IS ABSOLUTELY NECESSARY IF WE ARE TRULY DESIRING TO EVOLVE INTO A NEW STATE OF BEING, A NEW LIFE, A NEW STORY. THE LIFE DESIGN THAT CONTAINS OUR ULTIMATE DESIRES MANIFESTED. IT IS A PERSONAL CHOICE TO DO THIS. WE EACH HAVE FREE WILL, WE EACH HAVE TO DECIDE FOR OUR OWN SELF TO APPLY THE SELF DISCIPLINE TO EXECUTE THIS TRANSFORMATIVE PROCESS. IT'S NOT 'PAIN FREE' FOR ANYONE, BUT IT IS ABSOLUTELY WORTH IT. IF ANYONE DOES NOT HAVE THE WILLINGNESS TO GO DEEP WITHIN AND DO THIS PERSONAL INNER WORK, THAT IS YOUR / THEIR FREE WILL TO MAKE THAT DECISION, BUT IT ALSO ILLUMINATES THE FACT THAT YOU / THEY DO NOT HAVE A VERY STRONG DESIRE TO CHANGE AND WOULD RATHER STAY LIVING IN THE OLD STORY, WHERE EVERYTHING IS FAMILIAR AND COMFORTABLE. CHANGE IS UNCOMFORTABLE AND UNFAMILIAR FOR A SHORT TIME, BUT IT IS ENTIRELY WORTH IT LONG TERM.

IF YOU CANNOT STOP OVERTHINKING / ANXIETY / WORRY / NEGATIVE THINKING:

RELEASE THE NEED
'TO FIGURE IT ALL OUT' JUST RELEASE THE NEED TO CONTROL / UNDERSTAND.
YOU DO NOT HAVE TO FIGURE IT ALL OUT RIGHT NOW.
TAKE A NAP OR A NATURE WALK,
DO A GUIDED MEDITATION OR MEDITATE.
LISTEN TO A DR. WAYNE DYER AUDIO [THERE ARE MANY AVAILABLE ON YOUTUBE]
TAKE A SHOWER, TAKE A BATH.
CREATE A PIECE OF ART THAT RESONATES WITH THE CORE OF YOUR SOUL.
DO SOMETHING [ANYTHING HEALTHY] TO CHANGE THE PATH OF YOUR THOUGHTS.
MEDITATION IS GREAT BECAUSE IT ALLOWS RESISTANCE TO SUBSIDE.
EMBODY A [GENERALIZED] PEACEFUL FEELING TOWARDS YOUR FUTURE LIFE.
STOP FOCUSING ON THE DETAILS AND SEE THE BIGGER PICTURE - THAT IS HOW TO FLY.

KNOW THYSELF:
KNOW WHAT MAKES YOU FEEL YOUR BEST
& TURN TO THESE ACTS OF SELF LOVE.
[REFLECT ON THE SELF LOVE PAGE]

OBSERVE YOUR BODY LANGUAGE AND POSTURE.
THE WAY WE CARRY OURSELF DIRECTLY IMPACTS THE WAY WE FEEL.

TUNE INTO YOUR SENSES IN THIS PRESENT MOMENT.

AFFIRMATIONS:
I DO NOT HAVE TO FIGURE THIS OUT RIGHT NOW.
I DO NOT HAVE TO FIGURE IT ALL OUT RIGHT NOW.
THE ANSWER(S) I SEEK WILL COME TO ME IN THE RIGHT MOMENT(S).
SIMPLY THROUGH FOCUSING ON MY BREATH I CAN SHIFT MY FREQUENCY RIGHT NOW.
I AM IN A PEACEFUL ENERGY FREQUENCY.
IF I DON'T LIKE THE FREQUENCY I AM IN I AM FULLY CAPABLE OF
CHANGING IT RIGHT THEN AND THERE,
JUST AS EASILY AS I CAN CHANGE A RADIO STATION OR TELEVISION STATION.
I SIMPLY DEFINE WHAT FREQUENCY I DESIRE, EMBRACE MY POWER
AND SHIFT INTO THAT FREQUENCY.

IS WHAT YOU ARE OBSESSING OVER TRULY SIGNIFICANT WITHIN YOUR LIFE?
IS IT IN YOUR CONTROL?
IF YOUR MIND WAS STIMULATED BY ANOTHER TOPIC / SOMETHING ELSE TO DO WOULD
THIS HALT YOUR WORRY / STRESS / ANXIETY?

HAVING A WRITTEN VISION OF YOUR DESIRED LIFE DESIGN
ALLOWS YOU TO IGNITE THE FEELINGS OF THAT AS HERE NOW. THIS IS
SUCH A POWERFUL TOOL THAT TAKES YOU OUT OF THE MINDSET OF RELIVING
THE PAST OR WORRYING ABOUT THE FUTURE. IT ALLOWS YOU TO TRULY
SAVOR THE PRESENT MOMENT, TO TASTE INFINITY AND TO CONSCIOUSLY
IMAGINE AND IGNITE THE VIBRATION OF YOUR DESIRES AS HERE NOW.

"WORRY IS A MISUSE OF THE IMAGINATION.' - DAN ZADRA

OVERTHINKING OFTEN LEADS TO DWELLING ON WORST CASE SCENARIOS,
THUS, OUT OF ALL POSSIBLE OUTCOMES IN REGARDS TO THIS TOPIC OVERTHINKING
OFTEN LEADS TO MANIFESTING THE WORST OUTCOME, THIS IS BECAUSE THAT IS
WHAT IS BEING FOCUSED UPON WITH SO MUCH ENERGY.
EVEN IF THIS IS A SIGNIFICANT TOPIC, CHOOSE TO TAKE THE ACTION YOU CAN TAKE
AND THEN TRUST YOU ARE GOING TO RECEIVE THE PERFECT SOLUTION THAT IS IN
ALIGNMENT WITH THE HIGHEST GOOD FOR ALL. HAVE FAITH IN THIS OUTCOME.
DO NOT DOUBT AN AMAZING OUTCOME IS POSSIBLE, AND DO NOT ALLOW YOUR MIND
TO OBSESS OVER FEARING THE WORST CASE SCENARIOS YOUR MIND CREATES.
YOU DO HAVE THE POWER TO SHIFT YOUR ATTENTION TO SOMETHING ELSE.
WHEN YOU ALLOW YOURSELF TO RELAX AND MOVE OUT OF LOW-VIBRATIONAL,
OBSESSIVE THOUGHTS YOU ALLOW THE SPACE FOR GUIDANCE TO FLOW
INTO YOUR BEING AND FOR MIRACLES TO MANIFEST WITHIN YOUR LIFE.

IF YOU ARE DEPRESSED YOU ARE LIVING IN THE PAST.
IF YOU ARE ANXIOUS YOU ARE LIVING IN THE FUTURE.
IF YOU ARE AT PEACE YOU ARE LIVING IN THE PRESENT.
— LAO TZU

FEELING FEAR, DOUBT, ANXIETY, WORRY, ETC. IS A PURE SIGN THAT YOU ARE EITHER
MENTALLY LIVING IN THE FUTURE, THE PAST OR DISCONNECTED FROM THE
KNOWINGNESS THAT YOU ARE A DIVINE BEING WHO IS FULLY CAPABLE OF EMBODYING
FAITH IN THE UNSEEN FORCES AVAILABLE TO GUIDE AND SUPPORT YOUR PERSONAL
JOURNEY IN ALL MOMENTS. IF THIS IS STEMMING FROM THE PAST, OR SOMETHING THAT
HAS JUST OCCURRED, CHOOSE TO RECOGNIZE THAT THE PAST IS UNCHANGEABLE, BUT
YOUR PERSPECTIVE WITHIN THE PRESENT MOMENT IS CHANGEABLE. EVEN THE
SLIGHTEST SHIFT IN PERSPECTIVE WILL WORK MIRACLES. IF SOMETHING HAS OCCURRED
THAT HAS MADE YOU FEEL LESS THAN YOUR BEST, SHIFT PERSPECTIVES AND RECOGNIZE
THAT THE UNIVERSE IS WORKING WITHIN YOUR LIFE. CHANGE IS A NATURAL AND
INEVITABLE PART OF LIFE. WHEN WE SET AN INTENTION THE ENTIRE UNIVERSE SUPPORTS
OUR INTENTION, AND SOMETIMES THIS REQUIRES CHANGES OR OCCURRENCES WE DO
NOT ENJOY OR UNDERSTAND AT FIRST. IF WE RESIST CHANGE OR RESIST ADMITTING WE
WERE WRONG IN A PREVIOUS DECISION MADE, WE RISK SABOTAGING OUR ENTIRE
LIFETIME WITH LOW VIBRATIONAL ENERGY. IF WE FLOW WITH THE CHANGE, AND
CHOOSE TO SHIFT PERSPECTIVE WE ARE ABLE TO UNCOVER DEEPER MEANINGS AND
GUIDANCE THAT WILL IN TURN HELP US BETTER MANAGE THE CHANGE AND BREAK
THROUGH TO THE BEAUTY THAT AWAITS US THE OTHER SIDE. WORRYING ABOUT THE
FUTURE SEVERELY CRIPPLES OUR POTENTIAL TO LIFE A TRULY FULFILLING LIFE. WHEN
WE FEEL ANXIETY AND WORRY IT IS MOST OFTEN FROM OVERTHINKING, BECAUSE
OVERTHINKING MOST OFTEN LEADS TO DIGGING UP THE MULTIPLE WORST CASE
SCENARIOS. THE 'YA BUT, WHAT IF ___' IS A PERFECT EXAMPLE, AND SO IS 'BUT, I JUST
WANT TO BE PREPARED SO THAT I AM NOT CAUGHT OFF GUARD', AS WELL AS ALL
OTHER STATEMENTS LIKE THESE. THE MIND COMES UP WITH MANY EXCUSES FOR
CONTINUING THE CYCLES OF FAMILIAR EMOTIONS. WORRYING ABOUT THE FUTURE IS A
LOW VIBRATIONAL FEELING, AND THE UNIVERSE RESPONDS TO THIS FREQUENCY WITH
EVENTS AND CIRCUMSTANCES THAT MATCH THAT FREQUENCY.
WHAT YOU SPEND TIME AND ENERGY FEARING YOU ATTRACT TO YOU.
EVERYTHING YOU THINK ABOUT AND IMAGINE YOU ATTRACT TO YOU.
CHOOSE WISELY, GODDESS. HARNESS YOUR POWER IN EACH PRESENT MOMENT.

SHIFTING PERSPECTIVES IS CRUCIAL, DOING SO ALLOWS FOR THE EMBODIMENT OF HIGH VIBRATIONAL FEELINGS, WHICH EQUAL HIGH VIBRATIONAL EVENTS AND CIRCUMSTANCES IN THE NEAR FUTURE. WE MUST HAVE IMMENSE FAITH AND EMBODY THE FEELINGS THAT ARE IN HARMONY WITH OUR FAITH IN THE UNIVERSE SUPPORTING OUR INTENTION TO RECEIVE THE OUTCOME THAT WILL BLESS OUR LIFE, AND THE HIGHEST GOOD OF ALL. THERE IS NO EXCUSE TO SPEND TIME IN WORRY, ANXIETY, DOUBT, FEAR OR ANYTHING ALIKE. WE EACH HAVE THE POWER IN ANY MOMENT TO SHIFT OUR PERSPECTIVE. IT IS A CHOICE, YOUR ONLY LIMIT IS YOU. ALL EXCUSES STEM FROM ANALYTICAL CHATTER AND EGOTISTICAL DESIRES. EACH INDIVIDUAL MUST FIND THE SELF-DISCIPLINE TO SHIFT PERSPECTIVES AND EMBODY FAITH. WHEN WE ARE FULLY TUNED INTO THE INFINITE NATURE OF OUR SOUL WE ARE ABLE TO RECOGNIZE THAT THERE IS NO NEED TO WORRY OR FEEL ANXIETY TOWARDS ANYTHING AT ALL. EMBODY PEACE WHILE HOLDING FAITH IN THE INTENTIONS YOU HAVE SET. DO NOT SABOTAGE YOUR INTENTIONS WITH FEAR AND WORRY. SET INTENTIONS FOR ANYTHING AND EVERYTHING.

RATHER THAN BECOMING STRESSED OR ANXIOUS ABOUT ANYTHING OR ANY SITUATION THAT WILL TAKE PLACE IN THE FUTURE WRITE DOWN YOUR ABSOLUTE IDEAL OUTCOME FOR THE GIVEN SITUATION, OR LEAVE IT UP TO THE UNIVERSE ENTIRELY: ASK THE UNIVERSE TO PROVIDE YOU WITH THE OUTCOME THAT WILL BLESS YOUR LIFE IN THE MOST PEACEFUL AND LOVING WAY. INCREASINGLY KNOW AND **FEEL** THIS BLESSED OUTCOME AS YOUR TRUTH. **FEEL** THAT, FOR CERTAIN, THE OUTCOME WILL BRING YOU MANY BLESSINGS. KNOW THIS BLESSED OUTCOME IS INEVITABLE. DISREGARD THOUGHTS OR FEELINGS THAT ATTEMPT TO TELL YOU OTHERWISE. LEAVE NO ROOM FOR DOUBT. THIS IS JUST AS ANY OTHER DESIRE/GOAL. KNOW AND **FEEL** THAT EVERYTHING IS TAKEN CARE OF AND HAS NO CHOICE BUT TO MANIFEST ON THE EXACT VIBRATIONAL FREQUENCY YOU EMBEDDED YOUR INTENTION WITHIN.

FOCUS YOUR THOUGHTS, ENERGY, EMOTIONS AND FEELINGS ON WHAT YOU DO WANT, NOT WHAT YOU DO NOT WANT.

GODDESS, YOU ARE PURE POWER

ALIGN YOURSELF AND IMMERSE YOURSELF

WITHIN THE IMMENSITY OF ABUNDANCE THE UNIVERSE HAS TO OFFER MORE

THAN EVER. REMIND YOURSELF, HOWEVER YOU CAN, TO REMAIN IN THE

MOMENT AND CERTAIN OF YOURSELF.

FEEL THE POTENCY OF YOUR INTERNAL GODDESS POWER

EMANATING THROUGHOUT

EVERY SINGLE FIBER OF YOUR BEING AND EXISTENCE.

HERE IS A SIMPLE ENERGY HEALING TECHNIQUE
THAT WORKS IMMEDIATELY TO PROVIDE RELIEF:
PLACE ONCE HAND ON YOUR FOREHEAD
AND YOUR OTHER HAND ON THE BACK OF YOUR HEAD.
THEN, BREATHE DEEPLY
[YOU CAN FOLLOW THE BREATHING TECHNIQUE BELOW]

PLACE THE TIP OF YOUR TONGUE
ON THE ROOF OF YOUR MOUTH,
RIGHT BEHIND YOUR FRONT TEETH.
BREATH IN THROUGH NOSE FOR THE COUNT OF 4.
HOLD FOR THE COUNT OF 7.
SLOWLY RELEASE YOUR BREATH FROM MOUTH FOR THE COUNT OF 8.

TUNE INWARD TO EXPERIENCE WHAT THE UNIVERSE WITHIN YOU AND YOUR
SOUL HAS TO OFFER. WHEN WE ALLOW OURSELVES TO TUNE INWARD AND
CONNECT INTO THE INFINITE NATURE OF OUR SOUL WE EFFORTLESSLY CALM
ANY WORRY, ANXIETY, DOUBT, FEAR .. ETC. IN ORDER TO REAP THE MOST
IMPORTANT MESSAGES AND INSIGHTS THAT EXIST WITHIN WE MUST QUIET
ANALYTICAL CHATTER AND EGOTISTICAL DESIRES .. RELEASING THE NEED TO
CONTROL. AND THUS, SURRENDERING, ALLOWING THE UNIVERSE AND OUR
OVERSOUL TO TAKE OVER AND SUPPORT THE INTENTIONS WE HAVE SET WITHIN
OUR LIFE, AS WE HOLD ABSOLUTE FAITH WE ARE ABLE TO RECEIVE THE GIFTS OF
THE PRESENT MOMENT .. AH-HA MOMENTS ILLUMINATE OUR EXPERIENCE,
MIRACLES APPEAR AND OUR MINDS EYE VISION BECOMES VERY CLEAR

GODDESS LIFE DESIGNER

ASK FOR SIGNS FROM THE UNIVERSE
& BELIEVE YOU WILL RECEIVE THEM.

ASK FOR SIGNS SPECIFIC TO YOURSELF
TO BE PLACED IN YOUR LIFE
& MADE OBVIOUS TO YOU
THAT THEY ARE YOUR SIGNS.
BE MINDFUL & PRESENT IN EACH MOMENT,
SO THAT YOU ARE ABLE TO RECEIVE THEM.

ALWAYS HANDWRITE
EACH OF YOUR DESIRES IN
THE PRESENT TENSE,
AND GIVE THANKS IN ADVANCE,
AS THOUGH THEY HAVE
ALREADY COME TRUE.
THIS TRAINS YOUR
SUBCONSCIOUS MIND TO
ACCEPT THIS AS YOUR TRUTH
AND FURTHER SUPPORT YOU.
EVERYTHING WILL BEGIN TO **FEEL**
MORE NATURAL
AND EFFORTLESSLY ALIGN.

FEEL IT VIBRATING IN
EVERY FIBER OF YOUR BEING
AS ALREADY HERE.
MEDITATE ON THIS,
YOU MUST KNOW WHAT IT WILL FEEL
LIKE TO HAVE YOUR GOAL MANIFEST AS
TRUTH IN THE PHYSICAL PLANE.
IGNITE ALL 6 SENSES,
IN NO PARTICULAR ORDER.
JUST FOCUS ON THE
TRUE FEELINGS WITH EACH
SENSE AND ALIGN EFFORTLESSLY
WITH INSPIRED FLOW.

1. WHAT IS YOUR
OVERALL INTUITIVE VIBE
WHILE EXPERINCING
THIS GOAL FULFILLED?

2. SEE
3. HEAR
4. SMELL
5. TASTE
6. TOUCH

MEDITATE
ON THE FEELINGS OF
ALL 6 SENSES IN THE
FEELING OF YOUR GOAL
REACHED & FULFILLED.
[[AT LEAST ONCE A DAY]]

EVER-INCREASINGLY BE
IN A MINDSET OF GRATITUDE
& RECEPTIVITY.
TRULY **FEEL** SATISFIED
TO ATTRACT YOUR DESIRES.

YOUR END GOAL
IS DETERMINED BY YOU,
WITH CRYSTAL CLEAR
DEFINITION AND CERTAINTY.
THE UNIVERSE PROVIDES THE
'HOW & WHEN' DETAILS
AS YOU MOVE FORWARD WITH
INSPIRED ACTION, WHILE EMBODYING
THE FEELINGS
OF YOUR DESIRES AS AN
ALREADY FULFILLED FACT.
YOU ARE BECOMING A MASTER OF LIFE
MAPPING AND DESIGNING.
KNOW THAT YOU WILL NOW RECEIVE
UNEXPECTED GUIDANCE,
INSPIRATION
& MIRACLES.

FINANCIAL MANIFESTATIONS

KNOW WHAT YOU WILL DO WITH YOUR INCREASE IN FINANCES.
HAVING CLARITY IS CRUCIAL.

MAKE A LIST OF WHAT YOU DESIRE AND WHAT YOU WILL BE USING YOUR MONEY FOR.
ASK YOURSELF HONESTLY:
IF EVERY SINGLE THING IN LIFE / ON PLANET EARTH WAS FREE ..
WOULD I STILL DESIRE THESE THINGS?
REVISE YOUR LIST AS YOU PLEASE.

TOTAL THE COSTS SO THAT YOU KNOW EXACTLY HOW MUCH YOU ARE SETTING YOUR
INTENTION FOR. THEN REWRITE IT OUT: WITH X AMOUNT OF MONEY I WILL [FILL IN THE BLANK].

OUR BELIEFS AROUND FINANCES
ARE SOMETHING WE HAVE BUILT BASED UPON
THE BELIEFS OF THE PEOPLE WHO HAVE BEEN AROUND US OUR ENTIRE LIFE.
WE CAN CHANGE OUR FINANCIAL SITUATION
BY CHANGING OUR FINANCIAL MINDSET AND BELIEF SYSTEM.
[YOU MAY DESIRE TO REFLECT ON THE SUBCONSCIOUS BELIEFS PAGES]

JOURNAL EVERYTHING YOU DESIRE.
THERE IS NO JUDGEMENT,
WE HAVE INFINITE ABUNDANCE AVAILABLE TO US ALL,
FINANCIAL ABUNDANCE IS A VIBRATIONAL FREQUENCY
THAT MUST BE MATCHED INTERNALLY BEFORE IT IS
MANIFESTED EXTERNALLY [PHYSICAL REALITY].

**CREATE A LIST OF FINANCIAL I AM AFFIRMATIONS & SUBCONSCIOUS QUESTIONS
THAT RESONATE WITH YOUR PERSONAL DESIRES.**
[REFLECT ON PAGE 21 FOR DETAILS]

EXAMPLES:
I AM ALIGNED WITH THE ENERGETIC FREQUENCY OF ABUNDANCE.
WHAT MIRACLES HAVE OCCURRED WITHIN MY LIFE TO BRING ME SO MUCH ABUNDANCE?
I AM NOW FINANCIALLY STABLE, AND I WILL CONTINUE TO BE
THROUGHOUT MY ENTIRE HUMAN LIFETIME.
HOW WILL MY BELIEFS AND ENTIRE LIFE CHANGE NOW THAT I HAVE BEEN
FINANCIALLY BLESSED WITH ALL THIS ABUNDANCE?
I HAVE MORE THAN ENOUGH, I AM EVER-SO-GRATEFUL.
I AM LIVING THE LIFE I DESIRE BECAUSE I AM WORTHY.
I AM GENUINELY GRATEFUL IN KNOWING ABUNDANCE IS CONTINUOUSLY
FLOWING INTO MY LIFE THROUGHOUT MY ENTIRE LIFETIME.
I AM ABLE TO PROVIDE QUALITY LIVING CONDITIONS TO EVERYONE I LOVE.

I ELIMINATE PROCRASTINATION AND FEAR WITH ACTION AND LOVE.

MY SUBCONSCIOUS ONLY LISTENS TO MY HIGHER SELF

OBSERVE YOUR THOUGHTS AND FEELINGS IN REGARDS TO MONEY.

DO SO WITHOUT JUDGEMENT
IN EACH MOMENT THE TOPIC MAY ARISE,
FROM THIS MOMENT ON.

DO YOU FIND YOURSELF FEELING DISCOURAGED AROUND THE TOPIC OF FINANCES?

DO YOU FIND YOURSELF FEELING ENVY, JEALOUSY OR OTHER LOW EMOTIONS
TOWARDS OTHERS WITH FINANCIAL ABUNDANCE?

DIRECT YOUR FOCUS TO THE PIT OF YOUR STOMACH,
THINK ABOUT YOUR PRESENT FINANCIAL STATUS.
DO YOU FEEL:
HIGH VIBRATIONAL THOUGHTS, EMOTIONS AND FEELINGS?
NEUTRAL THOUGHTS, EMOTIONS AND FEELINGS?
OR LOW VIBRATIONAL THOUGHTS, EMOTIONS AND FEELINGS?

RECOGNIZE THAT IN ORDER TO CHANGE YOUR FINANCIAL SITUATION
YOU MUST CHANGE THE FREQUENCIES YOU EMBODY WITHIN
WHEN THINKING OF YOUR FINANCIAL SITUATION.

A WONDERFUL AND SIMPLE WAY TO DO THIS IS TO
PRACTICE FEELING GENUINE GRATITUDE FOR ALL PAST, PRESENT AND FUTURE MONEY
THAT HAS BEEN, IS AND WILL BE WITHIN YOUR LIFE.
GENUINE GRATITUDE IS A MAGNET FOR MIRACLES.
PRACTICE FEELING GENUINE GRATITUDE TOWARDS MONEY IN ALL WAYS POSSIBLE,
EVEN FEEL GRATEFUL THAT OTHERS HAVE FINANCIAL ABUNDANCE.
BE PLAYFUL WHILE PRACTICING GENUINE GRATITUDE, THIS ALLOWS YOU TO STEER CLEAR OF
EMBODYING THOUGHTS AND FEELINGS STEMMING FROM DESPERATION OR FORCE.

EMBODYING THE HIGH VIBRATIONAL FREQUENCY OF GENUINE GRATITUDE
AROUND THE TOPIC OF MONEY WILL BEGIN TO BENEFIT YOUR LIFE NO MATTER WHAT YOUR
INCOME SITUATION IS IN THESE MOMENTS / FUTURE MOMENTS.

ASSESS:
DO YOU EMBODY THE FEELING STATE OF ' I NEED MORE MONEY',
OR DO YOU EMBODY THE FEELING STATE OF
'I HAVE EVER-INCREASING FINANCIAL ABUNDANCE, I HAVE MORE THAN ENOUGH.'

THE FIRST IS AN EMBODIMENT OF NEED, OF LACK,
THEREFORE MORE CIRCUMSTANCES WILL MANIFEST
THAT PROVE THIS EMBODIED FREQUENCY OF NEED, OF LACK.
THE SECOND IS AN EMBODIMENT OF ABUNDANCE,
THEREFORE MORE CIRCUMSTANCES WILL MANIFEST THAT PROVE THIS EMBODIED
FREQUENCY OF ABUNDANCE AND EVER-INCREASING GROWTH.
ANYONE CAN CONSCIOUSLY HARNESS THEIR FEELING STATE [THEIR FREQUENCY] IF THEY
TRULY DESIRE TO APPLY THE SELF-DISCIPLINE AND DEFY PAST OR PRESENT
EXTERNAL ENVIRONMENTS AND CIRCUMSTANCES.

REMEMBER: "MONEY IS A GREAT SERVANT BUT A BAD MASTER." – FRANCIS BACON

SPEND MONEY GRATEFULLY. ALWAYS. NO EXCEPTIONS. WHETHER YOU ARE BUYING SOMETHING FOR YOURSELF THAT YOU TRULY WANT AND ARE EXCITED ABOUT, OR IF YOU ARE BUYING FOOD AND PERSONAL HYGIENE, OR EVEN IF YOU'RE PAYING BILLS, ETC. WHATEVER IT MAY BE, TRAIN YOURSELF TO ALWAYS DO SO GRATEFULLY.

ESTABLISH AND MAINTAIN A POSITIVE RELATIONSHIP WITH MONEY. ENERGY GOES WHERE THOUGHTS, FEELINGS AND ATTENTION FLOW. GENUINE GRATITUDE THAT YOU FEEL WITHIN YOUR BEING IS A MAGNET FOR MIRACLES, MONEY IS NO EXCEPTION. THIS TAKES PRACTICE, SO DON'T BE HARD ON YOURSELF. WHEN OPPORTUNITIES ARISE TO PRACTICE SPENDING MONEY GRATEFULLY, HARNESS THEM! BEGIN TO OBSERVE YOUR FEELING STATE WHENEVER YOU SPEND MONEY, ON ANYTHING AT ALL. THE MORE YOU BEGIN TO APPRECIATE MONEY AND FEEL GENUINE GRATITUDE FOR EVERY SINGLE WAY IT SERVES YOU, THE BETTER RELATIONSHIP YOU WILL HAVE WITH IT. AND THUS, THE MORE EFFORTLESS IT BECOMES FOR YOU TO ATTRACT IT INTO YOUR LIFE. WHAT ARE YOUR MONEY BELIEFS? DO YOU BELIEVE FINANCIAL ABUNDANCE IS ONLY FOR A SELECT FEW? OR DO YOU BELIEVE THERE ARE COUNTLESS OPPORTUNITIES FOR ANYONE TO ACHIEVE FINANCIAL ABUNDANCE? DO YOU OFTEN SAY 'I/WE CANNOT AFFORD THIS'? RECOGNIZE BY SAYING THIS [OR ANYTHING ALIKE] YOU ARE AFFIRMING TO YOUR SUBCONSCIOUS MIND AND THE ENTIRE UNIVERSE THAT YOU ARE IN LACK. AND THUS, YOUR FREQUENCY [FEELING STATE] OF LACK WILL BE REFLECTED BACK INTO YOUR LIFE AS REAL CIRCUMSTANCES THAT PROVE YOUR LACK. IN STATING YOU ARE IN LACK YOU MANIFEST MORE REASONS TO FEEL LACK AND MORE PROOF THAT YOU ARE IN FACT LACKING. THIS DOESN'T MEAN YOU SHOULD SPEND ALL YOUR MONEY TO PROVE YOU HAVE MONEY. IT MEANS EMBODY AND SPEAK 'I HAVE ENOUGH, I HAVE MORE THAN ENOUGH' WITHOUT HAVING TO ACTUALLY BUY WHATEVER IT IS. PREDOMINANTLY EMBODY THE FREQUENCY YOU DESIRE THE UNIVERSE TO MATCH. WHEN WE THINK ABOUT, SPEAK ABOUT AND SPEND MONEY WITH GENUINE GRATITUDE EMBODIED WITHIN OUR BEING THIS TRAINS US TO EVER-INCREASINGLY EMBODY AND EMIT THE FREQUENCY THAT WE ARE ABUNDANT. THE FREQUENCY THAT WE ARE GENUINELY GRATEFUL AND APPRECIATE HOW MONEY SERVES US. THEREFORE, WE WILL RECEIVE MANIFESTATIONS THAT MAKE US FEEL GENUINELY GRATEFUL, MANIFESTATIONS THAT AFFIRM WE ARE ABUNDANT.

PHYSICAL BODY / HEALTH MANIFESTATIONS

I AM NOT MY BODY. IN MY PUREST FORM I AM DIVINELY PERFECT, I AM AN ETERNAL BEING.

WHILE HERE ON EARTH I HAVE A HUMAN BODY,
AND WITH THAT BODY I AM ABLE TO DO MANY AMAZING THINGS.

I DECIDE HOW I LOVE MY BODY.
I DECIDE WHAT MAKES ME FEEL MY BEST IN REGARDS TO MY PHYSICAL APPEARANCE.

A SIMPLE FORMULA
FOR ANY DESIRED PHYSICAL BODY CHANGES AND/OR HEALTH CHANGES:

BE CLEAR ON THE PHYSICAL CHANGES / HEALTH CHANGES THAT YOU DESIRE.
WRITE THEM OUT.

DO NOT GO ABOUT THIS STATING WHAT YOU DO NOT WANT ANYMORE,
INSTEAD STATE WHAT YOU DO WANT.
YOU DO NOT WANT TO MANIFEST MORE OF WHAT YOU DO NOT WANT, RIGHT?
FOCUS SOLELY ON WHAT YOU DO IN FACT DESIRE.

CREATE PRESENT TENSE STATEMENTS FOR THESE CHANGES.
TRAIN YOURSELF TO KNOW THAT THIS IS NOW YOUR REALITY,
EVEN BEFORE ANY CHANGES HAVE OCCURRED.
VISUALIZE YOURSELF WITH THOSE CHANGES AS REALITY.
EMBODY THE CHANGES WITHIN EVERY FIBER OF YOUR BEING.
THE CHANGES YOU DESIRE ARE YOURS.

CREATE A PLACEBO FOR THE CHANGES YOU DESIRE.
DO RESEARCH,
BUT DO NOT OBSESS OVER THE METHOD YOU ARE WORKING WITH.
JUST BELIEVE THAT DOING (FILL IN THE BLANK WITH YOUR PLACEBO)
WILL CREATE THE CHANGE YOU DESIRE.
DOING THIS IN COMBINATION WITH TRAINING YOUR SUBCONSCIOUS MIND
THROUGH REVIEWING YOUR PRESENT TENSE STATEMENTS
AND EMBODYING THE CHANGES AS ALREADY PRESENT
WILL CREATE THE CHANGES YOU DESIRE.

DO NOT COUNTER YOUR PROCESS WITH DOUBTS OR NEGATIVITY..
THIS WILL BLOCK YOUR DESIRED CHANGES.
YOU MUST FULLY BELIEVE AND EMBODY THESE CHANGES AS HERE NOW,
EVEN BEFORE THEY ARE PRESENT.

AN OUTSTANDING BOOK PERTAINING TO HEALTH / THE PHYSICAL BODY:
'ENERGY MEDICINE:
BALANCING YOUR BODY'S ENERGIES FOR OPTIMAL HEALTH, JOY, AND VITALITY'
BY DONNA EDEN, WITH DAVID FEINSTEIN, PH.D.

Manifesting Love

WE ARE PURE LOVE AT OUR CORE, AND THAT IS WHY LOVE IS THE GREATEST EMOTION WE CAN FEEL
AS HUMAN BEINGS. EACH INDIVIDUAL'S DEFINITION OF HUMAN LOVE WILL BE DIFFERENT,
AND THAT IS PERFECT. THERE IS NO MOLD FOR WHAT LOVE MUST MEAN TO ALL OF US.
WE GET TO DEFINE OUR TRUEST DEFINITION OF THE WORD FOR OUR OWN SELF
AND BE THE EMBODIMENT OF THAT WITHIN OUR OWN LIFE. HOW BEAUTIFUL.

THERE ARE MANY FORMS OF LOVE EXISTING WITHIN OUR WORLD.
ALWAYS KNOW THAT YOU ARE ENTIRELY WHOLE AND PURE LOVE ALL ON YOUR OWN.
BE SURE THAT YOU CAN FIRST LOVE YOURSELF ENTIRELY BEFORE ATTEMPTING TO LOVE ANOTHER.
ALSO BE SURE THAT YOUR POTENTIAL 'LOVER' CAN LOVE THEIR OWN SELF ENTIRELY BEFORE ATTEMPTING TO
LOVE YOU. KNOW THAT YOU DO NOT HAVE TO HAVE A ROMANTIC PARTNER TO BE HAPPY, FIND YOUR
DEFINITION OF LOVE, EMBODY THAT AND ATTRACT A LIFE FILLED WITH THAT DEFINITION OF LOVE.
BE CLEAR ON WHAT EXACTLY YOU ARE DESIRING: A SHORT TERM EXPERIENCE? A LIFE LONG PARTNER? ETC.
WHEN IT COMES TO MANIFESTING A ROMANTIC PARTNER WE OFTEN TIMES HAVE OUR EYES AND HEART SET ON
A SPECIFIC PERSON. WRITE DOWN ALL OF THE QUALITIES YOU BELIEVE THIS SPECIFIC PERSON HAS [THE
REASONS WHY YOU ARE ATTRACTED TO THEM AND DESIRE THEM]. IF YOU DON'T HAVE A SPECIFIC PERSON IN
MIND THEN WRITE DOWN ALL THE QUALITIES YOU WOULD LOVE TO HAVE IN A ROMANTIC PARTNER. INCLUDE:
PHYSICAL QUALITIES, MENTAL QUALITIES, SPIRITUAL QUALITIES, LIFE VALUES, ETC. EVEN INCLUDE THE THINGS
THAT YOU WILL DO TOGETHER AND THE BOUNDARIES THAT YOU AGREE ON WITHIN YOUR RELATIONSHIP. LIST
ALL OF THE THINGS THAT ARE IMPORTANT TO YOU. **FEEL** AMAZING WHILE YOU ARE DOING THIS, REALLY GET
INTO YOUR OWN STATE OF PURE LOVE. ONCE YOU HAVE FINISHED WRITING - CLOSE YOUR EYES AND IMAGINE
THIS PERSON - ONLY NOW, BLUR OUT THIS PERSON'S FACE AND NAME IN YOUR MIND - THIS IS IMPORTANT TO
DO BECAUSE THE PERSON YOU THINK YOU WANT MAY NOT ACTUALLY BE THE PERSON YOU BELIEVE THEY ARE,
AND THERE **IS** A PERSON OUT THERE WITH THOSE EXACT QUALITIES YOU DESIRE YOUR PARTNER TO HAVE. SO,
DO NOT LIMIT YOURSELF! USE THE BLUR TECHNIQUE. FOR A FEW MINUTES THINK ON HOW AMAZING YOUR
ROMANTIC RELATIONSHIP WITH THIS PERSON **FEELS**. THEN, THANK YOUR DIVINE LIFE SOURCE FOR SENDING
YOU THIS PERSON, OR SOMEONE EVEN MORE PERFECT FOR YOU! LET GO AND KNOW THAT YOUR DIVINE LIFE
SOURCE IS BRINGING YOU THIS PERFECT PERSON IN THE MOST PEACEFUL AND LOVING WAY. THERE IS NO NEED
TO WONDER WHERE THEY ARE OR WHEN THEY WILL APPEAR. JUST CONTINUE TO **FEEL** GOOD EACH DAY BY
DOING THE THINGS YOU LOVE, THE THINGS THAT MAKE YOU **FEEL** YOUR BEST. EMBODY THE PERSON THAT
YOU WILL BE IN THIS RELATIONSHIP RIGHT NOW AND THROUGHOUT EACH MOMENT OF YOUR DAY.
EVER-INCREASINGLY FEEL AS IF YOUR MOST SATISFYING RELATIONSHIP IS ALREADY HERE NOW.
MAKE THIS FUN. **FEEL** THAT YOU ARE IN LOVE. DO NOT WAIT FOR THE RELATIONSHIP TO ARRIVE IN ORDER TO
BEGIN EMBODYING THE WAY YOU WILL THINK, ACT, **FEEL**, DRESS, BEHAVE AND CARRY YOURSELF
IN YOUR ROMANTIC RELATIONSHIP. DO IT ALL NOW, BE THAT PERSON NOW.

IF YOU ALREADY HAVE A ROMANTIC PARTNER [THIS ALSO APPLIES TO ANY RELATIONSHIP, NOT JUST
ROMANTIC] AND WANT TO MANIFEST MORE LOVE WITHIN YOUR RELATIONSHIP DO SO BY GETTING REALLY
CLEAR ON WHAT LOVE MEANS TO YOU, AND WHAT MAKES YOU FEEL LOVED THE MOST. FOCUS ON WHAT YOU
LOVE THE MOST ABOUT THIS PERSON AND TELL THEM, EXPRESS YOUR LOVE TO THIS PERSON IN THE UNIQUE
WAYS THAT MAKES THEM FEEL THE MOST LOVED. STUDY THEM, GET TO KNOW THEM BETTER. BY SHOWING THEM
THAT YOU APPRECIATE AND LOVE THEM IT WILL BEGIN TO BE REFLECTED BACK TO YOU FROM THEM. DO NOT
GO ABOUT THIS EXPECTING THEM TO SHOW YOU MORE LOVE, BUT RATHER,
EMBODY AND RADIATE THE QUALITY OF LOVE AND RESPECT THAT YOU DESIRE TO RECEIVE BACK INTO YOUR
LIFE. DO TELL THEM ALL THE AMAZING THINGS YOU LOVE AND APPRECIATE ABOUT THEM.

GRATITUDE WORKS MIRACLES IN ALL AREAS OF LIFE - LOVE IS NO EXCEPTION.

QUICK REFERENCE: THE 8 MOON PHASES OF EACH CYCLE

NEW MOON
THIS IS WHEN I DECIDE THE DESIRE I WILL BE MANIFESTING THIS MONTH.

CRESCENT MOON
I TRULY TAKE TIME TO RELAX & JOURNAL MY FEELINGS
ON WHAT MY DESIRE **FEELS** LIKE AS MANIFESTED IN MY LIFE.
[WHAT FREQUENCY DO I NEED TO BE IN TO MATCH MY DESIRES FULFILLMENT?]

FIRST QUARTER MOON
I TAKE MY BIG ACTION STEP TOWARD MY DESIRE.
I CONTINUE TO EVER-INCREASINGLY **FEEL** MY DESIRE AS ALREADY MANIFESTED.

GIBBOUS MOON
I TAKE TIME TO RELAX & TRUST THAT THE UNIVERSE HAS MY BACK.
EVERYTHING IS BEING ALIGNED IN DIVINE PERFECT TIME.
I CONTINUE TO EVER-INCREASINGLY **FEEL** MY DESIRE AS ALREADY MANIFESTED.

FULL MOON
I CONTINUE TAKING DAILY INSPIRED ACTION TOWARDS MY DESIRE.
I CONTINUE TO EVER-INCREASINGLY **FEEL** MY DESIRE AS ALREADY MANIFESTED.

DISSEMINATING MOON
I RELAX & GIVE GENUINE THANKS
AS MY DESIRE MANIFESTS INTO TRUE FORM.
I AM GRATEFUL THAT EVERYTHING IS IN ALIGNMENT WITH
THE HIGHEST GOOD FOR ALL.

THIRD QUARTER MOON
I GIVE BACK NOW, AS I HAVE ABUNDANTLY MANIFESTED MY DESIRE INTO MY LIFE.
THIS IS A GREAT TIME FOR [EXTRA] SELF LOVE RITUALS,
TO KEEP INSPIRATION & SELF APPRECIATION GOING STRONG.

BALSAMIC MOON
I AM GRATEFUL
FOR ALL THAT I HAVE ACHIEVED & RECEIVED.
I AM FEELING PHENOMENAL & INSPIRED,
AS I RELAX DEEPER INTO MY APPRECIATION, CONFIDENCE, SUCCESS,
INFINITE LOVE,
&
ALIGNMENT
WITH THE UNIVERSE.
I AM ALWAYS DIVINELY GUIDED & SUPPORTED.

THE DETAILS & QUESTIONS TO INSPIRE
SUCCESS FOR EACH INTENTION YOU SET USING S.M.A.R.T.:

S

I PROVIDE ABSOLUTE CLARITY ON THE DETAILS FOR WHAT IT IS I DESIRE.
THIS KEEPS ME FOCUSED AND MOTIVATED,
THE UNIVERSE LOVE TO RESPOND TO **SPECIFIC** DETAILS,
IT WANTS TO GIVE US OUR DESIRES--SO WE MUST KNOW THE DETAILS OF WHAT WE WANT
IN ORDER TO HAVE THAT MANIFESTED AS OUR REALITY.

ANSWER THESE 5 QUESTIONS:
(1) WHAT DO I WANT TO ACCOMPLISH?
(2) WHY IS THIS IMPORTANT?
(3) WHO IS INVOLVED?
(4) WHERE IS IT LOCATED?
(5) ARE THERE RESOURCES/LIMITS?

M

MY SET INTENTION MAKES ME FEEL **MOTIVATED** TO TAKE ACTION.
IS **MEANINGFUL** TO MY DESIRED LIFE DESIGN,
AS WELL AS
MEASURABLE IN TERMS OF TRACKING PROGRESSION.

ANSWER THESE 3 QUESTIONS:
(1) HOW MUCH?
(2) HOW MANY?
(3) HOW WILL I KNOW WHEN MY INTENTION HAS MANIFESTED?

A

MY SET INTENTION IS **ATTAINABLE**.

(1) THIS CAN BE DETERMINED BY ASSESSING MY PERSONAL BELIEF SYSTEM,
AND ASKING MYSELF WHAT I BELIEVE I AM TRULY CAPABLE OF ACHIEVING.
I BELIEVE I AM CAPABLE OF ACHIEVING _____ ALONGSIDE THE UNIVERSES FULL SUPPORT,
THE ENTIRE UNIVERSE IS WORKING WITH ME AND FOR ME TO BRING THIS TO ME,
BECAUSE WHEN I MOVE THE UNIVERSE MOVES WITH ME.
THE UNIVERSE AND I ARE A POWERFUL COMBO.
I AM GRATEFUL MY FAITH IS EVER-INCREASING.
I ALWAYS SEE THE BEST RESULTS WHEN I BELIEVE WITH EVERY FIBER OF MY BEING.
(2) ALSO, DO I HAVE ACCESS TO THE RESOURCES I NEED
IN ORDER TO BE ACTIONABLE TOWARDS THIS INTENTION AT THIS TIME?

R

I HAVE DETERMINED HOW MUCH THIS INTENTION MATTERS TO ME.
I AM CERTAIN THIS INTENTION **RESONATES** WITH MY DESIRES FOR MY LIFE DESIGN.

I AM ABLE TO ANSWER YES TO THESE QUESTIONS:
(1) DOES THIS SEEM WORTHWHILE?
(2) IS THIS THE RIGHT TIME?
(3) DOES THIS ALIGN WITH MY OTHER EFFORTS/NEEDS?

T

MY INTENTION IS **TIME SENSITIVE**
AND MOVING ME **TOWARDS** THE LIFE DESIGN I DESIRE.

DETERMINING QUESTIONS:
(1) WHAT IS THE APPROXIMATE TIME FRAME FOR THE MANIFESTATION OF THIS INTENTION?
(2) WHAT INSPIRED ACTION STEPS CAN I COMPLETE BY SPECIFIC DATES?
(3) WHAT CAN I DO TODAY TO MOVE ME TOWARDS THE MANIFESTATION OF MY INTENTION?

SIMPLY WRITING YOUR INTENTIONS ON PAPER MAKES THEM MUCH MORE LIKELY TO MANIFEST.

BLUEPRINT FOR MANIFESTING LONG TERM GOALS

REFLECT ON THE JOURNALING YOU HAVE DONE SO FAR,
THEN IN YOUR OWN JOURNAL,
JOURNAL ALONGSIDE FOLLOWING PROMPTS:
SPACE IS ALSO PROVIDED HERE TO WRITE SUMMARIES OF EACH,
SO YOU CAN EASILY REFLECT ON THROUGHOUT THE YEAR

WHAT ARE YOUR LIFETIME GOALS / DESIRES?
IMAGINE YOU ARE 95 YEARS OLD AND REFLECTING BACK ON YOUR LIFE ..
WHAT ARE YOU SO INCREDIBLY HAPPY YOU ACHIEVED / DID IN YOUR LIFETIME?

THINK ABOUT THIS IN A PLAYFUL STATE OF MIND,
REMEMBER, THIS IS YOUR LIFE AND YOU CAN EDIT IT AS FREQUENTLY AS YOU DESIRE TO!

THINK ABOUT WHAT IS FUN [IN YOUR PERSPECTIVE] DON'T OVER THINK IT .. JUST FLOW ..
WHAT DO YOU LOVE? WHAT'S FUN TO YOU? IF YOU HAD AN ENTIRE DAY / WEEK / MONTH
/ YEAR / LIFETIME TO DO EVERYTHING YOU COULD EVER WISH FOR / DREAM OF /
IMAGINE WHAT WOULD YOU DO?? BE PLAYFUL AND HAVE FUN WITH THIS, JUST MAKE-
BELIEVE FOR A MOMENT, AND DWELL ON WHAT INTERESTS YOU! WHAT IS SO DEEPLY
SATISFYING TO YOU PERSONALLY? BE REAL ABOUT THIS, BE OPEN AND RAW WITH
YOURSELF AT LEAST THIS ONCE IN YOUR LIFETIME.

WHERE WOULD YOU ABSOLUTELY LOVE TO SEE YOURSELF IN 7 YEARS?
WHERE WOULD YOU LOVE TO SEE YOURSELF IN 3 YEARS?
ALSO THINK ABOUT THESE IN A PLAYFUL STATE OF MIND.
REMEMBER, THIS IS YOUR LIFE AND YOU CAN EDIT IT AS FREQUENTLY AS YOU DESIRE TO!

7 YEARS: [STEPPING STONE FOR YOUR LIFETIME DESIRES]

3 YEARS: [STEPPING STONE FOR YOUR 7 YEAR DESIRES]

ONE YEAR GOAL [SOLAR GOAL]:

KEEP THIS GOAL IN ALIGNMENT WITH
WHERE YOU WOULD LOVE TO SEE YOURSELF IN 3 YEARS.
THINK ABOUT YOUR DESIRES,
ARE ANY OF THEM TOO BIG FOR ONE 30 DAY MOON CYCLE?
IF SO, MAKE THEM A ONE YEAR GOAL!
[OR A 3 MONTH GOAL, 6 MONTH GOAL OR 9 MONTH GOAL - NEXT PAGE]

ALIGN
EACH MOON CYCLE
ACCORDINGLY
WITH YOUR ONE YEAR GOAL.
USE THE 3, 6 & 9 MONTH GOALS AS
STEPPING STONES,
BULLET POINTS,
DUE DATES,
[[ALIGNMENT TOOLS]]
TO GET YOU TO YOUR ONE YEAR GOAL.
MAKING SURE YOU ARE KEEPING YOUR MOON CYCLE GOALS
A
L
I
G
N
E
D
EACH CYCLE IS CRUCIAL.

START WITH YOUR LARGER GOALS ON THE PREVIOUS PAGE, THEN YOUR 9, 6 & 3 MONTH GOALS
AS A BREAKDOWN OF YOUR ONE YEAR GOAL. THEN, REFLECT ON THESE GOAL PAGES
AS YOU COMPOSE YOUR NEW MOON DESIRES FOR EACH INDIVIDUAL MOON CYCLE.

WHAT IS YOUR 9 MONTH GOAL?
IS IT IN ALIGNMENT WITH [A STEPPING STONE TO] YOUR ONE YEAR GOAL?

WHAT IS YOUR 6 MONTH GOAL?
IS IT IN ALIGNMENT WITH [A STEPPING STONE TO] YOUR 9 MONTH GOAL?

WHAT IS YOUR 3 MONTH GOAL?
IS IT IN ALIGNMENT WITH [A STEPPING STONE TO] YOUR 6 MONTH GOAL?

INTENTION SETTING

ONLY SET INTENTIONS WHEN YOU ARE ABSOLUTELY FEELING IT.
[MAKE SURE YOU ARE IN A GOOD SPACE: BODY, MIND AND SOUL]

THE NEW MOON IS A GREAT TIME, AS THE GODDESS LIFE DESIGNER IS FORMULATED AROUND SETTING
INTENTIONS AT THE NEW MOON, BUT YOU CAN SET INTENTIONS WHENEVER YOU PERSONALLY DESIRE
TO. IT IS VERY IMPORTANT TO BE HONEST WITH YOURSELF: IF YOU ARE FEELING OFF IN ANY WAY [AT ALL]
SIMPLY WAIT FOR ANOTHER DAY. THERE IS NO RUSH AT ALL, INTENTION SETTING SHOULD BE ENJOYED
ENTIRELY. EVEN IF YOU ARE IN THE MIDST OF SETTING AN INTENTION AND IF YOU FEEL DOUBT THAT
YOUR INTENTION WILL MANIFEST, OR ANY FEELINGS OF FEAR [AT ALL] FOR ANY REASON —
ACKNOWLEDGE THESE FEELINGS AND STOP WHAT YOU ARE DOING.
RESPECT YOUR FEELINGS: CLEAN YOUR SPACE AND WALK AWAY FROM THE RITUAL,
DO SOMETHING ELSE TO SHIFT YOUR MINDSET ENTIRELY. BEGIN AGAIN ON A DIFFERENT DAY.
THIS IS VERY IMPORTANT BECAUSE THE ENERGY YOU EMBODY WHILE SETTING YOUR INTENTION IS VERY
STRONG AND FOCUSED. YOU ARE ASKING FOR THIS SAME ENERGY FREQUENCY TO MANIFEST INTO YOUR
LIFE AS EVENTS AND CIRCUMSTANCES. YOU DO NOT WANT TO EMANATE LOW VIBRATIONAL ENERGY
[FEAR, DOUBT, ETC] BECAUSE YOU DO NOT WANT TO RECEIVE LOW VIBRATIONAL MANIFESTATIONS THAT
MAKE YOU FEEL THESE WAYS, RIGHT? YES, WE DO NOT INSTANTLY MANIFEST OR MANIFEST THINGS WE DO
NOT PREDOMINATELY FEEL. BUT, WHEN TAKING THE TIME TO DO AN INTENTION SETTING RITUAL WE ARE
PUTTING A LOT MORE ENERGY, FOCUS, PASSION AND INTENT DIRECTLY INTO THOSE FREQUENCIES IN
THOSE MOMENTS. WHEREAS IN DAY TO DAY MOMENTS WE ARE NOT RITUALLY CONCENTRATING OUR
POWER IN SUCH A SIGNIFICANT WAY. THAT IS WHY THIS IS IMPORTANT.
BEFORE YOU RETURN AGAIN, ASK YOURSELF HONESTLY:
WHAT IS MY DOUBT OR FEAR ARISING FROM?
REFER TO THE SUBCONSCIOUS BELIEFS PAGES.
REMEMBER:
STARTING SMALLER, WITH SOMETHING THAT YOU DO NOT FEEL DOUBT OR FEAR TOWARDS MANIFESTING
DOES NOT MEAN YOU ARE INCAPABLE OF MANIFESTING LARGER.
IT COMES DOWN TO WHAT YOU WHOLEHEARTEDLY BELIEVE YOU ARE CAPABLE OF
WITHOUT RESISTANCE. YOUR ONLY LIMIT IS YOU, AND EVERY HUMAN HAS [OVER THE COURSE OF THEIR
LIFE] FORMED LIMITING BELIEFS IN ONE ASPECT OF LIFE OR ANOTHER. TAKE YOUR POWER BACK
THROUGH LETTING GO OF THOSE LIMITING BELIEFS, AND BUILD YOUR CONFIDENCE THROUGH
ACHIEVING SMALL SUCCESSES. YOU CAN THEN MANIFEST YOUR LARGER DESIRES ON THE FOUNDATION
OF YOUR SMALLER SUCCESSES. A GREAT WAY TO DO THIS IS TO START SETTING SMALL INTENTIONS
FOR YOUR DAILY TO-DO LIST EACH MORNING.

IF YOU ARE WANTING TO GET RID OF, RELEASE, ETC.
SEE PAGE 100, AND THEN ASSESS:
WHAT IS IT THAT YOU DO WANT IN ITS PLACE?
OR WHAT IS THE POSITIVE YOU CAN FOCUS ON THAT IS WITHIN YOUR DESIRED SOLUTION?
FOCUS ON WHAT YOU DO WANT, NOT WHAT YOU DON'T WANT.
YOU DO NOT WANT TO MANIFEST MORE OF WHAT YOU DO NOT WANT,
SHIFT YOUR FOCUS ONTO WHAT YOU DO IN FACT WANT TO MANIFEST / SEE MORE OF.
THESE ARE A FEW EXAMPLES [BUT THIS CONCEPT APPLIES TO ANYTHING]
I NO LONGER WANT TO BE SICK, FEEL ANXIETY, HAVE _____ ADDICTION, BE IN DEBT, ETC.
TURN THESE STATEMENTS INTO:
I AM NOW AT MY OPTIMAL HEALTH, I AM ALWAYS AT PEACE,
MY LIFE RADIATES SERENITY, I AM EVER-INCREASINGLY BECOMING MORE
AND MORE MINDFUL AND PRESENT WITHIN MY LIFE AND AS A RESULT I FEEL
ABSOLUTELY AT PEACE AND THINK ONLY ON THE THINGS I LOVE AND APPRECIATE.
I AM STRONG, I AM THE EMBODIMENT OF FREEDOM AND THIS FEELS AMAZING BECAUSE
I AM NOW ABLE TO FULLY HARNESS MY POWER AND DESIGN THE LIFE I DESIRE.
I AM NOW FINANCIALLY ABUNDANT, MY FINANCES KEEP INCREASING BY THE THOUSANDS,
I ALWAYS HAVE NEW CREATIVE IDEAS FLOWING INTO MY MIND, I AM SO GRATEFUL.
[[[MEDITATE ON HOW THIS MAY APPLY TO YOUR INTENTION]]].

KNOW THAT YOUR PERSONAL DESIRES ARE IN YOUR HEART FOR A REASON — THEY ARE FOR YOU.
DO NOT FEEL SOME TYPE OF WAY ABOUT ASKING FOR WHAT IT IS YOU REALLY WANT. KNOW THAT WHAT
YOU REALLY WANT IS ALSO WANTING YOU AND THE ENTIRE UNIVERSE WANTS YOU TO HAVE WHAT YOU
DESIRE — THAT IS WHY YOU ARE DESIRING IT IN THE FIRST PLACE. SO, DO NOT BE AFRAID TO SET
INTENTIONS FOR ALL OF YOUR DESIRES ~ HOWEVER, DO NOT EXPECT TO SEE YOUR BIGGEST
DESIRES MANIFEST INSTANTLY, OR IN A SHORT AMOUNT OF TIME [IN ONE MOON CYCLE] ~ THEY MIGHT,
BUT BIG DESIRES OFTEN TAKE LONGER. THE UNIVERSE MUST REORGANIZE TO BRING THIS DESIRE TO YOU,
AND MEANWHILE YOU MUST DO YOUR PART IN ALIGNING YOUR FREQUENCY WITH THIS DESIRE
FULFILLED, WHILE ALSO TAKING INSPIRED ACTION TO GENERATE ENERGY EXCHANGE SO THAT YOUR
DESIRE CAN COME TO YOU. IT IS ALSO IMPORTANT TO NOT PUT YOUR DESIRES ON A PEDESTAL. IF YOU
FEEL THEY ARE HIGHER THAN YOU ~ SOMETHING YOU ARE NOT WORTHY OF RECEIVING, YOU FEEL
NEEDY OF THEM OR THEY HOLD TOO MUCH IMPORTANCE TO YOU, THEN YOU ARE CREATING
RESISTANCE ~ PUSHING THEM AWAY FROM YOU ~ BECAUSE YOU ARE NOT EMBODYING [BEING] THE
PERSON WHO HAS THIS DESIRE FULFILLED. YOUR DESIRE FULFILLED MUST FEEL NORMAL TO YOU
~ AS IF YOU ALREADY HAVE THIS WITHIN YOUR LIFE, AND ARE ENTIRELY WORTHY OF IT.
SHIFT INTO FEELING THE KNOWINGNESS THAT YOUR DESIRE IS NOT HIGHER THAN YOU,
YOUR DESIRE IS HERE WITH YOU, IN THIS LIFETIME, RIGHT NOW.

IT IS IMPORTANT TO KNOW THAT YOU HAVE A WINDOW OF TIME TO SET YOUR INTENTION.
[THE NEW MOON PHASE LASTS A FEW DAYS, NOT JUST ONE]
YOUR FEELING STATE IS MORE IMPORTANT THAN THE TIMING OF YOUR INTENTION SETTING RITUAL.
BEGIN YOUR INTENTION SETTING RITUAL WHEN YOU ARE FEELING GOOD AND READY.

BE CERTAIN WHAT YOU ARE ASKING FOR IS WHAT YOU REALLY DO IN FACT WANT,
AS YOU PARTAKE IN YOUR INTENTION SETTING RITUAL YOU ARE INVOKING THE ENTIRE UNIVERSE
TO CONSPIRE ON YOUR BEHALF TO BRING THIS TO YOU. FEEL INTO THE DETAILS WHEN SETTING YOUR
INTENTIONS. SPEND TIME MEDITATING ON WHAT YOU TRULY DESIRE BEFORE YOU
BEGIN YOUR INTENTION SETTING RITUAL, FEEL INTO YOUR HEART-SPACE: IS THIS EXACTLY WHAT YOU
WANT TO MANIFEST WITHIN YOUR LIFE? FEEL INTO THIS DESIRE FULFILLED, CLOSE YOUR EYES AND
VISUALIZE YOURSELF AND YOUR ENTIRE LIFE WITH THIS DESIRE FULFILLED. THIS IS A GREAT WAY TO
DETERMINE WHETHER OR NOT YOU REALLY DO WANT IT, OR IF YOU NEED TO BE MORE SPECIFIC. CAN
YOU ENVISION YOURSELF EXPERIENCING THESE FEELINGS OF YOUR DESIRE FULFILLED EVERY SINGLE DAY?
DO THESE FEELINGS RESONATE WITH THE CORE OF YOUR SOUL? DO THESE FEELINGS FEEL FORCED? DO
THEY FEEL NEGATIVE, AT ALL? OR DO THEY FEEL REALLY GOOD, AT THE CORE OF YOUR BEING?
YOU HAVE TO BE CLEAR ABOUT WHAT IT IS YOU WANT. THINK OF PLACING AN ORDER [WHETHER THAT
BE FOR CLOTHING ONLINE OR FOOD AT A RESTAURANT OR ANYTHING ELSE] YOU DON'T NEGLECT TO
SPECIFY THE DETAILS FOR WHAT YOU DESIRE. AND THEREFORE, YOU KNOW WHAT IS GOING TO ARRIVE
TO YOU. DO THE SAME WITH ANY DESIRES YOU ARE SETTING THE INTENTION TO MANIFEST.
YOU DO NOT HAVE TO OBSESS OVER ALL THE SPECIFICS, BUT DO BE CLEAR.
WHAT YOU TRULY WANT IS THE FEELING YOUR DESIRES FULFILLMENT WILL BRING TO YOU,
SO FOCUS ON EMBODYING THAT EXACT FEELING STATE OF YOUR DESIRE FULFILLED.

YOU ARE NOW HARNESSING, ANCHORING AND DIRECTING THE IMMENSITY OF YOUR POWER
WITH DELIBERATE, FOCUSED INTENT. YOU ARE A POWERFUL MAGNET,
KNOW THAT YOU ARE ATTRACTING THAT WHICH YOU EMBODY.
INFUSE YOUR BEING AND THIS PRACTICE WITH LOVE AND CARE.
RECOGNIZE THAT YOU ARE AN IMMENSELY POWERFUL BEING.
BE MINDFUL AND LOVING WITH YOUR POWER.

YOUR DESIRES FULFILLMENT
IS MOST LIKELY NOT GOING TO BE A MONOTONE, BLAND 'OH, YES, IT IS HERE'
SO, REALLY FEEL INTO HOW IT TRULY IS GOING TO FEEL.
[THIS IS VERY IMPORTANT]

HOW WOULD YOU THINK / ACT / FEEL IF YOU KNEW FOR CERTAIN
YOUR DESIRES WERE GUARANTEED TO MANIFEST?
WHAT FREQUENCY DOES MY DESIRES FULFILLMENT IGNITE?
HOW CAN I BETTER IGNITE ALL OF MY SENSES?

OVER TIME YOU WILL DEVELOP YOUR OWN
UNIQUE INTENTION SETTING RITUAL THAT FEELS ABSOLUTELY RIGHT FOR YOU.
AND THAT IS THE MOST IMPORTANT FACTOR:
THAT THE INTENTION SETTING RITUAL FEELS RIGHT WITHIN ALL FIBERS OF YOUR BEING.

USE THIS INTENTION SETTING RITUAL IS FOR LARGER INTENTIONS
[SUCH AS: NEW MOON INTENTIONS AND OTHER LONG TERM DESIRES].
SMALLER INTENTIONS SUCH AS DAILY INTENTIONS
CAN BE SET WHILE BLESSING YOUR DAY / VISUALIZING YOUR DAY IN THE MORNING.

THESE PAGES ARE INTENDED TO BE USED AS A GUIDELINE FOR AN INTENTION SETTING RITUAL,
TAKE WHAT RESONATES WITH YOU AND DISCARD ANYTHING THAT DOES NOT.
ALSO, ADD IN ANYTHING THAT DOES RESONATE WITH YOU PERSONALLY.
REMEMBER, YOUR FEELING STATE WHILE SETTING YOUR INTENTION IS WHAT MATTERS THE MOST.
A GREAT TIME TO SET AN INTENTION IS AT THE END OF THE DAY
[OR ANYTIME YOU DO NOT HAVE MAJOR RESPONSIBILITIES TO TEND TO AFTER]
RELAX AND ALLOW YOUR SUBCONSCIOUS TO MARINATE IN YOUR INTENTION.
IT IS BENEFICIAL TO ALLOW AT LEAST AN HOUR OF RELAXATION AFTER PARTAKING IN
AN INTENTION SETTING RITUAL, THE LONGER THE BETTER.
[YOU MAY ALSO RECEIVE INSPIRATION OR GUIDANCE WITHIN YOUR DREAMS]
OR TAKE A NAP OR GO INTO NATURE. PARTAKE IN ANYTHING THAT YOU PERSONALLY
LOVE THAT ALLOWS YOU TO RELAX. THIS ALLOWS YOUR BODY, MIND AND SOUL
TO FULLY MARINATE IN THE INTENTION YOU HAVE NOW SET.

**ALSO: DOING SOMETHING YOU PERSONALLY LOVE BEFORE YOUR INTENTION SETTING RITUAL
IS A GREAT WAY TO GET YOUR VIBRATIONAL FREQUENCY BALANCED AND ALIGNED.**

MAKE SURE YOUR SPACE IS CLEAR [PHYSICALLY, SPIRITUALLY, EMOTIONALLY]
BURN SAGE OR PALO SANTO [OR DIFFUSE ESSENTIAL OILS]

SET ENVIRONMENT
EXAMPLES:
CANDLES READY,
ESSENTIAL OILS DIFFUSING,
LIGHTING ADJUSTED AS PLEASURABLE,
MUSIC, TONES OR FREQUENCIES ON [EXAMPLE: 528 OR 432 HERTZ],
DRINKING WATER AVAILABLE,
PERMANENT WRITING UTENSILS READY,
YOUR CHOICE OF PAPER READY,
HEALING CRYSTALS,
HERBS,
FLOWERS / ROSES,
ANYTHING ELSE YOU DESIRE.

MAKE SURE YOU HAVE REVIEWED THE S.M.A.R.T. FORMULA BEFORE BEGINNING.
HAVE YOU CLEARLY DECIDED WHAT YOUR DESIRE IS?

ALSO ASK YOURSELF: WHAT IS IT I WANT TO FEEL?
THE REASON I DESIRE _____ IS BECAUSE I WANT THE FEELINGS THAT BRINGS.
THESE FEELINGS ARE _____.

THEN,
CLEANSE YOUR AURA.
YOU CAN DO SO HOWEVER YOU PLEASE. [SEE PAGES 15-17 FOR IDEAS]
A SIMPLE AND RELAXING WAY TO DO SO:
SHOWERING OR BATHING
AND SCRUBBING YOUR BODY WITH EPSOM SALT / HIMALAYAN SALT / DEAD SEA SALT.
MEDITATE ON CLEANSING YOUR AURA WITH A VIOLET FLAME.
THIS FLAME WILL DISSOLVE ANY DENSE / HEAVY ENERGY CORDS.
ONCE YOU HAVE DONE SO RISE YOUR ENTIRE BODY [WITH COLD WATER IF YOU ARE ABLE].
[RETURN THE WATER TO WARM] AND TAKE A FEW MINUTES TO CLOSE YOUR EYES
AND VISUALIZE YOUR DESIRED LIFE DESIGN, AND THE INTENTION YOU ARE GOING TO BE SPECIFICALLY
FOCUSING ON MANIFESTING DURING THIS RITUAL.
FEEL INTO IT, EXPERIENCE IT .

ONCE YOU HAVE CLEANSED YOUR AURA AND YOU ARE IN YOUR SACRED SPACE
WITH EVERYTHING AS YOU DESIRE IT TO BE FOR THE DURATION OF YOUR RITUAL,
BEGIN BY ENVISIONING PROTECTIVE WHITE LIGHT / A VIOLET FLAME ALL AROUND YOU,
A GENTLE MIST OR FLAME
EMANATING THROUGHOUT EVERY FIBER OF YOUR BEING AND YOUR AURA.
FEEL YOUR ENERGY CONNECTING YOU TO EARTH,
ENVISION YOUR ENERGY DEEPLY ROOTED INTO THE SOIL,
CONNECTING UP AND INWARD TO YOUR HEART-SPACE,
BREATHE DEEPLY ~ INTO THE DEPTHS OF YOUR BEING ~
~ PAUSE ~
TUNE INTO THE ENERGY, THE MAGICK, AROUND YOU AND WITHIN YOU.
~ EXHALE ALL THAT DOES NOT SERVE YOUR HIGHEST GOOD ~
— FEEL YOUR INNER POWER —
FEEL YOUR CONNECTION TO YOUR DIVINE LIFE AND POWER SOURCE,
KNOW YOU ARE PROTECTED, GUIDED AND SUPPORTED BY YOUR LIFE SOURCE.
THE SAME ORGANIZED INTELLIGENCE THAT HAS CREATED
INFINITE NUMBERS OF PLANETS AND GALAXIES
~ NUMBERS BEYOND BILLIONS ~
IS INFUSING YOU, PROTECTING YOU AND FUELING YOU
WITH THAT EXACT CREATIVE POWER,
ALLOWING YOU TO MANIFEST A LIFE PERFECTLY ALIGNED
WITH YOUR OWN SOUL'S DEEPEST DESIRES.
~ YOU ARE PERFECTLY ALIGNED RIGHT NOW ~
AND IN EACH OF MOMENT OF YOUR RITUAL.
TRUST YOUR INTUITION ENTIRELY AS YOU MOVE INTO SCRIPTING YOUR INTENTION.
YOUR POWER IS NOW STRONG AND FOCUSED. YOUR POWER IS EMANATING MAGICKALLY
AND BEAUTIFULLY THROUGHOUT ALL FIBERS OF YOUR BEING.

FROM HERE BEGIN YOUR INTENTION SCRIPTING,
DO SO ON YOUR CHOICE OF PAPER,
IN PERMANENT INK.

BE IN A VIBRATIONAL FREQUENCY OF PEACE,
AND EMBODY SACRED RESPECT.
ALLOW YOURSELF TO BE INTUITIVELY GUIDED.
DO NOT GO INTO DETAIL FOR HOW / WHEN YOUR DESIRE WILL COME.
FOCUS ON THE FEELING OF THE END RESULT.
ALLOW SOURCE TO WORK ITS MAGICK IN PROVIDING THE EXACT HOW AND WHEN DETAILS.

IF YOU THINK 'YA, BUT ___' THAT IS A PERFECT SIGN THAT YOU NEED TO LET GO AND ALLOW YOUR
INTUITION TO GUIDE YOU INTO YOUR OWN BEST LIFE, WITHOUT LIMITATION.

REMEMBER: IN PERFORMING YOUR INTENTION SETTING RITUAL YOU ARE
INVOKING THE ENTIRE UNIVERSE [THE ORGANIZED INTELLIGENCE OF ALL LIFE THAT IS PERMEATING
THROUGHOUT ALL FIBERS OF EXISTENCE] AND ASKING IT TO PROVIDE THE PATH FOR YOUR DESIRE TO
COME INTO YOUR LIFE. WHICH IS WHY IT IS IMPORTANT TO INTEND THAT YOUR DESIRE'S
MANIFESTATION WILL COME IN THE MOST PEACEFUL AND LOVING WAY, AS WELL AS FOR THE HIGHEST
GOOD OF ALL SOULS. YOU ARE DIRECTING YOUR FOCUS, INTENTION AND FEELING STATE ON THIS
DESIRE'S FULFILLMENT THROUGHOUT YOUR ENTIRE INTENTION SETTING RITUAL. IGNITING YOUR BODY,
MIND AND SOUL, YOUR ENVIRONMENT AND EACH OF YOUR SENSES. YOUR FEELING STATE ~ YOUR
ENERGY FREQUENCY ~ IS WHAT YOU ARE FOCUSING IMMENSE AMOUNTS OF INTENT AND ENERGY ON
MANIFESTING INTO YOUR OWN LIFE. YOU ARE NOW ANCHORING IN THE FREQUENCY FOR THE
DIRECTION IN WHICH YOUR ENERGY WILL NOW FLOW FROM THIS POINT FORWARD ~ IT IS VERY
IMPORTANT TO IGNITE AND EMBODY THE FEELING STATES YOU WILL EXPERIENCE WITH YOUR DESIRE
ALREADY FULFILLED. BE IN VIBRATIONAL HARMONY WITH YOUR DESIRE'S COMPLETE MANIFESTATION
TO BRING THAT INTO YOUR LIFE. BE ON THE ENERGY FREQUENCY THAT IS IN PERFECT ENERGETIC
HARMONY WITH YOUR DESIRE FULFILLED ~ NOT THE FREQUENCY OF WISHING FOR IT. THE FREQUENCY
OF FULLY HAVING IT, THE FREQUENCY OF EXPERIENCING THE COMPLETE FULFILLMENT OF IT.

THE FOLLOWING PAGE PROVIDES AN EXAMPLE INTENTION SCRIPT. THAT DOES NOT MEAN YOU MUST
FOLLOW THE EXAMPLE TO THE T, OR AT ALL. IT IS MEANT TO SERVE AS AN EXAMPLE. I ADVISE THAT YOU
DO NOT LOOK AT IT [OR ANYTHING ELSE] AS YOU SCRIPT YOUR INTENTIONS. YOUR ENERGY PUT INTO
YOUR SCRIPT MUST BE ENTIRELY YOUR OWN AND TRUE TO YOUR DESIRE FULFILLED. DO NOT GET TOO
ANALYTICAL ABOUT IT. ACT ON INTUITION. IGNITE YOUR SENSES AND YOUR FEELING STATES
EXPERIENCED WITH YOUR DESIRE FULFILLED. GIVE THANKS AND TRULY FEEL INTO EXACTLY HOW YOU
WILL FEEL WITH YOUR DESIRE FULFILLED, FEEL THE GENUINE GRATITUDE YOU WILL TRULY EXPERIENCE
WHEN YOU ARE REFLECTING ON THE RECENT FULFILLMENT OF YOUR DESIRE.

UPON CONCLUDING YOUR RITUAL:
THANK YOUR DIVINE LIFE SOURCE, HIGHEST VIBRATIONAL ANGELS AND SPIRIT GUIDES,
AS WELL AS YOUR HIGHER SELF FOR GUIDING YOU INTO THE FULFILLMENT OF YOUR DESIRE. THEN,
INFUSE YOUR BODY, MIND, SOUL AND SPACE WITH BEAUTIFUL,
LOVING ENERGY INVITING IN EVEN MORE POSITIVE ENERGY FLOW.

FORMULA FOR INTENTION SCRIPTING

AN INTENTION SETTING AFFIRMATION:
I AM GRATEFUL FOR THE INTUITIVE AND DIVINE GUIDANCE THAT IS EVER-PRESENT WITHIN MY BEING AS I SET MY INTENTION. I FULLY TRUST THAT KNOW THAT I AM BEING GUIDED INTO MY OWN MOST FULFILLING FUTURE, AND WITHIN THAT I AM BENEFITTING THE HIGHEST GOOD OF ALL SOULS. I AM SO GRATEFUL FOR THE GUIDANCE I RECEIVE AS I SET AND SCRIPT MY INTENTION. I TRUST ALL IS IN ALIGNMENT NOW AS I REMAIN CONNECTED INWARD WITH MY HEARTBEAT, BREATH AND INNER POWER. I KNOW MY INTENTION IS NOW SET AS MY FUTURE TRUTH. I AM GRATEFUL FOR ALL BLESSINGS AND GUIDANCE I RECEIVE AS I AM PRESENT IN EACH MOMENT.

AN EXAMPLE INTENTION SCRIPT:

I AM RELAXING BY THE FIREPLACE IN MY BEAUTIFUL STONE AND BRICK HOME, IN THE MOST IDEAL AND BEAUTIFUL LOCATION I COULD EVER DREAM OF [DESCRIPTION OF DESIRE ACHIEVED]. I FEEL SO WARM INSIDE BECAUSE I AM ALWAYS BEING REMINDED OF HOW INFINITELY SUPPORTED I AM BY MY DIVINE LIFE SOURCE. SITTING HERE RIGHT NOW IS AN EXAMPLE OF HOW I KNOW THIS. MY DESIRES HAVE BEEN FULFILLED INTO MY REALITY, EXCEEDINGLY BEYOND THE LIMITS I ORIGINALLY DREAMED POSSIBLE. MY INTUITION HAS LOYALLY SERVED AS MY GUIDE, AND I CONTINUE TO TUNE INWARD AS I KNOW, FOR CERTAIN, I AM BEING GUIDED TOWARDS THE HIGHEST GOOD IN EVERY SINGLE MOMENT. I AM THANKFUL FOR MY LIFE, I AM GRATEFUL THAT I AM ABLE TO INSPIRE AND MOVE SO MANY BEAUTIFUL SOULS INTO THEIR OWN MOST BLISSFUL AND FULFILLING LIFE DESIGN. I SEE THE FLAMES INSIDE THE FIREPLACE DANCING AROUND AS I ENJOY THIS MOMENT OF REFLECTION AND WARMTH. I SMELL THE BURNING WOOD FRAGRANCES FILLING MY HOME. I TASTE THE TEA I AM SIPPING AND FOREVER AFTER IT WILL REMIND ME OF THIS MOMENT. I AM SO COMFORTABLE IN THIS MOMENT. THE INSIDE OF MY HEART IS REFLECTING WHAT IS OUTSIDE. MY BODY WRAPPED IN THESE PLUSH BLANKETS AND SOFT CLOTHES, MY HEART IS OVERFLOWING WITH GRATITUDE, GENEROSITY, AND LOVE. IT IS IN THESE MOMENTS OF RELAXATION, REFLECTION AND GRATITUDE THAT I FEEL THE MOST INSPIRATION AND LOVE. I EVER-INCREASINGLY KNOW AND FEEL THAT I AM FOREVER DIVINELY GUIDED, PROTECTED AND LOVED. THANK YOU DIVINE, FOR ALWAYS ALIGNING MY DESIRES WITH THE HIGHEST GOOD OF ALL SOULS. I AM SO GRATEFUL FOR RECEIVING MY DESIRE, AND I AM ALWAYS OPEN TO RECEIVING SOMETHING EVEN BETTER YOU MAY HAVE IN STORE. I AM SO GRATEFUL MY DESIRES HAVE COME INTO MY LIFE IN DIVINE, PERFECT TIMING.

[SIGN FULL NAME]

FOLLOWING THE DESCRIPTION OF YOUR DESIRE AS IF IT HAS ALREADY BEEN RECEIVED, MAKE SURE TO IGNITE AND WRITE ABOUT ALL OF YOUR SENSES FOR WHAT YOU ARE FEELING WITHIN THE FUTURE MOMENT YOU ARE WRITING ABOUT. YOUR INSPIRED ACTION STEPS AND EMBODIMENT OF EVER-INCREASINGLY FEELING AS IF YOUR DESIRE IS FULFILLED PLUS THE SUPPORT OF YOUR DIVINE LIFE SOURCE [PROVIDING THE EXACT HOW/WHEN DETAILS] EQUALS YOUR DESIRE MANIFESTED INTO YOUR REALITY.
AS YOU SCRIPT YOUR INTENTION FOCUS ENTIRELY ON IGNITING THE FEELING STATES AS IF YOUR DESIRED INTENTIONS HAVE ALREADY MANIFESTED WITHIN YOUR PHYSICAL REALITY -- IGNITING THESE FEELING STATES IS VERY CRUCIAL AND THE MOST IMPORTANT STEP.

FOR NEW MOON INTENTION SETTING:
YOU MAY DESIRE TO ADD:
' IT IS NOW THE END OF THIS THIS MOON CYCLE, I AM SO GRATEFUL '
NOTE:
YOU CAN PUT DATES FOR LONG TERM INTENTIONS, IF YOU WOULD LIKE TO.
I PERSONALLY ENJOY USING THE PHRASE 'IN DIVINE, PERFECT TIMING' INSTEAD, BECAUSE THIS ALLOWS ME TO LET GO OF THE URGE TO OBSESS OVER THE HOW AND WHEN DETAILS. I WRITE DOWN MY LONG TERM GOALS IN SUMMARY ON THE 'BLUEPRINT FOR MANIFESTING LONG TERM GOALS' PAGES SO THAT I CAN REFLECT ON THE TIMELINE I AM INTENDING TO WORK WITH. DOING SO ALLOWS ME TO NOT FEEL THE NEED TO PUT SPECIFIC DATES WITHIN MY INTENTION SCRIPTS.
DO WHAT RESONATES WITH YOU,
THERE IS NO RIGHT OR WRONG WAY AS LONG AS YOU ARE DOING WHAT RESONATES WITH YOU AND WORKS BEST FOR YOU! HAVE FUN, BE IN A PLAYFUL SPIRIT.

I SURRENDER CONTROL

SURRENDER IS A LOVING BLISS YOU OWE TO YOUR SOUL

OVER THE CORSE OF HUMAN EXISTENCE MANY HAVE HAD RITUALS FOR LETTING GO.
BELOW IS A GENERAL EXAMPLE FOR AN ALCHEMY VESSEL / SPACE.

IN HER BOOK, 'CREATING YOUR HEART'S DESIRE',
SONIA CHOQUETTE TALKS ABOUT HAVING AN ALCHEMY BOX.
[I LOVE HER WORK, AND HIGHLY RECOMMEND ANY OF HER BOOKS]
SHE STATES:
'YOUR MIND DOES NOT EVER TRULY WANT TO SURRENDER CONTROL,
UNLESS YOU ACTUALLY DO SOMETHING THAT LETS YOUR MIND KNOW
YOU ARE NO LONGER IN CONTROL.
YOU HAVE TO DO A RITUAL,
BECAUSE THAT IS HOW THE MIND LEARNS TO SURRENDER CONTROL.
UNTIL YOU DO THE RITUAL,
YOUR MIND IS GOING TO KEEP GOING BACK TO IT.'

SO,
THE RITUAL CONSISTS, FIRST, OF CREATING A VESSEL.
WHICH CAN BE A BOX, OR ANYTHING YOU CHOOSE. A TRIANGLE IS USED WITHIN
THE JOHN OF GOD COMMUNITY TO REPRESENT FAITH, LOVE AND CHARITY.
IT DOESN'T HAVE TO BE A VESSEL, EITHER.
IT COULD ALSO BE A SACRED PLACE [BIG OR SMALL] OF YOUR OWN.

'ANCIENT CIVILIZATIONS WOULD PRAY AS A COLLECTIVE GROUP,
AND IF ANY ONE OF THE INDIVIDUALS HAD A SPECIAL REQUEST
THEY WOULD TAKE IT TO THE TEMPLE AND THEY WOULD LEAVE IT.
SOMETIMES THEY WOULD PUT IT IN A SPECIAL VESSEL, PRAY OVER IT, AND THEN LEAVE IT.
DOING THAT TOLD THEM THEY WERE PUTTING IT IN THE HANDS OF THE UNIVERSE.'
- SONIA CHOQUETTE

WE ARE EACH CAPABLE OF DOING THIS, THROUGH CREATING A SPECIAL VESSEL OR PLACE
[OR COMBINATION OF BOTH], WHERE WE EACH PLACE OUR SURRENDERED REQUESTS.

ONCE YOU HAVE SCRIPTED YOUR INTENTION YOU CAN UTILIZE YOUR OWN
ALCHEMY VESSEL / SPACE AS AN EXTENSION OF YOUR RITUAL OF MANIFESTATION.

YOUR PERSONAL ALCHEMY VESSEL IS TO BE DECIDED UPON BY YOU PERSONALLY,
DECORATE YOUR VESSEL BOTH INTERNALLY AND EXTERNALLY, TO BE MEANINGFUL AND SACRED,
WHATEVER THAT ENTAILS FOR YOU PERSONALLY.
BE PLAYFUL AND CREATIVE. IGNITE YOUR INNER GODDESS.
GROUND INTO MOTHER EARTH AND CONNECT WITH YOUR DIVINE LIFE SOURCE.
FEEL UNCONDITIONAL LOVE AS YOU CREATE / DECORATE YOUR ALCHEMY VESSEL.

SURRENDER RITUAL:

REFER TO THE INTENTION SETTING PAGES FOR INSPIRATION
IF YOU HAVE NOT DONE SO ALREADY.

[[ADD VARIOUS ELEMENTS AS YOU PLEASE TO IGNITE ALL YOUR SENSES]]
THE MOST CRUCIAL PORTION OF ANY RITUAL IS WITHIN THE INTENT, FOCUS
AND ENERGY FREQUENCY YOU ARE EMBODYING THROUGHOUT THE ENTIRETY
OF IT. ADDITIONAL ITEMS AND ELEMENTS UTILIZED ARE BENEFICIAL,
BUT YOUR INTENT, FOCUS AND ENERGY FREQUENCY EMBODIED
ARE WHAT WILL TRULY IMPACT THE OUTCOME OF YOUR RITUAL
AND GIVE MUCH MORE MEANING AND POWER
TO ANY ITEMS AND ELEMENTS YOU CHOOSE TO USE.

ONCE YOU HAVE PREPARED YOUR MINDSET, VIBRATION AND SPACE:

WRITE DOWN WHAT YOU WANT IN A PRESENT TENSE STATEMENT
OF GENUINE GRATITUDE AND SURRENDER IT TO YOUR VESSEL.
[IF YOU HAVE ALREADY COMPLETED AN INTENTION SETTING RITUAL
AND HAVE YOUR WRITTEN DESIRE: SURRENDER THIS TO YOUR VESSEL.]

AFTER A FEW DAYS OF MEDITATING ON YOUR COMPLETE SURRENDER,
BURN YOUR REQUEST. [SAFELY]
THIS IS TO SHOW THAT YOU HAVE FULLY SURRENDERED THE REST OF
THE WORK TO THE UNIVERSE / YOUR DIVINE LIFE SOURCE.

GO ABOUT YOUR DAILY LIFE IN THE FEELING STATE OF SATISFACTION,
OF GENUINE GRATITUDE, THE VIBRATIONAL FREQUENCY THAT IS
IN HARMONY WITH YOUR DESIRE FULFILLED,
THINK ON WHAT MAKES YOU FEEL GOOD NOW.
WHAT ARE YOU GENUINELY GRATEFUL FOR? WHY?
FEEL AMAZING WHILE ALLOWING YOUR DIVINE LIFE SOURCE TO DETERMINE
THE EXACT HOW AND WHEN DETAILS FOR YOUR DESIRES MANIFESTATION.
MATCH THE RADIANT FREQUENCY OF YOUR DESIRE FULFILLED.
TUNE INWARD ~ IN ANY GIVEN MOMENT AND ASK
YOUR HIGHER SELF / SPIRIT GUIDES / ANGELS / DIVINE LIFE SOURCE
'WHAT STEP OF INSPIRED ACTION WILL YOU HAVE ME TAKE NOW?'

IF YOU ARE SURRENDERING
SOMETHING YOU DESIRE TO REMOVE / RELEASE FROM YOUR LIFE:
DO NOT DO THIS AS AN INTENTION SETTING RITUAL.
IT IS A DIFFERENT PROCESS BECAUSE IT IS A RELEASE,
AND NOT SOMETHING THAT YOU ARE WANTING TO BRING IN MORE OF.
A GREAT TIME TO DO THIS IS WHILE THE MOON IS FULL OR WANING.
[WANING: ANY PHASE AFTER THE FULL MOON & BEFORE THE NEXT NEW MOON]

WRITE IT ALL DOWN ON PAPER.
ONCE YOU HAVE DONE SO, SHRED THE PAPER INTO MANY PIECES.
THEN, BURN THE PIECES IN A FIRE-SAFE BOWL. [SAFELY]
AS YOU DO THE ABOVE PROCESS: INHALE DEEPLY, PAUSE, FEEL INTO WHERE
WHAT YOU ARE RELEASING EXISTS WITHIN YOUR BODY, MIND AND
ENERGY FIELD. FEEL IT ALL DEEPLY, IMMERSE YOURSELF COMPLETELY.
THEN, EXHALE DEEPLY AND RELEASE ENTIRELY.
REPEAT THE BREATHING PORTION OF THIS RITUAL [AS MUCH AS YOU DESIRE]
UNTIL YOU KNOW AND FEEL THAT EVERY SINGLE PARTICLE
OF WHAT YOU ARE RELEASING IS NO LONGER EXISTING
WITHIN YOUR BODY, MIND AND ENERGY FIELD.

EVEN IF YOU REFLECT ON THIS AGAIN IN THE FUTURE, YOU WILL NOT DWELL
UPON IT OR FEEL THAT 'IT IS A PART OF YOU' ANY LONGER. IT HAS NOW BEEN
REMOVED FROM YOUR ENERGY FIELD AND WILL EVER-INCREASINGLY DISSIPATE
FROM YOU MIND AND YOUR LIFE, UNTIL THERE IS NOTHING LEFT AT ALL.

AFTER PARTAKING IN THIS RITUAL
ALLOW YOURSELF TO RELAX, PREFERABLY IN NATURE.
PARTAKING IN AN AURA CLEANSE IS ALSO A GREAT IDEA AT THIS TIME,
FOLLOWED BY A SELF-LOVE RITUAL, SUCH AS A BEAUTY BATH.
FILL THIS SPACE YOU HAVE CREATED
WITH PURE SOURCE ENERGY.

YOU ARE PURE LOVE AND MAGICK
KNOW THE POTENCY OF
YOUR POWER
WITHIN.

THE SOLAR YEAR

IS WILLING TO BE UNIQUELY DESIGNED BY YOU, GODDESS.
TAKING FORM ONE COMPLETED MOON CYCLE AFTER THE OTHER,
TO ULTIMATELY REACH YOUR

ONE YEAR [SOLAR] GOAL

ALSO: BE SURE TO REFER TO THE MORNING & END OF DAY PAGES EVERY SINGLE DAY.

THE SUN IS 93 MILLION MILES
(150 MILLION KM)
FROM EARTH

THE DISTANCE EARTH TRAVELS IN ITS
365 DAY ORBIT AROUND THE SUN:
92.96 MILLION MI
(149.60 MILLION KM).

TRAVELING AT A SPEED OF
APPROXIMATELY 67,000 MPH
(107,000 KM/H)

EARTH COMPLETES ONE FULL ROTATION
EVERY 24 HOURS
[CREATING DAY/NIGHT AS WE KNOW IT]
AT THE SPPEED OF
1000 MILES PER HOUR
(1600 KM/HR)

MOON CYCLE 13
SAGITTARIUS

MOON CYCLE 12
SCORPIO

MOON CYCLE 11
LIBRA

MOON CYCLE 10
VIRGO

MOON CYCLE 9
LEO

MOON CYCLE 8
CANCER

MOON CYCLE 7
GEMINI

MOON CYCLE 6
TAURUS

MOON CYCLE 5
ARIES

MOON CYCLE 4
PISCES

MOON CYCLE 3
AQUARIUS

MOON CYCLE 2
CAPRICORN

BEGIN
MOON CYCLE 1
SAGITTARIUS

GODDESS LIFE DESIGNER

GODDESS LIFE DESIGNER

MOON PHASES DEFINED

EACH OF THE MOON PHASES HAS BEEN GIVEN A PAGE

FOR REFLECTION, MEDITATION AND JOURNALING.

USE THESE PAGES AS A TOOL DURING

THE APPROPRIATE TIMES OF EACH MOON CYCLE

TO HARNESS, ALIGN AND **AMPLIFY**

YOUR CREATIVE MANIFESTATION POWERS.

NEW MOON

I NOW MEDITATE ON THE DESIRE I WILL BE MANIFESTING THIS MOON CYCLE.
I AM PLANTING THE SEED I DESIRE TO MANIFEST.

UTILIZE THE ENTIRE NEW MOON PHASE.
DO NOT BE IN A HURRY TO SET YOUR INTENTION.
THE NEW MOON PHASE LASTS A FEW DAYS.
1. MEDITATE ON THE PROMPTS FOR THE CURRENT NEW MOON.
2. DECIDE YOUR DESIRE WITH CLARITY
3. SET YOUR INTENTION

I REFLECT ON PAGE 88
I JOURNAL THE QUESTIONS THIS PAGE PROMPTS ME TO IN REGARDS TO
THE DESIRE I AM CHOOSING TO MANIFEST THIS MOON CYCLE.
I DO THIS FOR INSPIRATION, ALIGNMENT, STRUCTURE AND CRYSTAL CLEAR CLARITY
IN THE DETAILS OF THE DESIRE I HAVE DECIDED UPON.

ONCE I HAVE DETERMINED MY DESIRE FOR THIS MOON CYCLE,

I REFER TO THE INTENTION SETTING PAGES [92-97]

WHEN I HAVE COMPLETED THE WRITTEN FORMAT OF MY INTENTION,
I CREATE AN I HAVE ____ AFFIRMATION FOR MY DESIRE FULFILLED.

I RECITE THIS AFFIRMATION MULTIPLE TIMES EACH DAY,
SO THAT IT EVER-INCREASINGLY FEELS TRUE WITHIN
ALL ASPECTS OF MY LIFE AND ALL FIBERS OF MY BEING.

[ALSO REFLECT ON PAGE 98]

CRESCENT MOON

ALSO CALLED THE WAXING CRESCENT MOON

**I TAKE TIME TO RELAX AND JOURNAL MY FEELINGS
ON WHAT MY LIFE FEELS LIKE WITH MY DESIRE FULLY MANIFESTED.**

MEDITATE: OBSERVE ANALYTICAL CHATTER AND EGOTISTICAL DESIRES,
ALLOW THOUGHTS TO COME AND GO ~ JUST OBSERVE THEIR PRESENCE.
ONCE CALM,
CONNECT DOWN INTO MOTHER EARTH AND INWARD,
I FEEL MY INNER GODDESS POWER IN CONNECTION WITH THE DIVINE.
I FEEL INTO VIBRATION OF MY DESIRE FULFILLED
I ALLOW IDEAS, INSPIRATION AND GUIDANCE TO FLOW INTO MY MIND.

[MEDITATING / CALMING THE ANALYTICAL MIND IGNITES THE CREATIVE THETA BRAIN
WAVE STATE, WHICH ALLOWS IDEAS AND INSPIRATION TO FLOW]

I JOURNAL THE INSPIRED ACTION STEPS I WILL TAKE THIS MOON CYCLE.
WHAT FREQUENCY DO MY INSPIRED ACTION STEPS IGNITE?

AM I MINDFUL IN BEING OPEN TO RECEIVING SIGNS FROM THE UNIVERSE?

AM I TRULY ABLE TO FEEL MY DESIRES AS MY REALITY?
IF YES:
I CONTINUE TO EVER-INCREASINGLY FEEL THEM AS MY PRESENT REALITY.
IF NO:
WHAT DO I TRULY BELIEVE I AM CAPABLE OF
100% FEELING AS MY REALITY RIGHT NOW?
I FOCUS ON EMBODYING THE FEELINGS
OF WHAT I CAN IMAGINE AND FEEL AS MY PRESENT REALITY,
EVEN IF THAT MEANS STARTING WITH SOMETHING SMALLER RIGHT NOW.
GENERATING SMALL SUCCESSES TRULY BUILDS MY CONFIDENCE
IN MY MANIFESTATION CAPABILITIES!
PLUS, I HAVE MY ENTIRE LIFE TO MANIFEST!
KNOWING THIS KEEPS ME MOTIVATED NO MATTER WHERE I AM AT RIGHT NOW.

**I REMIND MYSELF TO TAKE A FEW MOMENTS OUT OF MY DAY
HERE AND THERE, JUST TO OBSERVE ALL MY SENSES AND BREATHE.**

I PARTAKE IN SELF LOVE.

MY MIND BECOMES RELAXED, FOCUSED & CLEAR.

NOW MY DESIRE HAS THE ATTENTION & SPACE TO MANIFEST AS REAL.

FIRST QUARTER MOON

**I NOW MOVE FORWARD WITH THE INSPIRED ACTION STEPS
THAT I DEFINED DURING THE CRESCENT MOON PHASE.**

I ALLOW MYSELF TO BE FLEXIBLE AND OPEN-MINDED
IN REGARDS TO MY DESIRE.
DOING SO ALLOWS ME TO BE OPEN TO RECEIVING
SOMETHING EVEN BETTER THAN I COULD EVER IMAGINE ON MY OWN.

I ALLOW POSITIVITY AND INSPIRATION TO FLOW INTO MY LIFE.

I PARTAKE IN THINGS THAT IGNITE MY FLOW STATE OF MIND.

I AM INSPIRED, I KNOW I AM DIVINELY GUIDED, SUPPORTED AND PROTECTED.

I BREATHE IN INSPIRING ENERGY FROM MY DIVINE LIFE SOURCE,

I PAUSE AND FEEL THE INFINITE ABUNDANCE AVAILABLE TO ME,

I EMANATE OUT MY BEING MY PUREST FORMS OF CREATIVE MAGICK.

I AM INCREASINGLY KNOWING AND FEELING MY DESIRE

HAS ALREADY MANIFESTED INTO MY REALITY.

GIBBOUS MOON

ALSO CALLED THE WAXING GIBBOUS MOON

I TAKE TIME TO RELAX
AND TRUST THAT MY DIVINE LIFE SOURCE IS FULLY SUPPORTING ME.
EVERYTHING IS BEING ALIGNED IN DIVINE, PERFECT TIMING.

I MEDITATE ON THE FEELINGS OF MY DESIRES FULFILLED.
I ADD EVEN MORE DETAIL INTO WHAT THEY FEEL LIKE
AS ALREADY MANIFESTED WITHIN EACH ASPECT OF MY LIFE.
I BRING IN MORE SENSES AND VITALITY, I BRING MY DREAMS TO LIFE.

HOW WILL I CARRY MYSELF NOW?
HOW WILL I DRESS, LOOK & BEHAVE NOW?
HOW WILL I SPEND MY TIME?
HOW **EXACTLY** HAS THIS CHANGED MY LIFE?
WHAT IS MY OVERALL VIBE IN EXPERIENCING THE TRUE FULFILLMENT OF MY DESIRES?
HOW DOES THIS REALLY **FEEL** HAVING THE
MANIFESTED FORM OF MY DESIRE EMANATING THROUGHOUT
EVERY SINGLE FIBER OF MY EXISTENCE?
HOW APPRECIATIVE AM I FEELING?!?

I WRITE A PRESENT TENSE JOURNAL SCRIPT FOR A DAY IN LIFE 'AS IF'
MY DESIRES HAVE ALREADY BEEN FULFILLED. I DO NOT FOCUS ON THE DETAILS FOR
HOW AND WHEN, BUT RATHER, HOW AMAZING MY LIFE IS NOW & HOW GRATEFUL I DO
IN FACT FEEL! DOING SO HELPS ME TO GET IN FLOW WITH THE AMAZING FEELINGS OF
THE PLEASURABLE DETAILS OF MY MANIFESTATION FULFILLED.
I **FEEL** MY DESIRE'S MANIFESTED FORM WITH **CLARITY**,
I AM NOW VERY FAMILIAR WITH THE FEELINGS MY DESIRE'S FULFILLED FORM BRINGS.

I AM IN A SELF LOVE PHASE, I TREAT MYSELF GENTLY.
I ALLOW MYSELF TO RELEASE THE URGE TO CONTROL,
I FOLLOW MY VISION WITH A BLISSFUL, PLAYFUL VIBRANCY
IN THE HEART OF MY BEING.
I FEEL GENUINE GRATITUDE, IN ADVANCE, FOR MY DESIRES MANIFESTED.
IN SURRENDERING TO A POWER GREATER THAN MYSELF,
I AM CREATING SPACE FOR LOVING BLISS TO FILL AND INSPIRE MY BEING.

FULL MOON

I CONTINUE TAKING INSPIRED ACTION AS I ILLUMINATE
ALONGSIDE THE MOON,
I CAN SEE WITH CLARITY,
THE WISDOM I ALREADY HOLD WITHIN ME.
EVERYTHING IS ALREADY WITHIN ME.

I AM BLOSSOMING FROM WITHIN.

I AM FEELING 'FULL' OF FAITH AND INSIGHT AT THIS TIME.

THE FULL MOON IS AN AMAZING TIME TO SURRENDER AND RELEASE FOR CLEANSING
ANY HOLDS FOR CONTROL I MAY HAVE IN REGARDS TO MY DESIRES.
I RELEASE THEM TO THE GREATEST WILL OF THE DIVINE SOURCE OF MY BEING,
I TRUST I AM BEING DIVINELY GUIDED AND SUPPORTED IN EACH MOMENT.

I REFLECT ON MY JOURNALING I HAVE DONE SO FAR THIS MOON CYCLE.

I CONTINUE TO MEDITATE AND DAYDREAM ON THE FEELINGS AND

EACH OF MY SENSES AS THOUGH MY DESIRES ARE COMPLETELY FULFILLED.

I ALLOW MYSELF TO ACT ON INSPIRATION.

I ALLOW MYSELF TO LOVE AND BE LOVE.

I AM DESIGNING THE LIFE I DESIRE THROUGH MY OWN PASSION AND BLISS.

I KNOW THAT MY DIVINE LIFE SOURCE IS SUPPORTING ME.

I ABSORB THE MOONLIGHT INTO MY SKIN, AURA AND ENTIRE BEING.

I PLACE ANY SPIRITUAL TOOLS / HEALING CRYSTALS / OILS / HERBS / WATER / BOOKS

IN THE DIRECT LIGHT OF THE FULL MOON,

TO BE INFUSED WITH POWERFUL AND LOVING ENERGY!

DISSEMINATING MOON

ALSO CALLED THE WANING GIBBOUS MOON

I ALLOW MYSELF TO RELAX AND REENERGIZE

AS I EMBODY THE VIBRATIONS OF RECEPTIVITY AND SATISFACTION.

I AM ALIGNED WITH MY DESIRE FULFILLED.

I PARTAKE IN MY FAVORITE FORMS OF SELF LOVE!

I MEDITATE ON MY LIFE'S PURPOSE NOW.
I REFLECT ON THE JOURNALING I HAVE DONE IN REGARDS TO
MY PASSIONS AND DESIRES. I EDIT MY LIFE DESIGN AS I PLEASE.
I GIVE THANKS FOR THE GUIDANCE I RECEIVE NOW,
ALLOWING ME TO EVOLVE TO MY TRUEST,
MOST FULFILLING POTENTIAL IN THIS LIFE.

ASSESS:
AM I HOLDING ON TO MY DESIRED OUTCOME TOO TIGHT??
DOING SO WILL RESTRICT MY DESIRES FROM FLOWING INTO MY LIFE,
I MUST TRUST THAT EVERYTHING I DESIRE IS COMING TO ME
IN THE MOST PEACEFUL AND LOVING WAY.
IT IS CRUCIAL THAT I CREATE THE SPACE FOR MY DESIRES TO ENTER INTO MY LIFE.
IF I AM ALWAYS OBSESSING OVER THE OUTCOME THEN I AM NOT
TRULY LETTING GO AND ALLOWING THE UNIVERSE TO DO ITS PART.
THE ART OF SURRENDER IS ABSOLUTELY CRUCIAL WITHIN MANIFESTATION.
IT FEELS AMAZING TO LET GO AND ALLOW.
IT IS EASIER TO LET GO THAN TO TRY TO CONTROL ALL THE LITTLE DETAILS,
AND CONSTANTLY WONDER WHERE MY DESIRE IS.
I LET GO AND I KEEP MY VIBRATIONS HIGH BY EVER-INCREASINGLY EMBODYING
THE FEELING STATES I WILL EXPERIENCE WITH MY DESIRES ALREADY FULFILLED.
& BY DOING THINGS I LOVE WHILE KEEPING THE VIBRATIONAL FREQUENCY OF MY
DAILY THOUGHTS & FEELINGS SO VERY HIGH, ON THE VIBRATION OF SATISFACTION.
THIS ALLOWS MY ENERGETIC FREQUENCY TO MATCH
THE FULFILLMENT OF MY DESIRED OUTCOME,
THUS ATTRACTING AN ENERGETIC MATCH [MY DESIRES]
-NOT THE FEELINGS OF LACK OR 'WELL, WHERE IS IT?'

I AM GRATEFUL THAT EVERYTHING IS
IN ALIGNMENT WITH THE HIGHEST GOOD FOR ALL.

MY VIBRATIONAL FREQUENCY IS IN PERFECT HARMONY WITH THE VIBRATIONAL
FREQUENCY OF MY DESIRE FULLY MANIFESTED IN MY LIFE, I AM GENUINELY GRATEFUL.

THIRD QUARTER MOON

ALSO CALLED THE LAST QUARTER MOON

I KNOW THAT MY EXTERNAL REALITY IS THE MANIFESTATION OF
THE FEELING STATES I HAVE PREDOMINANTLY EMBODIED
AND THE INSPIRED ACTION STEPS I HAVE TAKEN,
UP INTO THIS POINT IN TIME.

I AM GENUINELY GRATEFUL. I REFLECT ON MY GRATITUDE LISTS.
I RADIATE GRATITUDE TO THE PEOPLE WITHIN MY LIFE!
I CELEBRATE ALL OF MY GROWTH!

I ACTIVELY CLEANSE MY LIFE OF ANY TOXIC BELIEFS, MINDSETS,
RELATIONSHIPS, OLD CLUTTER, WORK SITUATIONS, ETC.
THAT NO LONGER BENEFIT MY LIFE DESIGN.
I REFLECT ON THE POWER IN CLEAN AND TIDY PAGES. I MAKE SURE MY ENTIRE BEING IS
CLEANSED OF ALL THAT IS NOT SERVING MY HIGHEST GOOD AND DESIRED LIFE DESIGN.
I ALSO REFLECT ON THE CORE VALUES & BOUNDARIES PAGES AND THE FORGIVENESS PAGES

WORDS OF WISDOM FROM DR. WAYNE DYER:
WHEN YOU CARRY AROUND RESENTMENT INSIDE OF YOU ABOUT ANYTHING OR ANYONE IT WILL
END UP HARMING YOU AND CREATING IN YOU A SENSE OF DESPAIR.
NO ONE EVER DIES FROM A SNAKE BITE; THE VENOM THAT CONTINUES TO POUR THROUGH YOUR
SYSTEM AFTER THE BITE IS WHAT WILL DESTROY YOU.

I ASSES ANY DOUBTS THAT I FEEL TOWARDS MY SUCCESS
AND MANIFESTATION CAPABILITIES.
I REFLECT INTO MY OWN SELF AND UNCOVER ANY LIMITING BELIEFS
I MAY HAVE LINGERING DEEP INSIDE OF ME.
I REFLECT ON THE SUBCONSCIOUS LIMITING BELIEFS PAGES.
I PERFORM A RITUAL OF RELEASE FOR SELF-LIMITING BELIEFS
AND BRING IN CONFIDENCE, LOVE AND FAITH IN THE FORCES UNSEEN.

BALSAMIC MOON

ALSO CALLED THE WANING CRESCENT MOON

I AM GRATEFUL FOR ALL THAT I HAVE ACHIEVED

AND RECEIVED THIS MOON CYCLE.

I EMBODY AN EVER-INCREASING FAITH IN MY OWN GROWTH.

I CELEBRATE ALL OF MY SUCCESSES BOTH BIG AND SMALL.

I AM IN A SELF LOVE PHASE, I ALLOW MYSELF TO RELAX AND REENERGIZE.

I AM BEING GENTLE AND AT PEACE WITH MYSELF IN THE LAST MOON PHASE,

THIS IS A WONDERFUL TIME TO PARTAKE IN AN IN-DEPTH AURA CLEANSE.

BY RESTING AND TAKING PART IN SELF LOVE RITUALS I PREPARE TO TAKE ACTION AGAIN.

I NOW LET GO [EVEN MORE]

OF ANYTHING I AM TRYING TOO HARD TO CONTROL WITHIN MY OWN LIFE.

I RECOGNIZE I MUST LET GO OF OBSESSING OVER

THE HOW AND WHEN DETAILS FOR HOW EACH OF MY DESIRES WILL MANIFEST.

IN DOING SO I ALLOW THE UNIVERSE FREEDOM AND SPACE TO MOVE WITH ME

IN WAYS MUCH GREATER THAN I COULD EVER PREDICT OR CONTROL.

I AM FEELING PHENOMENAL AND INSPIRED AS I RELAX DEEPER INTO MY

APPRECIATION, CONFIDENCE, SUCCESS, INFINITE LOVE

AND ALIGNMENT WITH THE UNIVERSE AND MY TRUEST SELF.

JOURNALING THROUGH THIS LIFE DESIGNER KEEPS ME GROWING

EVER-INCREASINGLY STRONGER. IT IS AN ACT OF SELF LOVE.

THE SPECIFIC
MOON CYCLES

ONE MOON CYCLE, FROM NEW MOON TO NEW MOON,

LASTS APPROXIMATELY 29.5 DAYS.

[ON AVERAGE] THE MOON IS 238,855 MILES (384,400 KM) FROM EARTH.

THE MOON TRAVELS AT 2,288 MPH (3,683 KM PER HOUR) AROUND THE EARTH.

DURING THIS TIME IT TRAVELS A DISTANCE OF 1,423,000 MILES (2,290,000 KM).

THE MOON TRAVELS AROUND THE EARTH 13 TIMES IN ONE YEAR.

THE MOON CHANGES ZODIAC SIGNS APPROXIMATELY EVERY TWO AND A HALF DAYS,

**EACH MOON CYCLE
OF 2019
HAS ITS OWN 2 PAGES.
AN OVERVIEW FOR
WHAT WE WILL BE WORKING WITH DURING
THAT PARTICULAR CYCLE,
& A REFERENCE TOOL FOR
THE DATES OF EACH PHASE OF THAT CYCLE.
USE THE MOON CYCLE PAGES ALONG WITH
THE MOON PHASE PAGES
WHEN CREATING YOUR NEW MOON INTENTION SCRIPT
FOR EACH OF THE NEW MOONS.**

THESE PAGES ARE PROVIDED TO KEEP YOU ALIGNED WITH
THE MOON CYCLES AND PHASES OF 2019.
PROVIDING AN INSPIRATIONAL OVERVIEW FOR
[BUT NOT IN-DEPTH DESCRIPTIONS OF]
THE ASTROLOGICAL INSIGHTS FOR EACH INDIVIDUAL CYCLE.
THERE ARE MANY OUTSTANDING SOURCES AVAILABLE ONLINE WHICH
PROVIDE WELL EXPLAINED, IN-DEPTH INSIGHTS AND INSPIRATION
DURING EACH PRESENT NEW AND FULL MOON.
IMMERSE YOURSELF IN WISDOM FROM THE SOURCES YOU PERSONALLY DESIRE ~

DEC. 2018 - JAN. 2019
MOON CYCLE

LUNAR
ALIGNMENT

NEW MOON IN SAGITTARIUS

AREAS OF FOCUS UNDER THE SAGITTARIUS NEW MOON:

WE NOW UNCOVER HOW WE CAN EXPRESS THE CHARACTERISTIC ENERGIES
OF THE ARCHER WITHIN OUR DESIRED LIFE DESIGN:

ALLOW YOURSELF TIME TO MEDITATE ON THESE AFFIRMATIONS FOR A FEW MOMENTS,
THEN JOURNAL WHAT YOU FEEL BEING BROUGHT TO ATTENTION WITHIN YOUR OWN BEING.
AFTER JOURNALING, REFLECT ON THE NEW MOON PAGE [PAGE 103].

I AM EXTRACTING MY LIFE PASSIONS AND DESIRES FROM THE CORE OF MY BEING.
I AM RIGHT NOW CURIOUS ABOUT_____. I HAVE ALWAYS BEEN CURIOUS ABOUT_____.
_____ IS WHAT LIVING A MEANINGFUL LIFE MEANS TO ME.
I AM NURTURING MY FAITH AND SURRENDERING MY URGES TO CONTROL
ANY AND ALL OUTCOMES, BIG OR SMALL.
I AM CONNECTED TO THE RIGHT PEOPLE, PLACES AND EXPERIENCES IN EACH MOMENT,
I TRUST THAT.
MY PERSONAL TRUTH EXPOSED AND ILLUMINATED WITH BLISS FEELS LIKE THIS:

BEGINNING ON THE NEW MOON DEC. 6-8, 2018

CRESCENT MOON DATES: DEC. 9-13, 2018

FIRST QUARTER MOON DATES: DEC. 14-16, 2018

GIBBOUS MOON DATES: DEC. 17-20, 2018

DEC. 2018 - JAN. 2019
MOON CYCLE

LUNAR
ALIGNMENT

FULL [COLD] MOON IN BEGINNING IN GEMINI, SUN IN SAGITTARIUS (OPPOSITE OF GEMINI) DEC. 21 AND TRANSITIONING INTO CANCER, SUN IN CAPRICORN (OPPOSITE OF CANCER) DEC. 22-23

WITH THE FULL MOON IN CANCER WE ARE ABLE TO INTUITIVELY
ILLUMINATE THE CHARACTERISTIC ENERGIES
OF THE CRAB WITHIN OUR LIFE:

REFLECT ON THE FULL MOON PAGE [PAGE 107].
THEN, MEDITATE ON THE FOLLOWING AFFIRMATIONS, JOURNAL WHAT YOU FEEL
BEING ILLUMINATED WITHIN YOUR OWN BEING.

AFTER JOURNALING,
YOU MAY DESIRE TO PERFORM A FULL MOON RITUAL
OF SURRENDER FOR ALL THAT IS NOT SERVING YOUR HIGHEST GOOD [SEE PAGE 100].

I AM ABLE TO BRING MORE PEACE INTO MY LIFE BY RELEASING:
I AM ABLE TO BRING MORE FEELINGS OF SAFETY AND SECURITY INTO MY LIFE BY
RELEASING THESE THOUGHTS AND FEELINGS:
TO LOVE MY HOME / SACRED SPACE ON AN EVEN DEEPER LEVEL
I CAN RELEASE THESE THINGS TO MAKE SPACE FOR NEW ENERGY:

[WINTER SOLSTICE IS DEC. 21, 2018]

FULL MOON DATES: DEC. 21-23, 2018

DISSEMINATING MOON DATES: DEC. 24-27, 2018

THIRD QUARTER MOON DATES: DEC. 28-30, 2018

FINISHING WITH THE BALSAMIC MOON DEC. 31, 2018 - JAN. 3, 2019

Jan. - Feb. 2019
Moon Cycle

Lunar
Alignment

New Moon in **Capricorn**

Areas of focus under the Capricorn New Moon:

We now uncover how we can express the characteristic energies
of the goat within our desired life design:

Allow yourself time to Meditate on these affirmations for a few moments,
then journal what you feel being brought to attention within your own being.
After journaling, reflect on the new moon page [page 103].

My determination to succeed is fueled by:
I am ambitious in pursuing my passions and desires.
I truly feel dedication in the core of my being because:
This is what keeps me motivated:

Beginning on the New Moon Jan. 4-7, 2019

Crescent Moon dates: Jan. 8-12, 2019

First Quarter Moon dates: Jan. 13-15, 2019

Gibbous Moon dates: Jan. 16-19, 2019

JAN. – FEB. 2019
MOON CYCLE

LUNAR
ALIGNMENT

FULL [WOLF] MOON IN LEO, SUN IN AQUARIUS (OPPOSITE OF LEO)

WITH THE FULL MOON IN LEO WE ARE ABLE TO INTUITIVELY
ILLUMINATE THE CHARACTERISTIC ENERGIES
OF THE LION WITHIN OUR LIFE:

REFLECT ON THE FULL MOON PAGE [PAGE 107].
THEN, MEDITATE ON THE FOLLOWING AFFIRMATIONS, JOURNAL WHAT YOU FEEL
BEING ILLUMINATED WITHIN YOUR OWN BEING.

AFTER JOURNALING,
YOU MAY DESIRE TO PERFORM A FULL MOON RITUAL
OF SURRENDER FOR ALL THAT IS NOT SERVING YOUR HIGHEST GOOD [SEE PAGE 100].

I FEEL _____ IS HINDERING MY CREATIVITY:
I AM LESS THAN CONFIDENT WHEN IT COMES TO _____.
I CAN NOW RELEASE THIS FEAR AND TRUST I WILL ALWAYS BE DIVINELY SUPPORTED.
THE ATTRIBUTES I AM EMBODYING THAT DO NOT SERVE MY HIGHEST GOOD:

FULL MOON DATES: JAN. 20-21, 2019

DISSEMINATING MOON DATES: JAN. 22-25, 2019

THIRD QUARTER MOON DATES: JAN. 26-28, 2019

FINISHING WITH THE BALSAMIC MOON JAN. 29 - FEB. 2, 2019

FEB. - MARCH 2019
MOON CYCLE

LUNAR
ALIGNMENT

NEW MOON IN **AQUARIUS**

AREAS OF FOCUS UNDER THE AQUARIUS NEW MOON:

WE NOW UNCOVER HOW WE CAN EXPRESS THE CHARACTERISTIC ENERGIES
OF THE WATER BEARER WITHIN OUR DESIRED LIFE DESIGN:

ALLOW YOURSELF TIME TO MEDITATE ON THESE AFFIRMATIONS FOR A FEW MOMENTS,
THEN JOURNAL WHAT YOU FEEL BEING BROUGHT TO ATTENTION WITHIN YOUR OWN BEING.
AFTER JOURNALING, REFLECT ON THE NEW MOON PAGE [PAGE 103].

THIS IS HOW I CAN ACTIVELY MAKE THINGS BETTER WITHIN MY LIFE:
TO BE THE CHANGE I WANT TO SEE IN THE WORLD WOULD REQUIRE THAT I:
BEING MY MOST AUTHENTIC SELF CONSISTS OF ME DOING THESE THINGS:
MY LIFE IS FULL OF PURE BLISS AND ENJOYMENT BECAUSE
EVERY DAY CONSISTS OF ME DOING THESE SPECIFIC THINGS:

BEGINNING ON THE NEW MOON FEB. 3-6, 2019

CRESCENT MOON DATES: FEB. 7-10, 2019

FIRST QUARTER MOON DATES: FEB. 11-13, 2019

GIBBOUS MOON DATES: FEB. 14-17, 2019

FEB. - MARCH 2019
MOON CYCLE

))((

LUNAR
ALIGNMENT

**FULL [SNOW] MOON BEGINNING IN LEO, SUN IN AQUARIUS (OPPOSITE OF LEO) FEB. 18
AND TRANSITIONING INTO VIRGO , SUN IN PISCES (OPPOSITE OF VIRGO) FEB. 19-20**

WITH THE FULL MOON IN VIRGO WE ARE ABLE TO INTUITIVELY
ILLUMINATE THE CHARACTERISTIC ENERGIES
OF THE VIRGIN WITHIN OUR LIFE:

REFLECT ON THE FULL MOON PAGE [PAGE 107].
THEN, MEDITATE ON THE FOLLOWING AFFIRMATIONS, JOURNAL WHAT YOU FEEL
BEING ILLUMINATED WITHIN YOUR OWN BEING.

AFTER JOURNALING,
YOU MAY DESIRE TO PERFORM A FULL MOON RITUAL
OF SURRENDER FOR ALL THAT IS NOT SERVING YOUR HIGHEST GOOD [SEE PAGE 100].

TO DEEPEN MY SELF LOVE I CAN RELEASE THESE
HABITS / THOUGHTS / FEELINGS:
I RELEASE ALL THAT FEELS HEAVY WITHIN MY LIFE AND BEING AT THIS TIME.
I AM NOW RELEASING ____ SO THAT I AM ABLE TO BECOME WHOLE
AND BALANCED WITHIN ____ ASPECTS OF MY LIFE.

FULL MOON DATES: FEB. 18-20, 2019

DISSEMINATING MOON DATES: FEB. 21-24, 2019

THIRD QUARTER MOON DATES: FEB. 25-27, 2019

FINISHING WITH THE BALSAMIC MOON : FEB. 28 - MARCH 4, 2019

MARCH - APRIL 2019
MOON CYCLE

)O(

LUNAR
ALIGNMENT

New Moon in **Pisces**

Areas of focus under the Pisces New Moon:

We now uncover how we can express the characteristic energies
of the two fish within our desired life design:

Allow yourself time to Meditate on these affirmations for a few moments,
then journal what you feel being brought to attention within your own being.
After journaling, reflect on the new moon page [page 103].

I contain an abundance of love.
This is what true love looks like to me:
I am loving to myself in these specific ways:
These are ways I can be more self loving:
I am always strengthening my connection with my inner divine Goddess,
to radiate more pure love and magick within my life.

Beginning on the New Moon March 5-7, 2019

Crescent Moon dates: March 8-12, 2019

FIRST QUARTER MOON DATES: MARCH 13-15, 2019

Gibbous Moon dates: March 16-19, 2019

MARCH - APRIL 2019
MOON CYCLE

‍

LUNAR
ALIGNMENT

FULL [WORM] MOON BEGINNING IN VIRGO , SUN IN PISCES (OPPOSITE OF VIRGO) MARCH 20
AND TRANSITIONING INTO LIBRA , SUN IN ARIES (OPPOSITE OF LIBRA) MARCH 21

THIS FULL MOON IS IN BOTH VIRGO AND LIBRA ~ YOU CAN INTEGRATE THE VIRGO PROMPTS
[SEE LAST MONTH'S FULL MOON PAGE] ALONGSIDE THE LIBRA PROMPTS BELOW.
APRIL'S FULL MOON WILL ALSO BE IN THE SIGN OF LIBRA.

WITH THE FULL MOON IN LIBRA WE ARE ABLE TO INTUITIVELY
ILLUMINATE THE CHARACTERISTIC ENERGIES
OF THE SCALES WITHIN OUR LIFE:

REFLECT ON THE FULL MOON PAGE [PAGE 107].
THEN, MEDITATE ON THE FOLLOWING AFFIRMATIONS, JOURNAL WHAT YOU FEEL
BEING ILLUMINATED WITHIN YOUR OWN BEING.

AFTER JOURNALING,
YOU MAY DESIRE TO PERFORM A FULL MOON RITUAL
OF SURRENDER FOR ALL THAT IS NOT SERVING YOUR HIGHEST GOOD [SEE PAGE 100].

I AM NOW RELEASING ___ SO THAT I AM ABLE TO EMANATE
FAIRNESS, PEACE AND HARMONY WITHIN MY LIFE.
I GIVE THANKS FOR ALL SUPPORTIVE RELATIONSHIPS IN MY LIFE,
I RELEASE ANY AND ALL RELATIONSHIPS THAT DO NOT SERVE MY HIGHEST GOOD.
I MEDITATE ON ALL YIN AND YANG ASPECTS OF MY BEING,
I RELEASE THE UNBALANCED ASPECTS OF MY INTERIOR ENERGIES
SO THAT I MAY HARMONIZE WITH MY DESIRE'S
VIBRATIONAL FREQUENCY.

[SPRING EQUINOX IS MARCH 20, 2019]

FULL MOON DATES: MARCH 20-21, 2019

DISSEMINATING MOON DATES: MARCH 22-26, 2019

THIRD QUARTER MOON DATES: MARCH 27-29, 2019

FINISHING WITH THE BALSAMIC MOON : MARCH 30 - APRIL 3, 2019

APRIL - MAY 2019
MOON CYCLE

ↃᏆC

LUNAR
ALIGNMENT

NEW MOON IN **ARIES**

AREAS OF FOCUS UNDER THE ARIES NEW MOON:

WE NOW UNCOVER HOW WE CAN EXPRESS THE CHARACTERISTIC ENERGIES
OF THE RAM WITHIN OUR DESIRED LIFE DESIGN:

THIS IS THE SIGN YOU'VE BEEN WAITING FOR: ARIES IS THE FIRST ZODIAC SIGN,
YOUR FRESH START IS HERE NOW!
BE OPEN TO RECEIVING NEW, BLISSFUL OPPORTUNITIES.
CHEERS TO NEW BEGINNINGS!

ALLOW YOURSELF TIME TO MEDITATE ON THESE AFFIRMATIONS FOR A FEW MOMENTS,
THEN JOURNAL WHAT YOU FEEL BEING BROUGHT TO ATTENTION WITHIN YOUR OWN BEING.
AFTER JOURNALING, REFLECT ON THE NEW MOON PAGE [PAGE 103].

I AM FEARLESS IN DEFINING AND ACTING UPON WHAT I DESIRE.
I LEAD MY LIFE IN THE DIRECTION OF MY CHOOSING BECAUSE I AM WORTHY.
THIS IS WHAT I CAN DO TO ELEVATE MY BRAVERY:
I AM ABUNDANTLY RECEIVING AS RESULT OF
THE FULFILLMENT OF MY INNERMOST DESIRES.

BEGINNING ON THE NEW MOON APRIL 4-6, 2019

CRESCENT MOON DATES: APRIL 7-10, 2019

FIRST QUARTER MOON DATES: APRIL 11-13, 2019

GIBBOUS MOON DATES: APRIL 14-17, 2019

APRIL - MAY 2019
MOON CYCLE

LUNAR
ALIGNMENT

**FULL [PINK] MOON BEGINNING IN LIBRA , SUN IN ARIES (OPPOSITE OF LIBRA) APRIL 18-19
AND TRANSITIONING INTO SCORPIO, SUN IN TAURUS (OPPOSITE OF SCORPIO) APRIL 20**

WITH THE FULL MOON IN LIBRA WE ARE ABLE TO INTUITIVELY
ILLUMINATE THE CHARACTERISTIC ENERGIES
OF THE SCALES WITHIN OUR LIFE:

REFLECT ON THE FULL MOON PAGE [PAGE 107].
THEN, MEDITATE ON THE FOLLOWING AFFIRMATIONS, JOURNAL WHAT YOU FEEL
BEING ILLUMINATED WITHIN YOUR OWN BEING.

AFTER JOURNALING,
YOU MAY DESIRE TO PERFORM A FULL MOON RITUAL
OF SURRENDER FOR ALL THAT IS NOT SERVING YOUR HIGHEST GOOD [SEE PAGE 100].

I AM NOW RELEASING ___ SO THAT I AM ABLE TO EMANATE
FAIRNESS, PEACE AND HARMONY WITHIN MY LIFE.
I GIVE THANKS FOR ALL SUPPORTIVE RELATIONSHIPS IN MY LIFE,
I RELEASE ANY AND ALL RELATIONSHIPS THAT DO NOT SERVE MY HIGHEST GOOD.
I MEDITATE ON ALL YIN AND YANG ASPECTS OF MY BEING,
I RELEASE THE UNBALANCED ASPECTS OF MY INTERIOR ENERGIES
SO THAT I MAY HARMONIZE WITH MY DESIRE'S
VIBRATIONAL FREQUENCY.

FULL MOON DATES: APRIL 18-20, 2019

DISSEMINATING MOON DATES: APRIL 21-24, 2019

THIRD QUARTER MOON DATES: APRIL 25-28, 2019

FINISHING WITH THE BALSAMIC MOON : APRIL 29 - MAY 2, 2019

MAY - JUNE 2019
MOON CYCLE

LUNAR
ALIGNMENT

New Moon in Taurus

Areas of focus under the Taurus New Moon:

We now uncover how we can express the characteristic energies
of the bull within our desired life design:

Allow yourself time to Meditate on these affirmations for a few moments,
then journal what you feel being brought to attention within your own being.
After journaling, reflect on the new moon page [page 103].

I allow myself to relax and be rewarded.
This is how I can relax even deeper, in order to create optimal space
and alignment for my desires to flow abundantly into my life:
I can ___ to comfort, please and soothe my unique soul,
doing so allows me to sink deeper in tune with my feeling based senses.
Getting me out of my head and into my body.
I appreciate Earth, as she is [also] a live and flourishing Goddess.
I eat whole food from her, I plant life into her.
I give thanks to her for supporting me throughout my entire lifetime.

BEGINNING ON THE NEW MOON MAY 3-5, 2019

CRESCENT MOON DATES: MAY 6-10, 2019

FIRST QUARTER MOON DATES: MAY 11-12, 2019

GIBBOUS MOON DATES: MAY 13-16, 2019

MAY - JUNE 2019
MOON CYCLE

LUNAR
ALIGNMENT

FULL [FLOWER] MOON IN SCORPIO, SUN IN TAURUS (OPPOSITE OF SCORPIO)

WITH THE FULL MOON IN SCORPIO WE ARE ABLE TO INTUITIVELY
ILLUMINATE THE CHARACTERISTIC ENERGIES
OF THE SCORPION WITHIN OUR LIFE:

REFLECT ON THE FULL MOON PAGE [PAGE 107].
THEN, MEDITATE ON THE FOLLOWING AFFIRMATIONS, JOURNAL WHAT YOU FEEL
BEING ILLUMINATED WITHIN YOUR OWN BEING.

AFTER JOURNALING,
YOU MAY DESIRE TO PERFORM A FULL MOON RITUAL
OF SURRENDER FOR ALL THAT IS NOT SERVING YOUR HIGHEST GOOD [SEE PAGE 100].

I AM IN CONTROL OF MY DESTINY,
I EMBODY THE POWER TO RELEASE WHAT IS NOT SERVING MY HIGHEST GOOD.
RELEASING __ WILL CREATE SPACE FOR MORE PASSION TO ENTER MY LIFE.
THESE THINGS ARE HINDERING MY MOTIVATION AND DETERMINATION:
I CAN RELEASE THESE BELIEFS TO BRING IN MORE INTIMACY
[INTERNALLY AND EXTERNALLY] WITHIN MY LIFE:

FULL MOON DATES: MAY 17-19, 2019

DISSEMINATING MOON DATES: MAY 20-24, 2019

THIRD QUARTER MOON DATES: MAY 25-27, 2019

FINISHING WITH THE BALSAMIC MOON : MAY 28 - JUNE 1, 2019

JUNE 2019
MOON CYCLE

LUNAR
ALIGNMENT

NEW MOON IN **GEMINI**

AREAS OF FOCUS UNDER THE GEMINI NEW MOON:

WE NOW UNCOVER HOW WE CAN EXPRESS THE CHARACTERISTIC ENERGIES
OF THE TWINS WITHIN OUR DESIRED LIFE DESIGN:

ALLOW YOURSELF TIME TO MEDITATE ON THESE AFFIRMATIONS FOR A FEW MOMENTS,
THEN JOURNAL WHAT YOU FEEL BEING BROUGHT TO ATTENTION WITHIN YOUR OWN BEING.
AFTER JOURNALING, REFLECT ON THE NEW MOON PAGE [PAGE 103].

I HAVE THE MOST FUN WHEN I AM:
I AM ABLE TO CREATE MORE PLAYFULNESS IN MY LIFE BY:
MY INNER CHILD LOVES ALL OF THESE THINGS:
I LOVE TO ENGAGE MY MIND IN THESE SPECIFIC WAYS:
I AM COMMUNICATING WELL, IN SUPPORT OF MY DESIRES.

BEGINNING ON THE NEW MOON JUNE 2-4, 2019

CRESCENT MOON DATES: JUNE 5-8, 2019

FIRST QUARTER MOON DATES: JUNE 9-11, 2019

GIBBOUS MOON DATES: JUNE 12-15, 2019

JUNE 2019
MOON CYCLE

LUNAR
ALIGNMENT

FULL [ROSE] MOON IN SAGITTARIUS, SUN IN GEMINI (OPPOSITE OF SAGITTARIUS)

WITH THE FULL MOON IN SAGITTARIUS WE ARE ABLE TO INTUITIVELY
ILLUMINATE THE CHARACTERISTIC ENERGIES
OF THE ARCHER WITHIN OUR LIFE:

REFLECT ON THE FULL MOON PAGE [PAGE 107].
THEN, MEDITATE ON THE FOLLOWING AFFIRMATIONS, JOURNAL WHAT YOU FEEL
BEING ILLUMINATED WITHIN YOUR OWN BEING.

AFTER JOURNALING,
YOU MAY DESIRE TO PERFORM A FULL MOON RITUAL
OF SURRENDER FOR ALL THAT IS NOT SERVING YOUR HIGHEST GOOD [SEE PAGE 100].

I ALLOW MY CURIOSITY TO WONDER FREELY.
I CAN RELEASE ___ TO CREATE SPACE FOR MORE ENERGY THAT IS TRUE TO MY OWN SOUL.
MY TRUTH EXPOSED AND ILLUMINATED FEELS LIKE THIS:
I ENTHUSIASTICALLY WELCOME AND EMBRACE CHANGE.

FULL MOON DATES: JUNE 16-18, 2019

[SUMMER SOLSTICE IS JUNE 21, 2019]

DISSEMINATING MOON DATES: JUNE 19-23, 2019

THIRD QUARTER MOON DATES: JUNE 24-26, 2019

FINISHING WITH THE BALSAMIC MOON : JUNE 27-30, 2019

JULY 2019
MOON CYCLE

LUNAR
ALIGNMENT

NEW MOON IN CANCER

AREAS OF FOCUS UNDER THE CANCER NEW MOON:

WE NOW UNCOVER HOW WE CAN EXPRESS THE CHARACTERISTIC ENERGIES
OF THE CRAB WITHIN OUR DESIRED LIFE DESIGN:

ALLOW YOURSELF TIME TO MEDITATE ON THESE AFFIRMATIONS FOR A FEW MOMENTS,
THEN JOURNAL WHAT YOU FEEL BEING BROUGHT TO ATTENTION WITHIN YOUR OWN BEING.
AFTER JOURNALING, REFLECT ON THE NEW MOON PAGE [PAGE 103].

I AM ABLE TO BRING MORE PEACE INTO MY LIFE BY:
I AM ABLE TO BRING MORE FEELINGS OF SAFETY AND SECURITY INTO MY LIFE BY:
I AM IN LOVE WITH MY HOME.
I HAVE A SACRED SPACE OF MY OWN.

BEGINNING ON THE NEW MOON JULY 1-3, 2019

CRESCENT MOON DATES: JULY 4-7, 2019

FIRST QUARTER MOON DATES: JULY 8-10, 2019

GIBBOUS MOON DATES: JULY 11-14, 2019

JULY 2019
MOON CYCLE

LUNAR
ALIGNMENT

FULL [THUNDER] MOON IN CAPRICORN, SUN IN CANCER (OPPOSITE OF CAPRICORN)

WITH THE FULL MOON IN CAPRICORN WE ARE ABLE TO INTUITIVELY
ILLUMINATE THE CHARACTERISTIC ENERGIES
OF THE GOAT WITHIN OUR LIFE:

REFLECT ON THE FULL MOON PAGE [PAGE 107].
THEN, MEDITATE ON THE FOLLOWING AFFIRMATIONS, JOURNAL WHAT YOU FEEL
BEING ILLUMINATED WITHIN YOUR OWN BEING.

AFTER JOURNALING,
YOU MAY DESIRE TO PERFORM A FULL MOON RITUAL
OF SURRENDER FOR ALL THAT IS NOT SERVING YOUR HIGHEST GOOD [SEE PAGE 100].

THE RELEASE OF FULL AMBITION TOWARDS MY DESIRED LIFE DESIGN IS HINDERED BY:
I CAN REMOVE ____ FROM MY LIFE
SO THAT I AM EVEN MORE DEDICATED AND MOTIVATED.

FULL MOON DATES: JULY 15-18, 2019

DISSEMINATING MOON DATES: JULY 19-22, 2019

THIRD QUARTER MOON DATES: JULY 23-26, 2019

FINISHING WITH THE BALSAMIC MOON : JULY 27-30, 2019

AUGUST 2019
MOON CYCLE

ⅮⅭ

LUNAR
ALIGNMENT

NEW MOON IN LEO

AREAS OF FOCUS UNDER THE LEO NEW MOON:

WE NOW UNCOVER HOW WE CAN EXPRESS THE CHARACTERISTIC ENERGIES
OF THE LION WITHIN OUR DESIRED LIFE DESIGN:

ALLOW YOURSELF TIME TO MEDITATE ON THESE AFFIRMATIONS FOR A FEW MOMENTS,
THEN JOURNAL WHAT YOU FEEL BEING BROUGHT TO ATTENTION WITHIN YOUR OWN BEING.
AFTER JOURNALING, REFLECT ON THE NEW MOON PAGE [PAGE 103].

I AM CONSTANTLY FINDING WAYS TO EXPRESS MY CREATIVITY, MY FAVORITE WAYS ARE:
MY AMBITION DRIVES ME TO TAKE THE ROADS LESS TRAVELED,
I AM CONFIDENT I WILL ALWAYS BE DIVINELY SUPPORTED.
MY PERSONAL STRENGTHS INCLUDE:
I AM ATTRACTING THE LOVE I DESIRE TO RECEIVE,
BY EMBODYING THOSE ATTRIBUTES WITHIN MYSELF FIRST, THEY ARE:

BEGINNING ON THE NEW MOON JULY 31 - AUG. 1, 2019

CRESCENT MOON DATES: AUG. 2-5, 2019

FIRST QUARTER MOON DATES: AUG. 6-8, 2019

GIBBOUS MOON DATES: AUG. 9-13, 2019

AUGUST 2019
MOON CYCLE

LUNAR
ALIGNMENT

FULL [STURGEON] MOON IN AQUARIUS, SUN IN LEO (OPPOSITE OF AQUARIUS)

WITH THE FULL MOON IN AQUARIUS WE ARE ABLE TO INTUITIVELY
ILLUMINATE THE CHARACTERISTIC ENERGIES
OF THE WATER BEARER WITHIN OUR LIFE:

REFLECT ON THE FULL MOON PAGE [PAGE 107].
THEN, MEDITATE ON THE FOLLOWING AFFIRMATIONS, JOURNAL WHAT YOU FEEL
BEING ILLUMINATED WITHIN YOUR OWN BEING.

AFTER JOURNALING,
YOU MAY DESIRE TO PERFORM A FULL MOON RITUAL
OF SURRENDER FOR ALL THAT IS NOT SERVING YOUR HIGHEST GOOD [SEE PAGE 100].

I CAN RELEASE THESE JUDGEMENTS:
TO BE THE CHANGE I WANT TO SEE IN THE WORLD WOULD REQUIRE THAT I REMOVE
THESE HABITS / BELIEFS / FEELINGS FROM MY OWN BEING AND MY OWN LIFE:
I CAN GIVE THESE THINGS TO OTHERS IN NEED:

FULL MOON DATES: AUG. 14-16, 2019

DISSEMINATING MOON DATES: AUG. 17-21, 2019

THIRD QUARTER MOON DATES: AUG. 22-24, 2019

FINISHING WITH THE BALSAMIC MOON : AUG. 25-28, 2019

SEPTEMBER 2019
MOON CYCLE

⊃○⊂

LUNAR
ALIGNMENT

New Moon in **Virgo**

Areas of focus under the Virgo New Moon:

We now uncover how we can express the characteristic energies
of the virgin within our desired life design:

Allow yourself time to Meditate on these affirmations for a few moments,
then journal what you feel being brought to attention within your own being.
After journaling, reflect on the new moon page [page 103].

I am always desiring the highest good for all souls.
I am physically well, I love my body because:
To show more love to my body I can:
I am financially stable and that feels amazing because:
I am balanced within all aspects of my life.
These things satisfy me on a soul level:

BEGINNING ON THE NEW MOON AUG. 29-31, 2019

CRESCENT MOON DATES: SEPT. 1-4, 2019

FIRST QUARTER MOON DATES: SEPT. 5-7, 2019

GIBBOUS MOON DATES: SEPT. 8-12, 2019

SEPTEMBER 2019
MOON CYCLE

LUNAR
ALIGNMENT

FULL [HARVEST] MOON IN PISCES, SUN IN VIRGO (OPPOSITE OF PISCES)

WITH THE FULL MOON IN PISCES WE ARE ABLE TO INTUITIVELY
ILLUMINATE THE CHARACTERISTIC ENERGIES
OF THE TWO FISH WITHIN OUR LIFE:

REFLECT ON THE FULL MOON PAGE [PAGE 107].
THEN, MEDITATE ON THE FOLLOWING AFFIRMATIONS, JOURNAL WHAT YOU FEEL
BEING ILLUMINATED WITHIN YOUR OWN BEING.

AFTER JOURNALING,
YOU MAY DESIRE TO PERFORM A FULL MOON RITUAL
OF SURRENDER FOR ALL THAT IS NOT SERVING YOUR HIGHEST GOOD [SEE PAGE 100].

I CAN DEEPER LOVE MYSELF BY RELEASING:
I CAN DEEPER LOVE OTHERS BY RELEASING:
I AM ALWAYS STRENGTHENING MY CONNECTION WITH MY INNER DIVINE GODDESS,
IN DOING SO I EVER-INCREASINGLY RADIATING PURE LOVE AND MAGICK.

FULL MOON DATES: SEPT. 13-15, 2019

DISSEMINATING MOON DATES: SEPT. 16-20, 2019

[AUTUMN EQUINOX IS SEPT. 23, 2019]

THIRD QUARTER MOON DATES: SEPT. 21-23, 2019

FINISHING WITH THE BALSAMIC MOON : SEPT. 24-27, 2019

SEPTEMBER - OCTOBER 2019
MOON CYCLE

))C(

LUNAR
ALIGNMENT

New Moon in **Libra**

Areas of focus under the Libra New Moon:

We now uncover how we can express the characteristic energies
of the scales within our desired life design:

Allow yourself time to Meditate on these affirmations for a few moments,
then journal what you feel being brought to attention within your own being.
After journaling, reflect on the new moon page [page 103].

I am emanating fairness, peace and harmony within my life
in these specific ways:
I am strengthening my support systems and my faith that the entire universe is
supporting me at all moments.
I give thanks for all supportive relationships in my life.
I meditate on all yin and yang aspects of my being
I journal what comes to me when I think of
the feminine and masculine energies within myself.
I give thanks.

BEGINNING ON THE NEW MOON SEPT. 28-29, 2019

CRESCENT MOON DATES: SEPT. 30 - OCT. 3, 2019

FIRST QUARTER MOON DATES: OCT. 4-6, 2019

GIBBOUS MOON DATES: OCT. 7-11, 2019

SEPTEMBER - OCTOBER 2019
MOON CYCLE
LUNAR
ALIGNMENT

Full [hunter's] moon in Aries, sun in Libra (opposite of Aries)

With the full moon in Aries we are able to intuitively
illuminate the characteristic energies
of the Ram within our life:

Reflect on the full moon page [page 107].
Then, Meditate on the following affirmations, journal what you feel
being illuminated within your own being.

After journaling,
you may desire to perform a full moon ritual
of surrender for all that is not serving your highest good [see page 100].

I lead my life in the direction of my choosing because I am worthy.
I can release ___ to elevate my bravery.
These things generate low / heavy energy levels within me:
I release them now.

FULL MOON DATES: OCT. 12-14, 2019

DISSEMINATING MOON DATES: OCT. 15-19, 2019

THIRD QUARTER MOON DATES: OCT. 20-22, 2019

FINISHING WITH THE BALSAMIC MOON : OCT. 23-26, 2019

OCTOBER – NOVEMBER 2019
MOON CYCLE

LUNAR
ALIGNMENT

New Moon in **Scorpio**

Areas of focus under the Scorpio New Moon:

We now uncover how we can express the characteristic energies
of the scorpion within our desired life design:

Allow yourself time to Meditate on these affirmations for a few moments,
then journal what you feel being brought to attention within your own being.
After journaling, reflect on the new moon page [page 103].

I am designing the life I desire to live.
The intense passion and desire I feel deep within
bring me motivation and determination in these ways:
my soul's deepest passions bring the most fulfilling forms of
love, wealth and abundance into my life.
This is Intimacy defined by me:
I am spirit having a human experience.
I embrace my intuition deeply at this time.
I allow release, I allow transformation, I embrace change.

BEGINNING ON THE NEW MOON OCT. 27-28, 2019

CRESCENT MOON DATES: OCT. 29 – NOV. 2, 2019

FIRST QUARTER MOON DATES: NOV. 3-5, 2019

GIBBOUS MOON DATES: NOV. 6-10, 2019

OCTOBER – NOVEMBER 2019
MOON CYCLE

LUNAR
ALIGNMENT

FULL [FROST] MOON IN TAURUS, SUN IN SCORPIO (OPPOSITE OF TAURUS)

WITH THE FULL MOON IN TAURUS WE ARE ABLE TO INTUITIVELY
ILLUMINATE THE CHARACTERISTIC ENERGIES
OF THE BULL WITHIN OUR LIFE:

REFLECT ON THE FULL MOON PAGE [PAGE 107].
THEN, MEDITATE ON THE FOLLOWING AFFIRMATIONS, JOURNAL WHAT YOU FEEL
BEING ILLUMINATED WITHIN YOUR OWN BEING.

AFTER JOURNALING,
YOU MAY DESIRE TO PERFORM A FULL MOON RITUAL
OF SURRENDER FOR ALL THAT IS NOT SERVING YOUR HIGHEST GOOD [SEE PAGE 100].

I CAN RELEASE ___ TO MORE DEEPLY COMFORT, PLEASE AND SOOTHE MY UNIQUE SOUL.
DOING SO ALLOWS ME TO SINK DEEPER IN TUNE WITH MY FEELING BASED SENSES.
ALLOWING ME TO MOVE OUT OF MY HEAD AND INTO MY BODY.
I APPRECIATE EARTH, AS SHE IS [ALSO] A LIVE AND FLOURISHING GODDESS.
I EAT WHOLE FOOD FROM HER, I GIVE THANKS TO HER.
I APPRECIATE ALL SHE PROVIDES TO ME WHILE I AM ON MY JOURNEY HERE.

FULL MOON DATES: NOV. 11-13, 2019

DISSEMINATING MOON DATES: NOV. 14-17, 2019

THIRD QUARTER MOON DATES: NOV. 18-20, 2019

FINISHING WITH THE BALSAMIC MOON : NOV. 21-24, 2019

NOVEMBER - DECEMBER 2019
MOON CYCLE

)(

LUNAR
ALIGNMENT

NEW MOON IN **SAGITTARIUS**

AREAS OF FOCUS UNDER THE SAGITTARIUS NEW MOON:

WE NOW UNCOVER HOW WE CAN EXPRESS THE CHARACTERISTIC ENERGIES
OF THE ARCHER WITHIN OUR DESIRED LIFE DESIGN:

ALLOW YOURSELF TIME TO MEDITATE ON THESE AFFIRMATIONS FOR A FEW MOMENTS,
THEN JOURNAL WHAT YOU FEEL BEING BROUGHT TO ATTENTION WITHIN YOUR OWN BEING.
AFTER JOURNALING, REFLECT ON THE NEW MOON PAGE [PAGE 103].

I AM EXTRACTING MY LIFE PASSIONS AND DESIRES FROM THE CORE OF MY BEING.
I AM RIGHT NOW CURIOUS ABOUT_____. I HAVE ALWAYS BEEN CURIOUS ABOUT_____.
_____ IS WHAT LIVING A MEANINGFUL LIFE MEANS TO ME.
I AM NURTURING MY FAITH AND SURRENDERING MY URGES TO CONTROL
ANY AND ALL OUTCOMES, BIG OR SMALL.
I AM CONNECTED TO THE RIGHT PEOPLE, PLACES AND EXPERIENCES IN EACH MOMENT,
I TRUST THAT.
MY PERSONAL TRUTH EXPOSED AND ILLUMINATED WITH BLISS FEELS LIKE THIS:

BEGINNING ON THE NEW MOON NOV. 25-27, 2019

CRESCENT MOON DATES: NOV. 28 - DEC. 2, 2019

FIRST QUARTER MOON DATES: DEC. 3-5, 2019

GIBBOUS MOON DATES: DEC. 6-10, 2019

NOVEMBER - DECEMBER 2019
MOON CYCLE
LUNAR
ALIGNMENT

FULL [COLD] MOON IN GEMINI, SUN IN SAGITTARIUS (OPPOSITE OF GEMINI)

WITH THE FULL MOON IN GEMINI WE ARE ABLE TO INTUITIVELY
ILLUMINATE THE CHARACTERISTIC ENERGIES
OF THE TWINS WITHIN OUR LIFE:

REFLECT ON THE FULL MOON PAGE [PAGE 107].
THEN, MEDITATE ON THE FOLLOWING AFFIRMATIONS, JOURNAL WHAT YOU FEEL
BEING ILLUMINATED WITHIN YOUR OWN BEING.

AFTER JOURNALING,
YOU MAY DESIRE TO PERFORM A FULL MOON RITUAL
OF SURRENDER FOR ALL THAT IS NOT SERVING YOUR HIGHEST GOOD [SEE PAGE 100].

I CAN RELEASE ___ TO ALLOW SPACE FOR MORE GENUINE FUN AND PLAYFULNESS IN MY LIFE.
I CAN RELEASE THESE LIMITING BELIEFS AND FILL THIS SPACE WITH EMPOWERING BELIEFS:
I CAN SURRENDER ____ TO ELEVATE MY VIBRATION INTO PEACE AND SATISFACTION.

FULL MOON DATES: DEC. 11-13, 2019

DISSEMINATING MOON DATES: DEC. 14-17, 2019

THIRD QUARTER MOON DATES: DEC. 18-20, 2019

[WINTER SOLSTICE IS DEC. 21, 2019]
FINISHING WITH THE BALSAMIC MOON : DEC. 21-24, 2019

BECOMING YOUR BEST SELF

IS

SIMPLY

EXTRACTING

AND EMBRACING

YOUR POTENTIAL OF

ALL THAT YOU ARE AND DESIRE TO BE.

SEEK TRUE AUTHENTICITY OVER SEEKING PERFECTION.

YOUR TRUEST AUTHENTICITY IS IN FACT ATTAINABLE, AND CONTAINS THE MOST REWARDING EXPERIENCES AND FEELINGS - FAR ABOVE AND BEYOND WHAT YOU CAN IMAGINE IN THESE MOMENTS RIGHT HERE. PERFECTION IS NOT ATTAINABLE, PERIOD. ALTHOUGH YOU MAY THINK REACHING PERFECTION WILL BE REWARDING, IT WON'T BE. CHASING PERFECTION WILL LEAVE YOU ALWAYS FEELING THAT THERE IS 'SOMETHING ELSE' YOU NEED IN ORDER TO BE PERFECT AND HAPPY. CHOOSE TO SWITCH YOUR PERCEPTION. WHEN YOU BEGIN TO DIG INTO WHAT YOUR DEEPEST AUTHENTICITY CONSISTS OF YOU WILL BE BLESSED WITH SO MUCH GENUINE BLISS, AND SO MUCH LIGHTHEARTED HAPPINESS. INSPIRATION WILL FLOW INTO YOUR MIND, BODY AND SOUL WITH GRACEFULNESS AND EASE. YOU WILL NO LONGER BE CONCERNED WITH REACHING 'PERFECTION' AND AT THE SAME TIME YOU WILL PARADOXICALLY BEGIN TO TRULY FEEL PERFECT.

THE FOLLOWING PAGES ARE DESIGNED AS **DAILY** JOURNALING AND INSPIRATION TOOLS.

THEY ARE UNIVERSAL AMONGST THE VARIOUS MOON PHASES AND CYCLES OF THE YEAR.
FOLLOWING THESE PAGES DAILY ALLOWS FOR
DESIGNING, ALIGNING AND MANIFESTING
ANY AND ALL DESIRES.

THE GODDESS LIFE DESIGNER IS FORMULATED IN ALIGNMENT WITH THE SUN AND THE MOON AS FOCAL POINTS FOR LIFE PLANNING AND INTENTION SETTING. I PERSONALLY LOVE THIS, AS WHAT BETTER WAY TO DESIGN OUR HUMAN LIFETIME THAN THROUGH UTILIZING THE FOCAL POINTS WE HAVE ALL BEEN GIFTED AND SHARE. NO MATTER WHERE WE ARE LOCATED ON PLANET EARTH WE ALL EXPERIENCE THE SUN AND THE MOON. I DO BELIEVE THE GODDESS LIFE DESIGNER SERVES AS A POWERFUL GUIDE IN MANIFESTING ANY SOUL'S DESIRED LIFE DESIGN. I HAVE FAITH THAT THE ALIGNMENT YOU FIND WITHIN WILL FLOW WITH YOUR LIFE VERY, VERY WELL. THAT BEING SAID, STILL ALWAYS TRUST YOUR INTUITION. BY THAT I MEAN, IF IT IS PRESENTLY A MOON PHASE THAT IS NOT THE NEW MOON AND YOU REALLY FEEL THE URGE TO PARTAKE IN AN INTENTION SETTING RITUAL, BY ALL MEANS DO SO! ALSO, IF IT IS PRESENTLY A MOON PHASE DESCRIBED AS AN ACTION PHASE AND YOU REALLY AREN'T FEELING LIKE TAKING ANY ACTION, BUT INSTEAD REALLY FEEL PULLED TO INDULGE IN RELAXATION, SELF-CARE OR SELF-REFLECTION, BY ALL MEANS DO SO! THERE IS MOST DEFINITELY A REASON YOU ARE EXPERIENCING THIS INTUITIVE FEELING, YOUR HIGHER SELF WANTS YOU TO RELAX SO THAT YOU CAN RECEIVE SOME INSIGHT OR MESSAGE THAT YOU WOULDN'T RECEIVE IF YOU WERE FORCING YOURSELF TO PUSH FORWARD IN ACTION. ONLY TAKE ACTION WHEN IT IS INSPIRED ACTION THAT IS ALIGNED WITH YOUR DESIRE AND FEELS RIGHT. RELAXATION, SELF-CARE AND SELF-REFLECTION ALLOW THE ANALYTICAL MIND TO CALM, AND THIS ALLOWS YOU TO BE FULLY AWARE OF YOUR INTUITIVE NUDGES, INSIGHTS AND IDEAS. INSPIRED ACTION STEPS THAT WILL GUIDE YOU INTO THE FULFILLMENT OF YOUR DESIRES WILL ARISE WITHIN YOU DURING THESE MOMENTS OF RELAXATION. LIKEWISE, IF IT IS PRESENTLY A PHASE OF RELAXATION AND YOU FEEL FUELED WITH INSPIRATION, BY ALL MEANS TAKE THOSE STEPS OF INSPIRED ACTION YOU ARE BEING PULLED TOWARDS! THE IMPORTANT THING TO ACKNOWLEDGE, THOUGH, IS THAT YOU ARE ACTIVELY PARTAKING IN BOTH RELAXATION AND INSPIRED ACTION. THERE MAY BE TIMES WHEN YOU FEEL THE INTUITIVE NEED TO BINGE ON ONE OR THE OTHER, BUT REMEMBER RELAXATION IS CRUCIAL FOR YOUR WELLBEING, AND INSPIRED ACTION [EVEN IF IT IS THE SMALLEST STEPS OF INSPIRED ACTION] BOOSTS YOUR CONFIDENCE IN YOURSELF AND YOUR LEVELS OF FAITH YOU HOLD IN THE DIVINE TO SUPPORT YOU AND GUIDE YOU INTO YOUR DESIRED LIFE DESIGN.

THE I AM INFUSED WITH LOVE: PERSONAL ABUNDANCE JOURNAL BY ZAEYLIN SATYA
IS AVAILABLE FOR PURCHASE TO COMPLIMENT THE UTILIZATION OF THE GODDESS LIFE DESIGNER.
IT IS PARTIALLY LINED, AND SIMPLY FOR THOSE WHO WOULD LIKE A MATCHING,
SAME SIZE DESIGN TO CREATE IN. [THERE ARE MULTIPLE COVER OPTIONS AVAILABLE]
IT IS SEPARATE FROM THE GODDESS LIFE DESIGNER SO THAT IT IS NOT TAKING UP A LARGE PORTION
OF THE GODDESS LIFE DESIGNER .. WHILE ALSO BEING FILLED IN A SHORT AMOUNT OF TIME.
SINCE THE GODDESS LIFE DESIGNER IS CREATED FOR ONE YEAR USE,
WE WOULD NEED QUITE A FEW EXTRA PAGES TO JOURNAL IN.
THIS WAY YOUR GODDESS LIFE DESIGNER STAYS CLEAN
AND FILLED ONLY WITH SIGNIFICANT TOOLS AND REFERENCES FOR YOUR LIFE AND YOUR DESIRES.
YOU CAN PURCHASE THE MATCHING, 116 PAGE, PARTIALLY-LINED JOURNAL AS OFTEN AS YOU FILL IT,
OR YOU CAN USE YOUR OWN FAVORITE JOURNAL / NOTEBOOK / PLANNER/ JOURNALING METHOD.
BE OPEN TO TRYING DIFFERENT METHODS.
YOUR POWERS OF MANIFESTING WILL INCREASE WHEN **YOU** ARE MOST COMFORTABLE ..
TRULY ENJOYING THE THINGS **YOU** ARE DOING EACH DAY --- JOURNALING INCLUDED.

A GODDESS LIFE DESIGNER WILL FORMULATED FOR EACH COMING YEAR.
DREAM. LIVE. BE GRATEFUL. GIVE.

THE GODDESS LIFE DESIGNER
DAILY TO-DO LIST:

REFLECT ON THE MORNING PAGES

REFLECT ON ANY OTHER PAGES / EXERCISES
YOU DESIRE TO THROUGHOUT YOUR DAY

REFLECT ON THE END OF DAY PAGES

BLESSINGS ARE ALWAYS ALIGNED WITH YOU

AND YOUR CREATIVE JOURNEY ♥

DAILY ALIGNMENT IS VERY IMPORTANT!

YOU ARE NOT GOING TO MASTER THE REST OF YOUR LIFE IN ONE DAY.

JUST RELAX.

MASTER THE DAY.

THEN JUST KEEP DOING THAT EVERY DAY.

HAVE YOUR LONG TERM BLUEPRINT,

AND SET INTENTIONS EACH NEW MOON.

~ STAY INSPIRED ~ REFLECT ON YOUR DESIRES REGULARLY ~

BUT,

EACH DAY INTEND TO DIRECT YOUR FOCUS AND ENERGY ON MASTERING THIS DAY.

MASTER EACH DAY AND AT THE END OF YOUR LIFE

YOU WILL HAVE MASTERED YOUR ENTIRE LIFE.

REPETITION AND CONSISTENCY CREATE THE ENTIRETY.

EITHER YOU RUN THE DAY, OR THE DAY RUNS YOU. -JIM ROHN

PROVIDE YOURSELF WITH AN ENVIRONMENT [INTERNALLY AND EXTERNALLY]

THAT WILL ALLOW YOU TO FLOW INTO YOUR DESIRED LIFE DESIGN.

SIMPLY REMOVE EVERYTHING THAT RESTRICTS YOU, EVERYTHING THAT DOES NOT HELP YOU

EVOLVE, AND SUPPLY YOURSELF WITH THE THINGS THAT WILL SUPPORT YOUR GROWTH.

HAVING A RITUAL IS GREAT, BUT SOMETIMES THIS CAN LEAD TO FEELING LIKE WE ARE JUST RUNNING

THROUGH THE MOTIONS, AND WE CAN EASILY BEGIN TO DISCONNECT FROM OUR INNER POWER

AND WISDOM WHEN THIS HAPPENS. SO, MAKE SURE YOU ARE DOING WHAT RESONATES WITH YOU

AND WHAT MAKES YOU FEEL YOUR BEST EACH INDIVIDUAL DAY.

THE FOLLOWING PAGES ARE DESIGNED TO GUIDE YOU INTO DESIGNING YOUR OWN PERSONALIZED

RITUAL SO THAT YOU ARE FEELING AMAZING IN THE MORNING, ALL THROUGHOUT THE DAY

AND ALSO AT THE END OF THE DAY.

FLOW WITH THEM,

DO NOT STRESS OUT OVER COMPLETING EVERYTHING ON THEM.

THEY ARE NOT MEANT TO ADD STRESS,

THEY ARE MEANT TO IGNITE HIGH VIBRATIONAL FEELINGS WITHIN YOUR ENTIRE BEING.

IF YOU MISS A DAY DO NOT FEEL DISCOURAGED. DO YOUR BEST TO STAY DEDICATED AS YOU WILL

REAP THE MOST OUT OF THE GODDESS LIFE DESIGNER THROUGH FOLLOWING THE DAILY

PAGES. THEY ARE DESIGNED TO PROVIDE YOU WITH GUIDANCE AND SUPPORT THAT WILL

ELEVATE YOUR VIBRATION AND THE MASTERY OF EACH OF YOUR DAYS.

THE FOLLOWING PAGE SERVES AS AN EXAMPLE FOR A MORNING RITUAL.

I FIND THAT IT RESONATES WELL WITH MY OWN LIFE.

AS ALWAYS, TAKE WHAT RESONATES WITH YOU, DISCARD WHAT DOES NOT

AND ADD ANYTHING ELSE YOU PERSONALLY DESIRE TO.

EVEN IF YOU ARE VERY BUSY / SHORT ON TIME IN THE MORNING

AND YOU ARE UNABLE TO PARTAKE IN A FULL MORNING RITUAL,

FIND A WAY TO IMPLEMENT THE FOLLOWING 6 PRACTICES:

DOING SO WILL DRASTICALLY IMPROVE YOUR DAY.

AND THUS, OVER TIME YOUR ENTIRE LIFE WILL BE IMPACTED.

1. FIND A FEW MINUTES TO PAUSE AND REFLECT ON THE CURRENT MOON PHASE

2. LISTEN TO A GUIDED MEDITATION IN THE SHOWER

[THE THETA BRAIN WAVE STATE IS NATURALLY IGNITED WHILE SHOWERING]

3. BLESS YOUR DAY [SEE NUMBER 1 ON THE FOLLOWING PAGE]

& SEND BLESSINGS TO YOUR LOVED ONE'S DAY(S)

4. SET YOUR INTENTION FOR THIS DAY

5. VISUALIZE YOUR DAY

6. FEEL GENUINE GRATITUDE WITHIN YOUR HEART-SPACE

FOCUS YOUR ATTENTION AND ENERGY ON FEELING GENUINE GRATITUDE FOR WHAT YOU HAVE,

AND FOR THE DESIRES YOU ARE MANIFESTING. FEEL THESE SENSATIONS IN EVERY FIBER OF YOUR BEING.

SET SIMPLE INTENTIONS EACH DAY, FOR YOUR POINTS OF FOCUS THIS DAY.

WHAT'S ON YOUR TO-DO LIST?

HOW CAN YOU IMPLEMENT SIMPLE INTENTIONS INTO THESE TO-DOS?

WHAT MANIFESTATIONS WOULD YOU LOVE TO SEE COME FROM THESE TO-DOS?

ALSO SET SIMPLE INTENTIONS FOR CONVERSATIONS AND INTERACTIONS.

UPON WAKING:

APPLY THE SELF-DISCIPLINE TO REFRAIN FROM

CHECKING ANY SOCIAL MEDIA, EMAIL, TEXT, NEWS, TV, AND ALL THINGS ALIKE.

WAIT UNTIL YOU HAVE FINISHED YOUR MORNING RITUAL ENTIRELY.

IN DOING SO, YOUR MORNING RITUAL

WILL BECOME SO MUCH MORE POTENT & FULFILLING

[BOTH SHORT & LONG TERM].

MORNING RITUAL

1. INHALE DEEPLY. PAUSE AND TENSE EVERY INCH OF YOUR BODY AS YOU FEEL ANY AND ALL PRESSURES AND TENSIONS OF LIFE ~ BODY, MIND AND SOUL ~ EXHALE AND VISUALIZE THE RELEASE OF ALL THIS PRESSURE AND TENSION DOWN INTO THE CORE OF MOTHER EARTH THROUGH A STRONG CORD THAT IS EMANATING ALL COLORS OF THE RAINBOW ~ THIS CORD IS TRANSMUTING THE ENERGY INTO HEALING, PEACEFUL, LOVING ENERGY. CONTINUE BREATHING DEEPLY AND FEEL UNCONDITIONAL LOVE AND PURE SOURCE ENERGY INFUSING EVERY SINGLE FIBER OF YOUR BEING ~ WASHING OVER YOU ~ FROM THE TOP OF YOUR HEAD ~ SLOWLY DOWN ~ ALL THE WAY THROUGH THE TIPS OF YOUR TOES. YOU ARE NOW FILLED WITH PURIFIED SOURCE ENERGY. YOU ARE VIBRANT ~ BODY, MIND AND SOUL ~ YOU ARE THRIVING WITHIN THIS HUMAN EXISTENCE. YOU ARE INTUITIVE AND PRESENT. YOU ARE DIVINELY GUIDED AND LOVED. YOU ARE PART OF THE WHOLE. ALL IS ONE. YOU ARE ON A DIVINE PATH FOR THE HIGHEST GOOD OF ALL SOULS. AS YOU CONTINUE BREATHING: INHALE AND FEEL YOUR BREATH TRAVELING FROM YOUR ROOT CHAKRA SLOWLY UP YOUR SPINE TO YOUR CROWN CHAKRA, PAUSE AND FEEL YOUR CONNECTION WITH THE DIVINE, THEN EXHALE YOUR BREATH DOWN AND OUT THROUGH YOUR HEART CHAKRA. REPEAT THESE AFFIRMATIONS: I AM BALANCED, I AM HARMONIOUS, I AM COMPLETE, I AM ATTUNED TO THE CYCLIC NATURE OF THE UNIVERSE. I AM SATISFIED, I AM IN THE VIBRATIONAL FREQUENCY OF PEACE. I AM GENUINELY GRATEFUL. I KNOW AND FEEL THAT I AM GUIDED AND PROTECTED BY MY HIGHEST VIBRATIONAL ANGELS AND GUIDES. I AM BLESSED WITH GRACE BY MY HIGHEST VIBRATIONAL ANGELS AND GUIDES. I AM FILLED WITH UNCONDITIONAL LOVE FROM MY DIVINE LIFE SOURCE. I AM SPIRIT HAVING A HUMAN EXPERIENCE, I AM DESIGNING THE LIFE I DESIRE TO LIVE WITHIN WHILE ON MY JOURNEY HERE. I FEEL DIVINELY INSPIRED. I AM SO GRATEFUL FOR THIS LIFETIME. MY DAY IS NOW BLESSED AND ALIGNED WITH MY DESIRED LIFE DESIGN. I AM FILLED WITH POWERFUL SOURCE ENERGY DIRECTLY FROM THE DIVINE ITSELF. THE DIVINE ORGANIZED INTELLIGENCE THAT PERMEATES THROUGHOUT THE ENTIRE UNIVERSE IS WITHIN ME AND WORKS MIRACLES FOR MY LIFE, AS WELL AS FOR THE HIGHEST GOOD OF ALL SOULS. I AM AT PEACE. I AM SATISFIED. I OBSERVE OTHERS AND ALLOW THEM TO BE AS THEY ARE WITHIN THEIR JOURNEY. I AM FULFILLED. I AM WHOLE. I AM PURE LOVE. I AM MAGICK. I AM PEACE.

2. DRINK WATER
MIX IN ONE-TABLESPOON APPLE CIDER VINEGAR OR LEMON JUICE

3. ENVIRONMENT SET
LIGHT CANDLES, DIFFUSE ESSENTIAL OILS, OPEN BLINDS, CURTAINS AND WINDOWS, TURN ON RELAXING TONES, FREQUENCIES OR MUSIC --- 432 HZ / 528 HZ, SHAMANIC DRUMMING, CHAKRA MUSIC, ETC.

4. REFLECT ON THE MORNING JOURNALING PAGES [THE FOLLOWING PAGES]

5. STRETCH / MOVE YOUR TEMPLE
WHILE LISTENING TO EMPOWERING AFFIRMATIONS OR HEALING FREQUENCIES
E.G. 528 HERTZ OR 432 HERTZ

6. EAT SOMETHING TO NOURISH YOUR TEMPLE AND DRINK YOUR COFFEE / TEA

7. GIVE THANKS IN ADVANCE FOR THE PERFECTLY ALIGNED GUIDANCE RECEIVED:
THEN, PULL FROM YOUR FAVORITE ORACLE / TAROT
AND / OR FLIP TO A RANDOM PAGE OF ANY SPIRITUAL TEXT.

8. READ SOMETHING SIMPLE AND INSPIRING!
OR LISTEN TO A PODCAST OR YOUTUBE INSPIRATION OR AN AUDIO BOOK.

Morning Journaling ..

I AM GRATEFUL FOR AWAKENING THIS MORNING,

MY LIFETIME IS FILLED WITH AND FUELED BY
THE BLISSFUL EXPERIENCES OF MY OWN DEEPEST DESIRES FULFILLED.

I AM THRIVING WITHIN MY PASSIONATE HUMAN EXISTENCE.

BEFORE JOURNALING TAKE A MOMENT, OR A FEW, TO DO SOME BREATHING

OR MEDITATION YOU FEEL DRAWN TO.

CONNECT WITH YOUR HEARTBEAT, BREATH & INNER POWER.

I AM SO GRATEFUL FOR ..

LIST AT LEAST FIVE THINGS,

THE MORE THE BETTER,

AS THE MORE YOU FEEL GENUINE GRATITUDE

THE MORE YOU WILL RECEIVE TO FEEL GRATEFUL FOR!

DEEPEN THE FEELINGS OF GENUINE GRATITUDE
BY ASKING YOURSELF:
WHY AM I GRATEFUL FOR THESE THINGS?

TAKE A FEW MINUTES TO CLOSE YOUR EYES AND VISUALIZE YOUR DESIRED LIFE DESIGN.

FEEL INTO IT, EXPERIENCE IT

♥ REFLECT ON THE CURRENT MOON PHASE'S PAGE ♥

TAKE 5 MINUTES TO BE STILL AND VISUALIZE THE IDEAL WAY YOUR DAY WILL UNFOLD.

SET AN INTENTION FOR THIS DAY.

I CHOOSE WHERE MY ENERGY GOES TODAY.

I INVITE ALL THINGS WONDERFUL INTO MY LIFE TODAY.

I CHOOSE MY THOUGHTS TODAY.

I CHOOSE TO EMBODY FAITH OVER FEAR IN EACH MOMENT OF THIS DAY.

I AM ALWAYS CONNECTED TO MY DIVINE LIFE SOURCE,
I AM THE EMBODIMENT OF INFINITE GODDESS POWER.

JOURNAL YOUR INITIAL & INTUITIVE RESPONSES

FOR EACH OF THE FOLLOWING PROMPTS:

HOW I AM FEELING?

WHAT I APPRECIATE ABOUT MYSELF:

DO I FEEL I AM WORTHY OF RECEIVING MY BEST DAY TODAY?

ALL THE THINGS I NEED TO LET GO OF IN ORDER TO MOVE FORWARD TODAY:

I CAN DO THESE 3 THINGS TO BRING ME CLOSER TO MY DESIRE TODAY:

**I ASK MY DIVINE SOURCE FOR GUIDANCE & SUPPORT
IN THE AREA(S) OF MY CHOOSING,
BECAUSE I KNOW MY SOURCE LOVES ENGAGEMENT FROM ME
AND ASSISTING ME WITH MY INSPIRATIONS, PASSIONS AND DESIRES.**

MY IDEAL DAY IS ALIGNED WITH ME NOW, I AM SO GRATEFUL.

THE VIBE I DESIRE TO BE TODAY:

THE VIBE I DESIRE TO BE AROUND TODAY:

THE MINDSET I DESIRE TO BE IN THROUGHOUT THIS DAY:

MEDITATION NOTES:

OTHER WRITING PROMPTS MY HIGHEST SELF IS PULLING ME TOWARDS:

ANY PROMPT THE UNIVERSE IS NUDGING INTO MY VIEW THIS DAY:.

**ONLY 10% OF OUR LIFE IS DETERMINED BY OUR CIRCUMSTANCES,
THE REMAINING 90% IS DETERMINED BY
THE ATTITUDE WE PERSONALLY CHOOSE TO EMBODY
WHILE PERCEIVING AND REACTING TO THE CIRCUMSTANCES.
RECOGNIZE THIS & BE MINDFUL IN EACH & EVERY MOMENT OF LIFE.**

LIVE THIS DAY AS IF IT WERE YOUR LAST. THE PAST IS GONE & THE FUTURE IS NOT GUARANTEED.
-WAYNE DYER.
I AM PERFECTLY GUIDED IN EACH MOMENT OF MY LIFE JOURNEY.

I THINK ABOUT HOW FAR I'VE COME AND I CELEBRATE THAT!
I DO NOT WAIT UNTIL I HAVE REACHED THE ACHIEVEMENT OF ALL MY ULTIMATE DESIRES
IN ORDER TO BE HAPPY AND CELEBRATE, I CELEBRATE AND I AM HAPPY NOW!
THIS SETS THE TONE, FOR ME TO ATTRACT MORE THINGS TO CELEBRATE AND BE HAPPY ABOUT!

I AM RIGHT NOW LIVING WITHIN THE REALITY IN WHICH I WILL RECEIVE MY DESIRED LIFE
DESIGN. EVERYTHING IS COMING TOGETHER, GRADUALLY, IN A TIMELY MANNER.
I AM GENUINELY GRATEFUL,
I AM FULLY ENJOYING EACH MOMENT OF THIS JOURNEY.

MAKING TIME TO DO THE THINGS THAT MAKE ME GENUINELY HAPPY IS A PRIORITY IN MY LIFE.

ALL THINGS GO SMOOTHER WHEN I AM PATIENT, BECAUSE I AM GENERATING LESS RESISTANCE.
I EMBODY PATIENCE AND STAY ALIGNED THROUGH EVER-INCREASINGLY EMBODYING THE
VIBRATIONAL FREQUENCY OF MY DESIRES FULFILLMENT WHILE I MOVE FORWARD WITH
INSPIRED ACTION. I TRUST AND KNOW THAT IN DOING SO
MY INTENTION [SEED] WILL SPROUT AND BLOSSOM
IN DIVINE, PERFECT TIMING.

I FEEL AMAZING TODAY AS I MINDFULLY OBSERVE MY THINKING PATTERNS,
I CHOOSE TO THINK ONLY ON THE THINGS I LOVE AND APPRECIATE WITHIN MY LIFE.
THROUGHOUT THE DAY I OBSERVE MY THOUGHTS AND ASSESS:
WHAT AM I MANIFESTING RIGHT NOW?
I AM AWARE THAT IN EVERY SINGLE MOMENT MY POWER OF MANIFESTATION IS AT WORK.

I AM PRESENT. I AM AWARE. I CONNECT WITH THE PEOPLE IN MY REALITY TODAY.
I TRUST THAT THE ENTIRE UNIVERSE IS CONSPIRING TO MAKE MY DREAMS COME TRUE
AND ALL OF MY DESIRES MANIFEST. I DON'T LOOK FOR SIGNS OR EXPECT ANYTHING OUT OF
ANYONE — I AM SIMPLY PRESENT AND AWARE BECAUSE I KNOW THE SIGNS,
THE PERFECT CIRCUMSTANCES AND THE RIGHT PEOPLE WILL ALL ALIGN AND APPEAR WHEN
I AM LEAST EXPECTING. I AM NOT GOING TO MISS OUT SIMPLY BECAUSE OF BEING DISTRACTED,
I WILL BE PRESENT AND AWARE IN EACH MOMENT OF THIS DAY.

MAKING TIME TO DO THE THINGS THAT ALLOW ME TO EMBODY
GENUINE PEACE AND SATISFACTION IS A PRIORITY IN MY LIFE.

SWITCH I WANT [MY DESIRE] TO I HAVE [MY DESIRE].
I REPEAT THIS I HAVE STATEMENT AS MUCH AS I POSSIBLY CAN.
THIS RETRAINS MY SUBCONSCIOUS MIND INTO ACCEPTING THIS AS MY TRUTH,
AND IGNITES THE FEELING STATES OF TRULY HAVING MY DESIRE WITHIN MY PHYSICAL LIFE.
I REFLECT ON THE SUBCONSCIOUS EMPOWERING BELIEFS I AM ESTABLISHING AS MY TRUTH.
♥   [REFLECT ON I AM AFFIRMATIONS AND EMPOWERING SUBCONSCIOUS QUESTIONS]

I REFLECT ON THE DESIRES I AM CURRENTLY MANIFESTING.

I GIVE THANKS IN ADVANCE FOR MY DESIRES, TRULY FEELING INTO THE SATISFACTION

I WILL FEEL ONCE MY DESIRES HAVE COMPLETELY MANIFESTED INTO MY LIFE.

I AM AWARE THAT THE EXACT DETAILS FOR HOW AND WHEN MY DESIRE WILL MANIFEST ARE

BEING TAKEN CARE OF FOR ME AS I MOVE FORWARD TAKING INSPIRED ACTION

AND HARMONIZING MY VIBRATIONAL FREQUENCY.

I MEDITATE ON MY VISION BOARD DAILY.

I DO NOT VISUALIZE JUST TO MANIFEST, I VISUALIZE TO KNOW

[AND MOST IMPORTANTLY TO FEEL] WITHIN MY BODY AND MIND THAT THESE THINGS

ARE ALREADY FULLY PRESENT WITHIN MY LIFE. I KNOW THIS AS TRUTH WITHIN MY MIND AND

BODY FIRST. THE PHYSICAL MANIFESTATION WILL COME SECOND, ONCE I HAVE FIRST MASTERED

KNOWING AND FEELING THEY ARE ALREADY WITHIN MY LIFE. FEELING THEY ARE PRESENT

WITHIN MY LIFE GENERATES THE VIBRATIONAL FREQUENCY THAT IS IN PERFECT HARMONY

WITH THE TRUE MANIFESTATION OF THEM WITHIN MY PHYSICAL LIFE.

TODAY I WILL DO THE THINGS THAT MAKE ME FEEL TRULY AMAZING.

I SAY NO TO ANYTHING THAT DRAINS MY ENERGY OR DOES NOT RESONATE WITH THE

FREQUENCY OF MY DESIRES FULFILLMENT. THIS RAISES MY VIBRATIONAL FREQUENCY.

I KNOW I AM A POWERFUL VIBRATIONAL MAGNET.

~~~ I AM ATTRACTING MY DESIRES AND MORE TO BE GRATEFUL FOR WITH EASE ~~~

~ I LIVE IN THE PRESENT MOMENT ~

I TAKE TIME EACH DAY TO VISUALIZE THE FUTURE LIFE DESIGN I DESIRE AS HERE NOW,

WITH ALL OF MY DESIRES FULFILLED, BUT THROUGHOUT THE REST OF MY DAY

~ I WILL SAVOR EACH MOMENT ~

NOT RELIVING THE PAST OR WORRYING ABOUT THE FUTURE.

I KEEP MY VIBRATIONAL FREQUENCY STRONG,

INFUSED WITH GENUINE GRATITUDE, SATISFACTION AND PEACE.

I AM ALIGNED WITH THE MANIFESTATION OF MY DESIRED LIFE DESIGN.

I MOVE MY BODY BECAUSE I LOVE MY BODY.

I NURTURE MY BODY WITH QUALITY FUEL AND HYDRATION.

I REGULARLY PARTAKE IN VARIOUS FORMS OF SELF LOVE.

I AM PRESENT. I AM THE EMBODIMENT OF FAITH.

JUST FOR TODAY I WILL FOCUS MY ATTENTION ON FEELING GENUINELY GRATEFUL.

AFTER YOUR MORNING RITUAL

TAKE CARE OF ALL COMPLICATED AND IMPORTANT TASKS OF THE DAY.
THIS WILL LEAVE YOU FEELING EMPOWERED THROUGHOUT THE REST OF YOUR DAY
~ ENJOYING EVERYTHING ELSE JUST A LITTLE BIT MORE.

FOCUS ON ONE THING AT A TIME THROUGHOUT THE DAY,
DOING SO INCREASINGLY STRENGTHENS YOUR POWER OF MANIFESTATION.
BREAK UP ANY LARGE TASKS WITH SMALLER TASKS.

GIVE YOURSELF PERIODS OF RELAXATION THROUGHOUT THE DAY.
[TIME AWAY FROM YOUR ELECTRONICS, WORK AND EXTERNAL STIMULATION]
CONNECT WITH YOUR HEARTBEAT, BREATH AND INNER POWER.

TRAIN YOURSELF TO OBSERVE WHETHER YOUR VIBRATION
IS ATTUNED IN EACH MOMENT - EVEN WHEN YOU'RE WORKING
IT IS IMPORTANT TO NOT HUSTLE ALL THE TIME.
RELAXING AND VISUALIZING YOUR DESIRED LIFE DESIGN AS HERE NOW, TRULY FEELING
INTO THE GENUINE GRATITUDE AND SATISFACTION THAT COMES WITH THIS FACT,
IS EQUALLY AS IMPORTANT AS TAKING ACTION.
UTILIZE THE POWER OF MANIFESTATION YOU HAVE WITHIN YOU.
ALLOW SPACE FOR INSPIRATION TO FLOW IN,
ALLOW YOURSELF TO FEEL SATISFIED AND GRATEFUL.
BE IN THE VIBRATION OF RECEIVING MORE AND MORE
TO FEEL SATISFIED ABOUT AND GRATEFUL FOR.

PROVEN OPTIMAL PRODUCTIVITY FORMULA:

WORK FOR 52 MINUTES, BREAK FOR 17 MINUTES.

[THERE ARE MANY STUDIES THAT SUPPORT THIS FORMULA,
YOU CAN DO YOUR OWN RESEARCH IF YOU WOULD LIKE.]

THERE IS POWER IN TAKING BREAKS!
GO ON A NATURE WALK WITHOUT ELECTRONICS AND VISUALIZE / DAYDREAM.

ASK YOUR HIGHER SELF, HIGHEST VIBRATIONAL ANGELS AND SPIRIT GUIDES
FOR GUIDANCE, PROTECTION, ASSISTANCE AND SIGNS [AS YOU PLEASE]
YOU DO HAVE TO ASK YOUR HIGHEST VIBRATIONAL ANGELS AND GUIDES
FOR THEIR ASSISTANCE,
THEY ABSOLUTELY LOVE TO BE OF ASSISTANCE!!!
BUT THEY CANNOT IMPEDE ON YOUR FREE WILL,
YOU MUST ASK IN ORDER TO RECEIVE.

'IF YOU GET TIRED LEARN TO REST, NOT TO QUIT.' — BANKSY

ALLOW YOURSELF TO BE ABLE TO SWITCH BETWEEN
YOUR PERSONAL MASCULINE AND FEMININE ENERGY THROUGHOUT EACH DAY.

FEEL INTO THAT FUTURE MOMENT ~ WHEN YOUR DESIRE IS ALREADY HERE.
HOW EXACTLY DOES THIS CHANGE YOUR LIFE?
HOW DOES THIS CHANGE YOUR MINDSET?
AND PERCEPTIONS?
FEEL INTO EXACTLY HOW YOUR LIFE WILL FEEL WITH YOUR DESIRE(S) MANIFESTED.
GET TO KNOW THESE FEELINGS WELL.

EMANATE ALL FEELINGS FROM YOUR HEART CENTER,
YOUR HEART CHAKRA.
THIS IS YOUR POTENT POWER CENTER,
THE CENTER FROM WHICH YOUR FEELING STATES RADIATE.

IF YOU ARE IN YOUR CROWN, THIRD-EYE OR THROAT CHAKRAS
THIS MEANS YOU ARE IN YOUR THOUGHTS.

IF YOU ARE IN YOUR ROOT, SACRAL OR SOLAR PLEXUS CHAKRAS
THIS MEANS YOU ARE IN YOUR EMOTIONS.

BE CONSCIOUSLY PRESENT IN YOUR FEELING STATE,
YOUR HEART CHAKRA.

YOUR HEART CHAKRA IS IN THE CENTER OF YOUR OTHER SIX CHAKRAS MENTIONED.
[SEE CHAKRA PAGE]

YOUR THOUGHTS AND EMOTIONS COMBINED GENERATE YOUR FEELING STATE,
YOUR PURE AND POWERFUL MANIFESTATION POWER.

EMBODYING HIGH VIBRATIONAL FREQUENCIES IS NOT THE SAME AS BEING HIGH ENERGY.
YOU CAN BE HIGH VIBRATIONAL AND FULL OF ENERGY, BUT YOU CAN ALSO BE HIGH VIBRATIONAL
AND CALM. EMBODYING HIGH VIBRATIONAL FREQUENCIES EQUATES TO THE FREQUENCIES OF
SATISFACTION, GENUINE GRATITUDE, UNCONDITIONAL LOVE AND PEACE. SOMETIMES YOU WILL BE
HIGH ENERGY AND EXCITED WHEN EMBODYING THESE FREQUENCIES. ESPECIALLY IN THOSE INTIAL
MOMENTS WHEN YOUR DESIRE MANIFESTS OR WHEN YOU RECEIVE UNEXPECTED GUIDANCE,
INSPIRATION OR SIGNS. THEN, AFTER THE INITIAL SPARK OF ENERGY THESE THINGS BRING INTO
YOUR BEING, YOUR ENERGY LEVELS OUT. YOU STILL FEEL REALLY GOOD, YOU FEEL GENUINELY
PEACEFUL AND SATISFIED. YOU ARE CALM AND AT PEACE BECAUSE YOU KNOW YOU ARE ABUNDANT
IN ALL AREAS OF LIFE, RECEIVING ALL OF YOUR DESIRES THROUGHOUT THIS LIFETIME. THE
EMBODIMENT OF PEACE IS ACTUALLY ONE OF THE HIGHEST VIBRATIONAL FREQUENCIES THAT CAN
BE EMBODIED [SEE PAGE 170]. THIS IS IMPORTANT TO KNOW, BECAUSE BEING HIGH ENERGY DOES
NOT ASSURE YOU ARE EMBODYING HIGH VIBRATIONAL FREQUENCIES. HIGH ENERGY CAN ALSO
EXIST WITH LOW VIBRATIONAL FREQUENCIES EMBODIED.

FEEL INTO THE FREQUENCIES YOU ARE EMBODYING IN EACH MOMENT:
DO THEY FEEL REALLY GOOD?
ARE YOU FEELING ABSOLUTELY SATISFIED AND UNCONDITIONALLY LOVED?
ARE YOU FEELING AN ENDLESS STREAM OF INSPIRATION?
ARE YOU FEELING GENUINELY GRATEFUL?
ARE YOU AT PEACE IN THIS MOMENT?
OR ARE YOU FEELING TENSE?
ARE YOU FEELING THE NEED TO ALWAYS BE DOING?
ARE YOU FEELING STUCK?
ARE YOU FEELING THAT YOU ARE FORCING YOURSELF TO PUSH FORWARD?
ARE YOU FEELING THAT YOU ARE FORCING YOURSELF TO BE ENERGIZED?
DOES YOUR ENERGY FEEL PURE? OR DOES IT FEEL CHAOTIC?
BE HONEST WITH YOURSELF WHEN ANSWERING THESE QUESTIONS.
WHILE IT IS TRUE THAT LIVING IN HIGH VIBRATIONAL FREQUENCIES WILL PROVIDE YOU WITH
ENERGY AND INSPIRATION, THIS ENERGY WILL BE BALANCED AND HARMONIOUS, NOT
UNBALANCED AND CHAOTIC. YOU WILL EXPERIENCE DIFFERENT ENERGY LEVELS THROUGHOUT
LIFE, BUT WHEN YOU ARE PREDOMINANTLY LIVING IN HIGH VIBRATIONAL FREQUENCIES YOUR
ENERGY LEVELS WILL NATURALLY BE MORE BALANCED AND HARMONIOUS.

END OF DAY RITUAL

1. SET ENVIRONMENT

RELAXING TONES OR FREQUENCIES, ADJUST LIGHTING, LIGHT CANDLES,

DIFFUSE ESSENTIAL OILS, BURN SAGE/PALO SANTO.

2. WEAR CLOTHES THAT MAKE YOUR VIBRATION FEEL REALLY GOOD,

GET COSY IF YOU LIKE TO.

3. PREPARE TO PUT YOUR PHONE AWAY FOR THE DAY.

FINISH DOING WHATEVER YOU NEED TO DO ON IT,

REDUCE ELECTRONICS AND UNNATURAL LIGHTING.

4. DRINK CAFFEINE FREE TEA / WATER, EAT LIGHT

5. TIDY UP YOUR LIVING SPACE

SO THAT YOU WAKE UP IN THE MORNING FEELING

REFRESHED, ORGANIZED, CLEAR MINDED AND INSPIRED!

DO THIS WHILE LISTENING TO A RELAXING AUDIO BOOK, PODCAST,

OR MUSIC/FREQUENCIES.

6. DO A CHAKRA ALIGNING / AURA CLEANSING MEDITATION

OR ANY OTHER MEDITATION YOU ARE RESONATING WITH.

7. REFLECT ON THE FOLLOWING END OF DAY PAGES

Goddess,

RELAXING INTO THE END OF THE DAY,
REFLECT ON AND JOURNAL ALONGSIDE THESE PROMPTS:

BEFORE JOURNALING TAKE A MOMENT, OR A FEW,
TO DO SOME BREATHING OR MEDITATION YOU FEEL DRAWN TO.
CONNECT WITH YOUR HEARTBEAT, BREATH & INNER POWER.

I AM GRATEFUL THIS DAY HAS BROUGHT ME:
[LIST AT LEAST 5 THINGS AND INCLUDE WHY]

HOW I LOVED MYSELF TODAY:

WHAT WAS THE BEST PART OF THIS DAY?

WHAT MAKES ME FEEL BEST ABOUT TODAY:

TOMORROW I CAN ___TO BOOST MY SELF LOVE AND VIBRATIONAL ALIGNMENT,

SO THAT I INCREASINGLY HARMONIZE WITH

THE VIBRATIONAL FREQUENCY OF MY DESIRES FULFILLED.

I BREATHE HEALING ENERGY INTO MY BODY,

I EXHALE ALL THAT DOES NOT SERVE MY HIGHEST SELF.

REPEAT.

I KNOW THAT MY DIVINE LIFE SOURCE IS ALWAYS SUPPORTING ME.

I KNOW THAT THE ENTIRE UNIVERSE IS CONSPIRING ON MY BEHALF,

TO BRING MY DESIRES INTO FRUITION,

IN DIVINE, PERFECT TIMING,

IN THE MOST PEACEFUL AND LOVING WAY,

FOR THE HIGHEST GOOD OF ALL SOULS.

I AM SO GRATEFUL.

I DISSOLVE ALL NEGATIVE ENERGY CORDS WITH THE EMBODIMENT OF

PEACE, UNCONDITIONAL LOVE AND GENUINE GRATITUDE.

I NOW FOCUS ON MYSELF

AND MINDING MY OWN BUSINESS.

I SET THE INTENTION TO HAVE A RESTFUL, REJUVENATING SLEEP TONIGHT.

I WELCOME INTUITIVE INSIGHTS AND INSPIRATION WITHIN MY NIGHTLY DREAMS.

WHATEVER MINDSET I AM IN AS I FALL ASLEEP

CREATES THE FREQUENCY OF DREAM I WILL EXPERIENCE.

WHILE ASLEEP I AM MARINATING IN MY SUBCONSCIOUS MIND.

I AM MINDFUL IN ATTUNING MY VIBRATIONAL FREQUENCY

TO THE FREQUENCY OF PEACE, GENUINE GRATITUDE AND PURE LOVE

5-10 MINUTES BEFORE AND ALL THE WAY INTO FALLING SLEEP

DOING SO IS VERY EFFECTIVE IN PROGRAMMING MY SUBCONSCIOUS MIND

TO SUPPORT THE MANIFESTATION OF MY DESIRED LIFE DESIGN.

A SIMPLE AND POTENT WAY TO DO SO:

I MEDITATE ON THE IMMENSE GENUINE GRATITUDE, SATISFACTION AND PEACE

I WILL FEEL WITH THE FULFILLMENT OF MY DESIRED LIFE DESIGN AS

A PRESENT MOMENT FACT. I GIVE THANKS UNTIL I FALL ASLEEP.

KEEP A DREAM JOURNAL AND WRITE ANY DREAMS DOWN AS SOON AS YOU AWAKEN,

WHETHER THIS BE DURING THE NIGHT OR IN THE MORNING.

DO NOT DISECT YOUR DREAMS RIGHT AWAY, WAIT UNTIL LATER IN THE DAY.

I GIVE THANKS.

I AM ALWAYS DIVINELY GUIDED.

I AM SAFE. I AM PROTECTED. I AM INFINITE. I AM ABUNDANT. I AM BLISSFUL. I AM BEAUTIFUL.

AS YOU ARE LAYING IN BED IMAGINE YOU ARE LIVING WITHIN YOUR DESIRED LIFE DESIGN.
~ IGNITE YOUR SENSES AND FEEL INTO ALL THE DETAILS ~
DELVE INTO YOUR IMAGINATION.
HOW GENUINELY GRATEFUL ARE YOU FEELING?
HOW SATISFIED, AT PEACE AND RELIEVED ARE YOU FEELING?
FEEL THESE SENSATIONS WITHIN EVERY FIBER OF YOUR BEING AS YOU TRANSITION INTO YOUR SLEEP. FEEL AS IF YOU ALREADY HAVE YOUR DESIRES WITHIN YOUR LIFE NOW.THIS IS SO POWERFUL, AS YOUR THOUGHTS UPON FALLING ASLEEP CREATE THE FREQUENCY OF DREAM IN WHICH YOUR SUBCONSCIOUS MIND WILL NOW MARINATE. TRAINING YOUR SUBCONSCIOUS MIND TO BE IN SUPPORT OF YOUR DESIRES IS SO POWERFUL. RATHER THAN THINKING ON WHAT YOUR ARE LACKING OR WHAT WORRIES YOU MAY HAVE OR WHAT MAY HAVE WENT 'WRONG' IN THE DAY AS YOU FALL ASLEEP. IF YOU ARE DOING THAT YOU ARE TRANSITIONING INTO THAT SUBCONSCIOUS STATE FOR THE NEXT 8 HOURS [GIVE OR TAKE] AND TRAINING YOUR MIND TO SUPPORT AND GIVE YOU MORE OF WHAT YOU DO NOT WANT. SO, THIS IS VERY CRUCIAL. PRACTICE LETTING GO OF ALL CONCERNS [BEFORE YOU MEDITATE ON FEELING AS IF YOUR DESIRES ARE YOUR PRESENT REALITY]. A SIMPLE TECHNIQUE: IMAGINE A STRONG, BRIGHT WHITE ENERGY CORD CONNECTING INTO THE CORE OF MOTHER EARTH, INHALE DEEPLY. PAUSE AND FEEL ALL OF YOUR LIFE'S PRESSURES AND TENSIONS. EXHALE COMPLETELY AS YOU ALLOW ALL CONCERNS / NEGATIVITY / TENSIONS / PRESSURES TO DRAIN DOWNWARDS OUT OF YOUR BEING AND INTO EARTH. AS THIS HEAVY ENERGY TRAVELS THROUGH THIS BRIGHT WHITE ENERGY CORD IT IS TRANSMUTED INTO PEACEFUL, LOVING, HEALING ENERGY.
THEN, VISUALIZE EVERY SINGLE FIBER OF YOUR ENTIRE BEING INCREASINGLY BEING INFUSED WITH PURE SOURCE ENERGY
VISUALIZE THIS LOVING, PEACEFUL CONSCIOUSNESS
DISSOLVING ANY REMAINING LOW VIBRATIONAL FREQUENCIES.
NOW YOU ARE PREPARED TO MEDITATE ON THE FEELINGS
AS IF YOUR DESIRES ARE ALREADY YOUR REALITY.
~ SWEET DREAMS ~

IF YOUR MIND CANNOT LET GO OF CONCERNS / NEGATIVITY / TO-DO LISTS / IDEAS .. ETC.
THEN WRITE THEM OUT ON PAPER OR IN YOUR PHONE ~ DO THIS SO YOUR MIND CAN
RELAX IN KNOWING THAT YOU HAVE NOT FORGOT ABOUT THESE THINGS,
BUT YOU ARE NOW ABLE TO DETACH FROM THEM AND TEND TO THEM LATER,
AS YOU PREPARE TO REST AND SLEEP.

[ADD IN] A SHOWER OR BATH AT ANY POINT DURING OR BEFORE
YOUR EVENING RITUAL
~ WASH OFF ALL HEAVY THOUGHTS / ENERGY,
FEEL YOUR AURA BEING CLEANSED AND RENEWED,
BECOME PRESENT.
FOCUS ON TUNING INTO AND EMBODYING
YOUR OWN PUREST FORMS OF AUTHENTICITY.
LISTEN TO YOUR SOUL.

I AM
WORTHY,
LOVE
&
LOVED.

THE REASONS WHY I LOVE AND APPRECIATE MYSELF:

ALL OF THE THINGS I AM GRATEFUL FOR IN LIFE:

HAVING A LIST OF THINGS YOU DO LOVE / APPRECIATE IS A GREAT TOOL.
WHENEVER YOU RECOGNIZE YOU ARE WITHIN A LOW VIBRATIONAL FEELING STATE
REFLECT ON THIS LIST AND THE HIGH VIBRATIONAL FEELING STATES
THESE THINGS BRING INTO YOUR BEING.

I GIVE THANKS IN ADVANCE EVERY SINGLE DAY FOR ALL OF THE THINGS I DESIRE IN MY LIFE.
MY ULTIMATE LIFE DESIRES LISTED:

THE FOLLOWING PAGES ARE PROVIDED FOR INSPIRATION

WHILE MANIFESTING YOUR DESIRED LIFE DESIGN.

REFLECT ON THEM AS OFTEN AS YOU PLEASE.

FOLLOWING THE INSPIRATIONAL PAGES

YOU WILL FIND ADDITIONAL INFORMATION

INCLUDING THE 12 UNIVERSAL LAWS,

AND HOW EACH LAW APPLIES TO MANIFESTING YOUR DESIRES.

Shift Your Perspective

IMAGINE FOR A FEW MOMENTS:

YOU JUST ARRIVED ON A NEW PLANET.

YOU ARE TOLD:

YOU ARE THE CREATOR OF YOUR REALITY HERE.

ALL YOU MUST DO IS:

1. DEFINE WHAT YOU DESIRE

TAKE THE TIME TO DEFINE AND DESIGN THE EXPERIENCE YOU DESIRE TO HAVE HERE.

2. BE OPEN TO RECEIVING DIRECTIONS IN REGARDS TO THE INSPIRED ACTION STEPS YOU WILL TAKE TO BRING ABOUT THE FRUITION OF YOUR DESIRED LIFE DESIGN,

IN ANY MOMENT ASK YOUR HIGHER SELF / ANGELS / GUIDES / SOURCE:

WHAT IS THE NEXT THING YOU WILL HAVE ME DO?

3. INCREASINGLY ALIGN YOUR VIBRATIONAL FREQUENCY SO THAT IT IS IN HARMONY WITH YOUR DESIRED LIFE DESIGN.

EMBODY THE THOUGHTS AND FEELINGS YOU WILL EXPERIENCE WITH YOUR DESIRE FULFILLED, THIS IS A PRESENT MOMENT PRACTICE. WHEN YOU LEARN TO HARNESS YOUR PRESENT MOMENT THOUGHTS AND FEELING STATES YOU GAIN CONTROL OF YOUR VIBRATIONAL FREQUENCY AND FULLY HARNESS YOUR INNATE POWER OF MANIFESTATION.

4. DETACH FROM THE NEED TO DETERMINE AND CONTROL THE EXACT HOW AND WHEN DETAILS.

TRUST THAT THE ORGANIZED INTELLIGENCE WHICH IS HOLDING THE ENTIRE UNIVERSE TOGETHER IS SUPPORTING YOU. IT DOES SO BY PROVIDING EVENTS AND CIRCUMSTANCES WITHIN YOUR LIFE THAT MATCH THE FREQUENCIES YOU EMBODY. THIS DIVINE INTELLIGENCE WILL WORK OUT THE DETAILS FOR HOW AND WHEN YOUR DESIRES WILL MAKE THEIR WAY TO YOU AS LONG AS YOU DO YOUR PART IN FOLLOWING THE ABOVE STEPS.

NOW APPLY THIS TO YOUR EXISTENCE ON PLANET EARTH. THIS IS YOUR REALITY.

I AM ABUNDANT.

I AM GUIDED, SUPPORTED AND PROTECTED.

I AM WISE.

I HOLD ALL I NEED WITHIN ME.

I MEDITATE ON THE SENSATIONS OF MY DESIRED LIFE DESIGN.

IT IS SIMPLY EASIER TO FEEL MY DESIRES AS HERE NOW,

THAN IT IS TO STRESS OR WORRY ABOUT LACK OR NOT HAVING.

IT FEELS SO MUCH BETTER TO FEEL INTO MY DESIRES FULFILLED,

THAN IT DOES TO FEEL THE LACK OF THEM.

I CLOSE MY EYES,

AND IT IS EASY FOR ME TO FEEL MY DESIRED LIFE DESIGN AS REAL RIGHT NOW.

I AM BALANCED AND IN HARMONY WITH THE CYCLIC NATURE OF THE UNIVERSE.

REMEMBER: KNOWLEDGE IS POTENTIAL POWER.

YOU HAVE TO APPLY WHAT YOU LEARN,

OR YOU WILL REMAIN UNCHANGED,

AND SO WILL YOUR ENTIRE LIFE.

SWITCH I HAVE TO ____ —> TO —> I GET TO ____ .

EVEN IF YOU DO NOT FEEL THIS WAY ABOUT THESE THINGS,

DO THIS TO SHIFT YOUR PERSPECTIVE, AND YOUR VIBRATION.

CHANGE THE WAY YOU ARE CARRYING YOURSELF

AND YOU WILL IMMEDIATELY NOTICE A DIFFERENCE IN THE WAY YOU FEEL.

I WRITE MY INTUITIVE INSIGHTS DOWN AS I RECEIVE THEM,

TO RECALL AND UTILIZE THEM WITHIN MY LIFE.

I AM WHOLE, LOVE & LOVED.

I TREAT MY TEMPLE WELL & NURTURE MY SOUL.

I AM GENTLE WITH MYSELF.

♥

MANIFESTING IS NOT:

I WANT ___, SO WHERE IS IT?

OR, I WANT ___ AND I FEEL IT IS MINE, SO WHERE IS IT?

MANIFESTING IS:

I HAVE DECIDED [WITH CLARITY ON THE DETAILS] THAT I WANT ___ AND I AM NOW ALIGNING MY FREQUENCY WITH THE FREQUENCY OF THIS DESIRE FULFILLED [I FEEL AS IF I HAVE IT], WHILE ALSO TAKING INSPIRED ACTION STEPS IN THE DIRECTION OF THIS DESIRE FULFILLED. THE LAW OF ACTION IS ONE OF THE TWELVE UNIVERSAL LAWS APPLYING TO MANIFESTATION. THIS CREATES ENERGY EXCHANGE THAT IS IN HARMONY WITH YOUR DESIRE'S FULFILLMENT.

[YOU MOVE AND THE ENTIRE UNIVERSE MOVES WITH YOU, TO SUPPORT YOU]

WHAT MAKES MANIFESTATION DIFFERENT THAN REGULAR ACTION OR CONSTANT HUSTLING IS THAT INSTEAD OF WORKING, WORKING, WORKING IN ORDER TO GET TO THE STATE OF FEELING FULFILLED, YOU ARE TAKING ALIGNED ACTION STEPS WHILE AT THE SAME TIME HARNESSING YOUR VIBRATIONAL FREQUENCY [FEELING STATE], SO THAT YOU ARE ALIGNED WITH THE FREQUENCY OF THE FULFILLMENT OF YOUR DESIRE. IN DOING SO THE ENTIRE UNIVERSE IS ABLE TO MATCH YOUR FREQUENCY EMITTED – SENDING YOU EVENTS AND CIRCUMSTANCES THAT MATCH YOUR VIBRATION – OF YOUR DESIRE FULFILLED – THE ENTIRE UNIVERSE IS CONSPIRING ON YOUR BEHALF TO BRING THE FULFILLMENT OF YOUR DESIRE, WHILE YOU FEEL AS IF, HOLD FAITH AND TAKE ACTION. THE ENTIRE UNIVERSE IS WORKING IN SUPPORT OF YOUR DESIRE BECAUSE YOU ARE EMANATING THE FREQUENCY OF YOUR DESIRE FULFILLED WHILE TAKING THOSE STEPS OF INSPIRED ACTION. IF YOU ONLY TAKE ACTION AND YOUR VIBRATION REMAINS IN THE FREQUENCY OF NOT YET HAVING – YOU WILL RECEIVE EVENTS AND CIRCUMSTANCES THAT PROVE YOU ARE NOT YET THERE, THAT YOU ARE STILL NEEDING TO DO MORE WORK AND OVERCOME OBSTACLES IN ORDER TO GET TO YOUR DESIRE'S FULFILLMENT. IT IS A VERY SIMPLE MINDSET SHIFT FROM 'I WANT' TO 'I HAVE' – WHILE AT THE SAME TIME TAKING THOSE STEPS OF ACTION. THE MIND IS A VERY, VERY POWERFUL TOOL. DO NOT UNDERESTIMATE IT'S POWER. IF YOU ARE THINKING / SPEAKING DOUBT [OR SELF-SABOTAGING THOUGHTS AND FEELINGS] YOU ARE STRIPPING YOUR POWER AWAY. BELIEVE IN YOURSELF. PROCEED AS IF SUCCESS IS INEVITABLE. KNOW THE ENTIRE UNIVERSE IS MOVING WITH YOU AND RESPONDING TO YOUR VIBRATIONAL FREQUENCY EMITTED.

Inspired Action

IF YOU FEEL STUCK OR DON'T KNOW WHAT STEPS OF INSPIRED ACTION TO TAKE:

RELAX, DO SOMETHING THAT DOESN'T REQUIRE MUCH OF YOUR ATTENTION / FOCUS.

GIVE GENUINE THANKS IN ADVANCE TO YOUR HIGHER SELF / THE DIVINE / YOUR ANGELS / YOUR GUIDES

[WHICHEVER YOU PREFER OR A COMBINATION] FOR THE INSPIRATION RECEIVED.

THEN, LET GO OF THINKING ON THIS AND THE INSPIRATION WILL COME WHEN YOU ARE LEAST EXPECTING IT.

TRYING TOO HARD TO 'FIND' THE SOLUTION OR STEPS OF INSPIRED ACTION TO TAKE BLOCKS THESE THINGS

FROM COMING TO YOU, SO RELAX. IT IS PERFECTLY FINE AND NECESSARY TO RELAX!!

IT ISN'T UNPRODUCTIVE TO RELAX, IT IS QUITE THE OPPOSITE.

OVER TIME YOU WILL REALIZE THIS FOR YOURSELF, IF YOU HAVEN'T ALREADY.

INSPIRED ACTION STEPS ARISE WHEN WE ALLOW OURSELVES TO BE STILL AND CONNECT WITH SPIRIT. WE BECOME INSPIRED WHILE IN STILLNESS WITH SPIRIT. FORCED ACTION COMES FROM THE NEED TO DETERMINE AND CONTROL THROUGH ANALYTICAL PROCESSING, THE EGOTISTICAL SELF.

WHEN WE ARE IN A HIGH VIBRATION OF FLOW, OR THAT OF PEACE AND SATISFACTION

WE ARE MORE OPEN TO RECEIVING GUIDANCE AND INSPIRATION FOR WHAT STEPS OF INSPIRED ACTION WE

MUST TAKE IN ORDER FOR OUR DESIRES TO MANIFEST INTO THE PHYSICAL.

MEDITATE ~ HOWEVER YOU PERSONALLY DESIRE TO,

OR GET INTO FLOW STATE BY DOING SOMETHING YOU TRULY LOVE TO DO.

YOU KNOW YOU ARE IN FLOW STATE WHEN YOU ARE DOING SOMETHING THAT MAKES YOU LOSE SENSE OF

TIME, SOMETHING THAT RESONATES WITH THE CORE OF YOUR BEING, SOMETHING YOU TRULY LOVE TO DO.

WHEN YOUR ACTION IGNITES FLOW STATE THAT IS A WONDERFUL SIGN

THAT YOUR ACTION IS IN FACT INSPIRED.

TAKING INSPIRED ACTION STEPS ALLOWS THE UNIVERSE TO MOVE WITHIN OUR LIFE IN WAYS WE ARE UNABLE TO PREDICT OR CONTROL. THAT IS WHY IT IS CALLED INSPIRED ACTION.

WHEN WE TAKE THE ACTION STEPS WE TRULY FEEL INSPIRED TO TAKE

WE ARE GUIDED INTO THE FULFILLMENT OF OUR DESIRE.

DO NOT BE AFRAID TO FAIL OR MAKE MISTAKES. KNOW THERE TRULY ARE NO LOSSES ~ ONLY WINS AND ONLY LESSONS. THE ONLY WAY TO TRULY FAIL IS TO REMAIN STAGNANT WITHIN OLD PATTERNS, TO REFUSE TO ACCEPT, RELEASE AND MOVE FORWARD. TAKE INSPIRED ACTION STEPS TOWARDS YOUR DESIRED LIFE DESIGN. RECREATE YOUR SUBCONSCIOUS MIND AND TAKE THE RISKS WITH AN EMBODIMENT OF FAITH AND KNOWINGNESS THAT ALL THINGS ARE LEADING YOU INTO THE LIFE DESIGN THAT YOU HAVE TAKEN THE TIME TO DEFINE. BECAUSE YOU HAVE SET THE INTENTION FOR YOUR DESIRED LIFE DESIGN THE ENTIRE UNIVERSE IS NOW CONSPIRING ON YOUR BEHALF ~ CREATING A PATH INTO YOUR DESIRED LIFE ~ GUIDING YOU THROUGHOUT EACH MOMENT, EVEN WHEN IT DOESN'T FEEL 'GOOD' ~ SWITCH YOUR PERSPECTIVE AND KNOW THIS TOO IS A CRUCIAL PART OF THE PATH THAT LEADS INTO YOUR DESIRES FULFILLMENT.

HOW DO YOU KNOW WHEN YOU ARE RESISTING?

YOU FEEL TENSE, YOU ARE NEGLECTING SELF LOVE, TIRED, AND ACTION FEELS FORCED.

HOW DO YOU KNOW WHEN YOU HAVE LET GO AND ARE ALLOWING?

YOU FEEL RELAXED AS YOU ARE IN HARMONY, PARTAKING IN SELF LOVE

AND ALSO ENJOYING TAKING INSPIRED ACTION.

WE ARE PURE ENERGY

THE PREDOMINANT ENERGY FREQUENCY WE EMBODY WE ATTRACT TO US.

**MOST PEOPLE ARE EMBODYING AN ENERGY FREQUENCY
IN RESPONSE TO THEIR ENVIRONMENT,
MEANING THEY ARE ALLOWING THE ENVIRONMENTS IN THEIR REALITY TO DETERMINE
THE PREDOMINANT ENERGY FREQUENCIES THEY EMBODY.
THEREFORE, CONTINUOUSLY ATTRACTING TO THEM [MANIFESTING] MORE AND MORE OF
THE SAME, DIRECT REFLECTIONS OF THEIR PAST AND PRESENT ENVIRONMENTS.**

TO HARNESS THIS INNATE INNER POWER
EACH INDIVIDUAL MUST PREDOMINANTLY EMBODY THE ENERGY FREQUENCY
THAT IS A MATCH TO THE ENERGY FREQUENCY OF THEIR DESIRE FULFILLED.

**THE PREDOMINANT ENERGY FREQUENCY EMBODIED, PLUS INSPIRED ACTION AND THE
SUPPORT OF THE ENTIRE UNIVERSE EQUALS THE DESIRED MANIFESTATIONS RECEIVED.**

IT IS NOT A QUESTION OF
'IF I CAN MANIFEST, IF YOU CAN MANIFEST OR IF THEY CAN MANIFEST'
WE ALL ARE ALREADY MANIFESTING, WE ALWAYS HAVE BEEN AND ALWAYS WILL BE.

**THE QUESTION IS WHETHER WE DECIDE TO APPLY THIS KNOWLEDGE
AND STOP EMBODYING THE FAMILIAR FREQUENCIES, THE REACTION BASED
FREQUENCIES. DROPPING THE OLD LIMITING BELIEFS AND NARRATIVES WE HAVE
PREVIOUSLY LIVED BY IN ORDER TO BEGIN CREATING A NEW STORY FOR OURSELF,
A NEW LIFE DESIGN, ONE THAT IS OF OUR OWN DEEPEST DESIRES FULFILLED.**

YOUR PREDOMINANT THOUGHTS, EMOTIONS AND FEELING STATE
ARE WHAT HOLD THE GREATEST INFLUENCE ON YOUR COMING MANIFESTATIONS.
MOMENTARY THOUGHTS, EMOTIONS AND FEELING STATES WE FEEL EVERY ONCE IN A WHILE
HAVE LITTLE IMPACT ON THE WHOLE. THIS IS WHY IT IS IMPORTANT TO EVER-INCREASINGLY
FOCUS YOUR THOUGHTS, EMOTIONS AND FEELINGS PREDOMINANTLY ON THE WAY YOUR
DESIRE IN ITS MANIFESTED FORM FEELS. AND NOT ON THE FEELINGS OF LACKING IT / NOT YET
HAVING IT / WANTING IT / FEARING IT WON'T COME / LACKING FAITH IN ITS ABILITY TO
MANIFEST WITHIN YOUR LIFE.

WHEN YOU DECIDE YOU ARE GOING TO TAKE CONTROL OF YOUR POWER THE BEST THING YOU CAN DO IS MONITOR YOUR FREQUENCY IN EACH MOMENT AND FIND THE WAY(S) THAT WORK FOR YOU PERSONALLY TO ALIGN YOUR FREQUENCY WITH THAT OF YOUR DESIRES ALREADY FULFILLED.

THERE IS NOTHING MORE SIGNIFICANT THAN MASTERING YOUR VIBRATIONAL FREQUENCY. YOUR THOUGHTS MOST OFTEN DETERMINE HOW YOU FEEL, SO FILL YOUR MIND WITH EVERYTHING THAT SUPPORTS YOU IN FEELING AS THOUGH YOUR DESIRES ARE ALREADY FULFILLED, AND REMOVE EVERYTHING THAT DOES NOT.

YOU ALREADY EXIST AND YOUR DESIRE ALREADY EXISTS. ALL YOU HAVE TO DO IS HARMONIZE YOUR FREQUENCY WITH THE FREQUENCY OF YOUR DESIRE ~ GET ON THE SAME FREQUENCY. THINK OF HOW EASILY YOU CAN TUNE THE RADIO TO A SPECIFIC STATION. DO THIS WITH YOUR FEELING STATE, YOUR VIBRATIONAL FREQUENCY.

THE URGE TO CONTROL STEMS FROM THE FEAR THAT ___ WONT MANIFEST, OR MANIFEST EXACTLY HOW YOU DESIRE IT TO. THE OPPOSITE OF FEAR IS FAITH. IN BELIEVING WHOLE HEARTEDLY THAT ___ WILL MANIFEST IS TO HOLD FAITH IN THE POWERS UNSEEN BY YOUR PHYSICAL HUMAN VISION. ONCE YOUR INTENTION HAS BEEN SET YOU MUST HOLD ABSOLUTE FAITH THAT THE OUTCOME WILL BE DELIVERED. LET GO OF THE NEED TO CONTROL AND MOVE FORWARD WITH ALIGNED INSPIRED ACTION.

'TRYING TO FORCE SOMETHING TO GO OUR WAY OFTEN LEADS TO RESULTS THAT ARE FAR FROM WHAT WE WANT.' - YUNG PUEBLO

YOUR DESIRE'S FREQUENCY IS NOT HARD TO MATCH. IN YOUR PUREST STATE, YOUR TRUEST STATE, YOU ARE THE HIGHEST VIBRATIONAL FREQUENCY. THE ONLY THING HOLDING YOU DOWN IS RESISTANCE, COMMONLY IN THE FORM OF LIMITING BELIEFS. GIVE YOURSELF PERMISSION TO RELEASE THEM WHEN THEY ARISE. IN HOLDING THIS INTENT YOU WILL GRADUALLY LET GO OF ALL RESISTANCE AND BECOME A HARMONIOUS VIBRATIONAL MATCH WITH YOUR DESIRES FULFILLMENT. YOU ARE A POWERFUL MAGNET, AND YOU ARE FULLY CAPABLE OF HARMONIZING WITH WHAT YOU DESIRE TO ATTRACT, DO SO THROUGH ADJUSTING YOUR VIBRATIONAL FREQUENCY.

BEING AT PEACE WITH ALLOWING YOUR DESIRE ADEQUATE TIME TO MANIFEST ALLOWS YOUR SUBCONSCIOUS TO MORE DEEPLY SUPPORT YOUR DESIRED MANIFESTATIONS. PARADOXICALLY, THEY WILL THEN MANIFEST EVEN FASTER.

DO NOT ALLOW YOUR VIBRATION TO BE A REACTION TO THE CIRCUMSTANCES OF YOUR PRESENT REALITY — HARNESS YOUR VIBRATION SO THAT IT IS IN HARMONY WITH THE VIBRATION OF YOUR DESIRED LIFE DESIGN.

TRUTHFULLY ASK YOURSELF:

AM I BEING IMPATIENT?

ACKNOWLEDGE THE ROOT OF YOUR IMPATIENCE.

ARE YOU AFRAID YOUR DESIRE WONT MANIFEST?

OR WON'T MANIFEST WHEN YOU WANT IT TO?

BOTH STEM FROM THE URGE TO CONTROL.

THE URGE TO CONTROL IS PROOF THAT YOU ARE EXPERIENCING A LACK OF FAITH,

YOU MAY NOT FULLY BELIEVE THAT YOUR DIVINE LIFE SOURCE WILL ACTUALLY PROVIDE FOR

YOU, THAT YOUR DIVINE LIFE SOURCE WILL IN FACT DETERMINE THE EXACT HOW AND WHEN

DETAILS FOR HOW YOUR DESIRE WILL BE PROVIDED TO YOU.

BUT, YOU MUST HAVE FAITH IN ORDER FOR THE PROCESS TO WORK .. RELEASE .. RELEASE ..

RELEASE ... RECEIVE. THE URGE TO CONTROL STEMS FROM THE FEAR THAT ____ WONT MANIFEST,

OR MANIFEST EXACTLY HOW WE DESIRE IT TO. THE OPPOSITE OF FEAR IS FAITH.

IN BELIEVING WHOLE HEARTEDLY THAT ___ WILL MANIFEST IS TO

HOLD FAITH IN THE POWERS UNSEEN BY OUR PHYSICAL HUMAN VISION.

MATCH YOUR VIBRATIONAL FREQUENCY TO YOUR DESIRE'S VIBRATIONAL FREQUENCY.

RESONATE WITH IT COMPLETELY, FOR THEN IT HAS NO OTHER OPTION

BUT TO MANIFEST WITHIN YOUR REALITY.

YOU DON'T ATTRACT WHAT YOU WANT. YOU ATTRACT WHAT YOU ARE. — DR WAYNE DYER

YOUR ONLY JOB IS TO:

1. DEFINE YOUR DESIRE [SET YOUR INTENTION]

2. TAKE INSPIRED ACTION IN ALIGNMENT WITH YOUR DESIRE

[IN ANY GIVEN MOMENT SIMPLY ASK YOUR HIGHEST SELF / THE DIVINE / YOUR ANGELS / GUIDES

'WHAT IS THE NEXT STEP OF INSPIRED ACTION I CAN TAKE?]

AND ALWAYS FOLLOW THE GUIDANCE YOU RECEIVE — AS LONG AS IT FEELS RIGHT WITHIN YOU.

3. EVER-INCREASINGLY EMBODY THE FEELING STATES YOU WILL EXPERIENCE WITH YOUR DESIRE

ALREADY FULFILLED [GET INTO RECEIVING MODE, THE ENERGY VIBRATION OF SATISFACTION]

ACT AS IF YOUR DESIRE IS IN FACT ALREADY YOURS. IT IS YOURS. YOU ASKED WITH AN

EMBODIMENT OF GENUINE, HEARTFELT INTENT, AND YOU SHALL RECEIVE. YOU MUST ALLOW

YOURSELF TO BELIEVE. YOU ARE A MIRACLE IN THE FLESH, BELIEVE IN YOUR POWER AND YOUR

DIVINE LIFE SOURCE'S SUPPORT ONE-HUNDRED PERCENT. BE GENUINELY GRATEFUL,

THIS INNATE CREATIVE POWER WITHIN YOU IS BEAUTIFUL.

DO NOT QUESTION HOW YOUR DESIRE WILL COME — STOP THOSE THOUGHTS IN THEIR

TRACKS. YOU CHOOSE YOUR DESIRE BUT THE EXACT DETAILS OF THE PROCESS AREN'T YOURS TO

DEFINE. KNOW WITHIN EVERY SINGLE FIBER OF YOUR BEING THAT ALL THINGS LEAD TO THE

FULFILLMENT OF YOUR DESIRES. SEE ALL EVENTS AND CIRCUMSTANCES IN THIS LIGHT,

NO MATTER WHAT. KNOW THAT THE EXACT DETAILS FOR HOW AND WHEN

YOUR DESIRE WILL MANIFEST ARE BEING WORKED OUT FOR YOU.

FOR DESIRES THAT ARE EXTREMELY LIFE CHANGING: ALLOW YOUR DIVINE LIFE SOURCE TIME TO ACCOMMODATE YOUR DESIRES. YOU CAN ACHIEVE WHATEVER YOU PLEASE, DO RECOGNIZE THAT YOU MUST BE PATIENT AND HOLD FAITH WHILE DOING SO. DO NOT TRY TO RUSH THE PROCESS OR FORCE ANYTHING. THIS IS WHY IT IS BENEFICIAL TO WORK WITH THE LONG TERM BLUEPRINT AND THEN USE THE MOON CYCLES AS STEPPING STONES ALONG THE PATH TO THE LARGER DESIRES. WHEN YOU ATTEMPT TO RUSH OR FORCE YOU END UP EMBODYING LOW VIBRATIONAL FREQUENCIES ~ LEADING TO LOW VIBRATIONAL MANIFESTATIONS, AND NOT YOUR DESIRES AT ALL. HOLD FAITH WHILE REMAINING PATIENT AS YOU MOVE FORWARD IN ALIGNMENT WITH YOUR DESIRES, TAKING INSPIRED ACTION AND EVER-INCREASINGLY FEELING AS IF THEY HAVE ALREADY BECOME YOUR REALITY. ADJUST SLOWLY .. ENJOY THE PROCESS .. SAVOR THE MOMENTS .. ENJOY WHERE YOU ARE AT NOW .. KNOW AND FEEL WHAT IS COMING TO YOU IN DIVINE, PERFECT TIME. YOU DO NOT ALWAYS NEED TO BE THINKING ABOUT YOUR DESIRES IN ORDER FOR THEM TO MANIFEST. REFLECTING ON THE FEELINGS OF YOUR DESIRES FULFILLED IN THE MORNING AND AT THE END OF YOUR DAY IS A GREAT WAY TO STAY ALIGNED. YOU CAN DO SO MORE OFTEN THROUGHOUT THE DAY IF YOU DESIRE, BUT YOU DO NOT HAVE TO. CHALLENGE YOURSELF TO FOCUS ON ONE THING AT A TIME THROUGHOUT THE DAY, AND FEEL PEACEFUL AS YOU DO SO. THIS WILL ELIMINATE FEAR / ANXIETY AND WILL STRENGTHEN YOUR FOCUS AND INCREASE YOUR VIBRATIONAL FREQUENCY. THE UNIVERSE KNOWS WHAT YOU DESIRE BECAUSE YOU HAVE SET YOUR INTENTION IN RITUAL, IT HAS NOT FORGOT.

IF DOUBT EVER STARTS TO ARISE: SEE IT AS AN OPPORTUNITY TO RISE ABOVE AND CELEBRATE THAT YOU ARE GROWING STRONGER BY TAKING CONTROL OF YOUR THOUGHTS, EMOTIONS AND FEELING STATES. DELIBERATELY PRACTICE FEELING AS IF YOUR DESIRE IS ALREADY IN YOUR LIFE.

HOW EXACTLY HAS THIS CHANGED YOUR LIFE?
HOW BLESSED ARE YOU FEELING?
HOW HAVE YOUR PERCEPTIONS CHANGED?
HOW EXACTLY WILL THIS MAKE YOU FEEL ONCE ___ IS MANIFESTED AS YOUR REALITY?
IF YOU ARE WORKING ON A PROJECT: HOW WILL IT FEEL WHEN YOU HAVE COMPLETED? WHAT WORDS CAN YOU USE TO DESCRIBE
YOUR INTENTIONS FOR THIS PROJECT'S COMPLETED FORM?
MEDITATE ON THOSE THOUGHTS AND FEELINGS
BECOME FAMILIAR WITH THE SENSATIONS.

THROUGHOUT EACH MOON CYCLE DEDICATE YOUR ATTENTION TO EMBODYING THE HIGH VIBRATIONAL ENERGY FREQUENCIES [FEELING STATES] YOUR MANIFESTATION FULFILLED WILL BRING INTO YOUR BEING AND ALL ASPECTS OF YOUR LIFE. LIVE THROUGH INCREASINGLY EMBODYING THIS AS YOUR MOST FREQUENT STATE OF BEING. DETACH FROM TRYING TO DETERMINE THE EXACT HOW AND WHEN IT WILL COME TO YOU WHILE YOU GO ABOUT LIFE IN THIS ENERGETIC FREQUENCY FEELING AS IF ___ IS ALREADY YOUR REALITY. YOU DO HAVE TO TAKE INSPIRED ACTION, AND NOT JUST WAIT AROUND FEELING. MOVE FORWARD IN LIFE TAKING INSPIRED ACTION IN ALIGNMENT WITH YOUR DESIRES. YOU CAN EASILY DEFINE THE INSPIRED ACTION STEPS YOU MUST TAKE BY ASKING YOUR HIGHER SELF [OR DIVINE LIFE SOURCE] DURING MEDITATION, OR IN ANY OTHER MOMENT: WHAT IS THE NEXT STEP OF INSPIRED ACTION YOU WILL HAVE ME TAKE? ALSO NOTE: IF YOUR DESIRE DOES NOT MANIFEST IN ONE CYCLE — DO NOT DISREGARD IT. CONTINUE PUTTING ENERGY TOWARDS IT THROUGH EVER-INCREASINGLY FEELING IT AS YOUR REALITY, IT WILL COME TO YOU IN DIVINE, PERFECT TIMING. KNOW THAT IT IS IN FACT COMING TO YOU. YOU ARE WORKING YOUR MAGICK THROUGH HARNESSING YOUR FEELING STATE IN EACH MOMENT, AND YOUR INTENTION WILL COME TO YOU. BE EXCITED TO SEE HOW YOUR LIFE AND POWER SOURCE WILL WORK ITS MAGICK IN DETERMINING THE EXACT HOW AND WHEN YOUR DESIRE WILL BE BROUGHT TO YOU.

I DESIRE WITH A PLAYFUL ATTITUDE I LET GO OF WONDERING
HOW AND WHEN MY DESIRES WILL APPEAR. INSTEAD, I AM EXCITED TO SEE HOW
MY DIVINE LIFE SOURCE WILL WORK ITS MAGICK IN BRINGING MY DESIRES TO ME
AS I MOVE FORWARD WITH ALIGNED INSPIRED ACTION.
ACTION ALONE IS 'DOING' IN ORDER TO MAKE SOMETHING HAPPEN,
INSPIRED ACTION IS 'DOING' WITH FEELINGS OF JOY AND INSPIRATION
[STEMMING FROM MY HEART AND INTUITION] FLOWING AND ALLOWING THINGS TO HAPPEN.

CONNECT WITH YOUR INNER CHILD ~ THAT PLAYFUL SPIRIT ~
DO THE THINGS YOU LOVED TO DO AS A CHILD OR ALWAYS WANTED TO DO AS A CHILD.

I DO NOT OBSESS OVER OUTCOMES I DESIRE,
INSTEAD I OBSESS ON FELING THE FEELINGS OF PEACE AND SATISFACTION MY DESIRES COMPLETE,
MANIFESTED FORM BRINGS INTO MY LIFE, AS ALREADY HERE NOW. I MEDITATE ON EXACTLY HOW THIS
FEELS, THIS IS HOW I HOLD FAITH WHILE DETACHING AND ALLOWING
I PRACTICE THE ART OF SURRENDER.
I AM THE EMBODIMENT OF FAITH.

INITIALLY YOU MIGHT THINK THAT YOU WANT EVERYTHING YOU COULD EVER DREAM OF OR IMAGINE
ALL AT ONCE, BUT THINK ABOUT IT FROM A LARGER PERSPECTIVE .. YOU DO NOT WANT IT ALL AT ONCE.
IT IS MUCH MORE PLEASURABLE AND REWARDING TO RECEIVE IT ALL IN A CONSTANT, ENDLESS,
EVER-FLOWING STREAM. IT IS MUCH MORE ENJOYABLE TO LIVE WITHIN A LIFE DESIGN THAT IS
CONSTANTLY FULFILLING, EXCITING AND REWARDING YOU WITH MORE AT EVERY TURN.

SURRENDER IS NOT 'GIVING UP' ON YOUR DESIRES.
SURRENDER IS LETTING GO OF THE NEED TO OBSESS OVER AND CONTROL THE DETAILS FOR EXACTLY
HOW AND WHEN YOUR DESIRES WILL COME INTO YOUR LIFE. SURRENDER IS DETACHING AND
ALLOWING THE ENTIRE UNIVERSE TO WORK WITH YOU, TO SUPPORT YOU, WHILE YOU HOLD FAITH.
YOUR JOB IS TO MOVE WITH INSPIRED ACTION IN ALIGNMENT WITH YOUR DESIRES AND MEDITATE ON
THE FEELINGS YOUR DESIRES FULFILLMENT BRINGS. EVER-INCREASINGLY ADJUST THE FEELING STATES
YOU EMBODY WITHIN YOUR DAILY LIFE SO THAT THEY ARE IN HARMONY WITH HOW YOU WILL FEEL
WITH YOUR DESIRES MANIFESTED. DO SO THROUGHOUT ALL ASPECTS OF YOUR LIFE. KNOW THAT YOUR
DESIRES ARE COMING TO YOU IN DIVINE, PERFECT TIMING. DO NOT EMBODY FEELING STATES OF NEED
OR LACK — FOR THOSE WILL ATTRACT TO YOU EVENTS AND CIRCUMSTANCES THAT PROVE YOU ARE
LACKING, AND YOUR DESIRES WILL MOVE FURTHER AWAY FROM YOU. YOU MUST BE IN HARMONY WITH
YOUR DESIRES FULFILLED, NOT THE LACK OF THEM / NEEDING THEM AND NOT HAVING THEM. THIS IS
VERY IMPORTANT TO UNDERSTAND. BE GENTLE WITH YOURSELF BECAUSE THIS IS NOT AN OVERNIGHT
CHANGE IN VIBRATION, OR A ONE-DAY CHANGE IN VIBRATION. IT WILL TAKE TIME TO MASTER, SO STAY
DEDICATED AND FIND THE WAYS THAT RESONATE WITH YOU PERSONALLY SO THAT YOU ARE ABLE TO
TRULY IGNITE THE FEELINGS STATES OF YOUR DESIRES FULFILLED. MASTER EACH DAY, AND THEN
CONTINUE DOING THAT AND YOU WILL EVOLVE AND GROW INTO THE VIBRATIONAL MATCH OF YOUR
DESIRES FULFILLED. SURRENDER INTO THE FREQUENCY OF SATISFACTION, GRACE AND PEACE

SIMPLE DAILY PRAYER/MEDITATION/AFFIRMATION SCRIPT:

I AM THANKFUL FOR _____.

FILL IN THE BLANK WITH EACH DESIRE YOU ARE MANIFESTING.

I TRUST THAT MY DIVINE SOURCE
IS PROVIDING ME WITH EXACTLY WHAT I NEED
IN EACH MOMENT OF THIS LIFETIME.

WHEN FEELING STUCK HANDLING A 'PROBLEM':

MY 'PROBLEM' IS _____.

IS THIS COMPLETELY OUT OF MY CONTROL?
IF YES, THEN I RELAX INTO EASE WITHIN MY FAITH IN THE DIVINE,
OR PERFORM A RITUAL TO SURRENDER.
IF NO, THEN MY IDEAL SOLUTION IS _____.
[IGNITE ALL SENSES INTO THE SOLUTION]

'NO PROBLEM CAN BE SOLVED
FROM THE SAME LEVEL OF CONSCIOUSNESS THAT CREATED IT.' - ALBERT EINSTEIN
STEP BACK FROM OBSESSING OVER ALL OF THE DETAILS
AND ALLOW YOURSELF TO BREATHE AS YOU RECONNECT WITH THE BIG PICTURE.

I CHOOSE TO LET GO WHEN I AM NOT IN CONTROL,
I TRUST THE UNIVERSE ALWAYS HAS MY BACK,
MAKING MOVES FOR ME EVEN WHEN I CANNOT SEE,
I AM CONFIDENTLY TRUSTING WHAT I CANNOT SEE.
I CHOOSE TO FOCUS ON THE FEELINGS OF MY IDEAL SOLUTION,
AS I HAVE FULL FAITH THAT
THE ENTIRE UNIVERSE IS SUPPORTING MY EVERY INTENTION I EMIT FROM MY BEING.
WHEN I MOVE, THE ENTIRE UNIVERSE MOVES WITH ME TO SUPPORT ME.
WHEN I HAVE DONE ALL I CAN DO,
I RELAX AND HOLD ABSOLUTE FAITH THAT MY DIVINE, CREATIVE LIFE SOURCE
LOVES ME AND IS TAKING CARE OF ME.

IF YOU ARE IN THE FREQUENCY OF LACK, NOT YET HAVING
OR DISAPPOINTMENT THAT YOUR DESIRE HAS NOT MANIFESTED YET
YOU ARE BLOCKING YOUR DESIRE FROM COMING TO YOU. YOU MUST MOVE INTO THE FREQUENCY OF
FULFILLMENT, SATISFACTION, ALLOWING, RECEIVING.

DO NOT CLING TO RESISTANCE, ALLOW YOURSELF TO LET GO AND ALLOW

HARNESS YOUR VIBRATION IN THESE MOMENTS . DO NOT WAIT FOR YOUR DESIRE TO MANIFEST BEFORE
FEELING LIKE YOU HAVE IT. YOU MUST FEEL IT FIRST — ALIGN YOUR VIBRATIONAL FREQUENCY WITH
THE VIBRATIONAL FREQUENCY OF ALREADY HAVING IT. MAKE THIS YOUR PREDOMINANT
VIBRATIONAL FREQUENCY YOU RESIDE IN EACH MOMENT.
YOU ATTRACT TO YOU EVENTS AND CIRCUMSTANCES
THAT MATCH YOUR FREQUENCY YOU ARE EMBODYING IN THIS MOMENT.

IF ONE ADVANCES CONFIDENTLY IN THE DIRECTION OF THEIR DREAMS, AND ENDEAVORS TO LIVE THE
LIFE WHICH THEY HAVE IMAGINED, THEY WILL MEET WITH A SUCCESS UNEXPECTED IN COMMON
HOURS. - HENRY DAVID THOREAU

DO NOT GET SO EXCITED TO SEE YOUR DESIRE MANIFEST THAT YOU SETTLE FOR LESS THAN WHAT YOU
INTENDED TO RECEIVE. WHEN YOU SAY YES TO ANYTHING AND EVERYTHING THAT COMES YOUR WAY YOU
END UP BLOCKING THE MANIFESTATION OF WHAT IT IS YOU TRULY DESIRE. USE DISCERNMENT, HAVE
BOUNDARIES AND A CLEAR DEFINITION OF WHAT YOUR DESIRE'S MANIFESTED FORM ENTAILS.

MY DAYDREAM/ DAILY THINKING IS A PREVIEW OF MY FUTURE REALITY.
I CHOOSE TO BE MINDFUL
IN ONLY THINKING AND DREAMING
ON THE THOUGHTS THAT PRODUCE THE FEELINGS I DESIRE TO MANIFEST AS MY REALITY.

'THE SECRET OF CHANGE IS TO FOCUS ALL OF YOUR ENERGY,
NOT ON FIGHTING THE OLD, BUT ON BUILDING THE NEW.' –SOCRATES

[ONE] OF THE PRINCIPAL REASONS WHY SO MANY FAIL TO GET WHAT THEY WANT IS BECAUSE THEY DO
NOT DEFINITELY KNOW WHAT THEY WANT, OR BECAUSE THEY CHANGE THEIR WANTS ALMOST EVERY
DAY. 'KNOW WHAT YOU WANT AND CONTINUE TO WANT IT. YOU WILL GET IT IF YOU COMBINE DESIRE
WITH FAITH. THE POWER OF DESIRE WHEN COMBINED WITH FAITH BECOMES INVINCIBLE.'
- CHRISTIAN D. LARSON (1874-1954) YOUR FORCES AND HOW TO USE THEM

REMEMBER:
YOU DO NOT PLANT THE SEED AND EAT THE FRUIT THE SAME DAY.
YOU ALSO CANNOT EXPECT TO GROW THE FRUIT IF YOU DO NOT PLANT THE SEEDS.
PLANT THE SEEDS OF WHAT YOU DESIRE, AND THEN .. DO NOT SABOTAGE YOUR DESIRES BY DOUBTING
THAT THEY WILL MANIFEST. WHEN PLANTING SEEDS IN A GARDEN YOU DO NOT START DOUBTING THE
SEEDS JUST BECAUSE THEY TAKE TIME TO GERMINATE. YOU ARE AWARE THAT THEY TAKE NURTURING,
LOVE AND TIME TO SPROUT. LIKEWISE DO NOT DO THIS WITH YOUR DESIRED MANIFESTATIONS.
SUPPORT THEM, NUTURE THEM, LOVE THEM, FEEL INTO THEM, BELIEVE IN THEM, IMMERSE YOURSELF
INTO HOW THEY WILL FEEL WITHIN YOUR LIFE, FALL IN LOVE WITH THEM BEFORE THEY ARE FULLY
FORMED. DO NOT DOUBT THEM OR FORGET TO NUTURE THEM,
THEY DO NEED YOUR LOVE AND CARE.

YOU CANNOT SEE AIR, GRAVITY, ELECTRICITY OR WIFI
AND YET YOU DO NOT DOUBT THEIR EXISTENCE..

YOU MUST HOLD FAITH IN THE UNSEEN FORCES THAT ARE WORKING FOR YOU,
AS YOU INTEND FOR THEM TO. YOU CONSCIOUSLY DO SO WITH YOUR
WORDS, THOUGHTS, EMOTIONS AND, MOST IMPORTANTLY,
YOUR FEELING STATE [VIBRATIONAL FREQUENCY].

FOR INSPIRATION: RESEARCH DR MASARU EMOTO'S STUDIES ON WATER,
AND ON RICE. DO THE RICE EXPERIMENTS AT HOME, JUST TO SHOW YOURSELF THE IMMENSITY OF
POWER THAT DOES EXIST WITHIN CONSCIOUSNESS AND INTENT.

'IF YOU LOOK AT WHAT YOU HAVE IN LIFE, YOU'LL ALWAYS HAVE MORE.
IF YOU LOOK AT WHAT YOU DON'T HAVE IN LIFE, YOU'LL NEVER HAVE ENOUGH.' —OPRAH WINFREY

Universal guidance to follow:

CHOOSE YOUR SEED.
BE CERTAIN OF WHAT YOU WANT. ORANGES CANNOT GROW FROM LEMON SEEDS. DON'T EXPECT THEM TO.

CHOOSE YOUR *desired life design.*
BE CERTAIN WITH YOURSELF ON WHAT IT IS YOU TRULY WANT.
USE DETAIL.

↓

PLANT YOUR SEED IN THE SOIL.
YOU KNOW WHICH PLANT YOUR SEED WILL GROW INTO,
BECAUSE YOU TOOK TIME TO CHOOSE IT YOURSELF.

PLANT YOUR IDEAL LIFE IN YOUR MIND.
KNOW THE DETAILS OF YOUR DESIRED LIFE DESIGN,
YOU ARE CERTAIN THIS IS WHAT YOU ARE GROWING WITHIN YOUR LIFE,
BECAUSE YOU TOOK TIME TO CHOOSE AND DEFINE YOUR LIFE AS YOU DESIRE IT TO BE.

↓

Water your seed.

Take inspired action towards, and in line with, your life design you desire.

↓

PROVIDE SUNLIGHT TO YOUR SEED.

DAYDREAM ON THE FEELINGS OF YOUR DESIRED LIFE DESIGN AS AN ALREADY ACHIEVED FACT.
GET FAMILIAR WITH THESE FEELINGS, ALWAYS FEEL THEM IN ORDER TO STAY INSPIRED.
POSITIVE FEELINGS FUEL GROWTH.
BY FEELING ANY DOUBT OR FEELINGS OF LACK YOU ARE SELF-SABOTAGING YOUR GARDEN
BY PLANTING AND GIVING ALL OF THE AVAILABLE SUNLIGHT TO NUMEROUS WEEDS.
THE WEEDS WILL GROW PROMINENTLY, FUELED BY YOUR NEGATIVE FEELINGS OF... THEM.
WITH ALL OF THESE WEEDS YOUR CHOSEN SEED WILL EITHER STRUGGLE TO GROW,
OR SIMPLY NOT GROW AT ALL.
FEELINGS OF DOUBT, LACK AND DWELLING ON ALL THAT COULD POSSIBLY GO WRONG ARE
THE WEEDS OF YOUR GARDEN.
IT IS CRUCIAL TO FOCUS ON WHAT YOU ARE STRIVING TOWARDS.
FEEL THE POSITIVE FEELINGS ASSOCIATED WITH THAT.

↓

NOW YOU CAN GROW YOUR DESIRED LIFE DESIGN SUCCESSFULLY INTO BLOSSOMING FORM.
ALLOW THE WATER + SUNLIGHT PROCESS TO REPEAT AND BECOME YOUR EVERY MOMENT STATE OF
BEING THROUGHOUT EACH DAY. THEN,
YOUR DESIRED LIFE DESIGN WILL BEGIN TO TAKE FULL BLOSSOM BEFORE YOUR EYES.

DIFFERENT FEELING STATES ATTUNE OUR BEING TO THE VIBRATIONAL FREQUENCY THAT IS IN HARMONIOUS WITH THAT FEELING STATE. WE HAVE THE FREE WILL TO EMBODY THE FREQUENCY WE DESIRE. IF IT SEEMS DIFFICULT, AS IF EXTERNAL CIRCUMSTANCES ARE THE CAUSE OF YOUR FEELING STATE [YOUR FREQUENCY YOU ARE ATTUNED TO] THAT IS BECAUSE YOU HAVE BEEN CONDITIONED YOUR ENTIRE LIFE TO BELIEVE LIFE IS HAPPENING TO YOU AND NOT RESPONDING TO YOU. THIS IS NOT 'YOUR FAULT' BUT IT IS YOUR RESPONSIBILITY TO BECOME EVER-INCREASINGLY AWARE AND CONSCIOUSLY EMBODY THE FREQUENCY YOU DESIRE TO LIVE WITHIN. YOUR SUCCESS IN CONSCIOUSLY MANIFESTING THE LIFE DESIGN YOU DESIRE IS RELIANT ON YOUR ABILITY TO LIVE IN THE PRESENT MOMENT. IN DOING SO YOU ARE ABLE TO BECOME CONSCIOUS OF YOUR FREQUENCY YOU ARE EMBODYING IN EACH MOMENT. IF YOU OBSERVE YOU ARE IN A LOWER FREQUENCY THAN YOU DESIRE TO MANIFEST: SET THE INTENTION TO MOVE INTO A HIGHER FREQUENCY THAT MATCHES YOUR DESIRED LIFE DESIGN, AND IN EACH MOMENT AFTER SETTING THIS INTENTION FOCUS ON EMBODYING GENUINE GRATITUDE FOR ANYTHING YOU DESIRE AND EVERYTHING YOU ALREADY HAVE TO BE GRATEFUL FOR. THE VIBRATION OF GENUINE GRATITUDE IS RESONATE WITH PEACE, JOY AND LOVE THEREFORE IT IS A MAGNET FOR MIRACLES.

THE APPROXIMATE
VIBRATIONAL FREQUENCIES OF VARIOUS FEELING STATES:
FREQUENCIES ARE MEASURED IN HERTZ [HZ]

PEACE: 600HZ

JOY: 540HZ

LOVE: 500HZ

PURPOSE: 400HZ

ACCEPTANCE: 350HZ

WILLINGNESS: 310HZ

NEUTRALITY: 250HZ

ANGER: 150HZ

FEAR: 100HZ

GRIEF: 75HZ

GUILT: 30HZ

SHAME: 20HZ

THE 12 UNIVERSAL LAWS

ARE BASED ON METAPHYSICAL, PHILOSOPHICAL AND QUANTUM PHYSICS PRINCIPLES
FUNCTIONING SINCE THE BEGINNING OF TIME.

QUANTUM PHYSICS PROVES THAT EVERY SINGLE THING,
WHEN BROKEN DOWN INTO THE SMALLEST PARTICLES, IS ONLY ENERGY.
AND THAT ENERGY IS VIBRATING IN CIRCULAR PATTERNS.
DIFFERENT THINGS AND DIFFERENT PEOPLE HAVE DIFFERENT ENERGY FREQUENCIES.

1. THE LAW OF DIVINE ONENESS

ALL THINGS ARE CONNECTED, WE ARE ALL EXPRESSIONS OF OUR DIVINE LIFE AND POWER
SOURCE [THE ORGANIZED INTELLIGENCE THAT PERMEATES THROUGHOUT THE ENTIRE
UNIVERSE]. ALL LIFE AND ENERGY COMES FROM THIS ONE SOURCE. SINCE WE ARE ONE,
WE EACH IMPACT THE ENTIRE COLLECTIVE. KNOWING THIS, PARTAKE IN YOUR PASSIONS
WITH THE INTENT TO IMPACT THE HIGHEST GOOD FOR ALL SOULS.

2. THE LAW OF VIBRATION.

'EVERYTHING IS ENERGY AND THAT'S ALL THERE IS TO IT. MATCH THE FREQUENCY OF THE
REALITY YOU WANT AND YOU CANNOT HELP BUT GET THAT REALITY. IT CAN BE
NO OTHER WAY. THIS IS NOT PHILOSOPHY. THIS IS PHYSICS' - EINSTEIN.
LIKE FREQUENCIES ATTRACT LIKE FREQUENCIES. SO, BE ON THE VIBRATION OF 'I HAVE MY
DESIRE' NOT THE VIBRATION OF 'I WANT MY DESIRE'.

3. THE LAW OF ACTION.

TAKING INSPIRED ACTION IS ABSOLUTELY CRUCIAL FOR YOUR DESIRE TO MANIFEST.
ACTION CREATES ENERGY EXCHANGE. TAKE YOUR INSPIRED ACTION
ON THE FREQUENCY OF YOUR DESIRE'S MANIFESTATION.

4. THE LAW OF CORRESPONDENCE.

'AS ABOVE, SO BELOW, AS WITHIN, SO WITHOUT, AS THE UNIVERSE, SO THE SOUL ...'
— HERMES TRISMEGISTUS
WHAT YOU THINK AND SPEAK GENERATES EMOTION.
THE COMBINATION OF THESE THOUGHTS/SPOKEN WORDS AND EMOTION
CREATES A FEELING ~ YOUR FEELINGS EMBODIED WILL BE MATCHED BY SOURCE. THUS,
PROVIDING YOU WITH HARMONIOUS EXTERNAL EVENTS AND CIRCUMSTANCES.
HARNESS YOUR THOUGHTS/SPOKEN WORDS AND FEELINGS AND YOU WILL HARNESS YOUR
LIFE. SHIFT YOUR PERCEPTION, EVEN JUST EVER-SO-SLIGHTLY TO GENERATE THE FEELINGS
YOU DESIRE TO RECEIVE MORE OF. FOCUS ON WHAT YOU WANT, NOT WHAT YOU DO NOT
WANT. THIS IS AN INSIDE JOB, NO ONE OUTSIDE OF YOU CAN DO THIS FOR YOU. IT REQUIRES
SELF-DISCIPLINE. EMBODY A MINDSET OF FAITH AND KNOWINGNESS OVER A MINDSET OF
FEAR OR DOUBT, IN EACH MOMENT. WHEN LOW VIBRATIONAL THOUGHTS AND FEELINGS
ARISE SIMPLY STOP THEM IN THEIR TRACKS AND REPEAT TO YOURSELF 'I AM SAFE, MY DIVINE
LIFE SOURCE, MY HIGHEST VIBRATIONAL ANGELS AND SPIRIT GUIDES, AS WELL AS MY
HIGHEST SELF ARE ALL PROTECTING ME AND LOVINGLY GUIDING ME. I HOLD FAITH IN THE
FORCES UNSEEN BY MY HUMAN VISION. I NEED NOT WORRY OR STRESS ABOUT ANYTHING,
BUT RATHER, EMBODY THE FEELINGS OF MY DESIRES FULFILLED.'

5. THE LAW OF CAUSE AND EFFECT.

YOU ARE THE MASTER DESIGNER OF YOUR LIFE.

IF IT DOES NOT SEEM THAT WAY RIGHT NOW, THAT IS SIMPLY BECAUSE YOU HAVE BEEN EMBODYING FAMILIAR THOUGHTS AND FEELINGS WHICH PRODUCE FAMILIAR EVENTS AND CIRCUMSTANCES WITHIN YOUR LIFE UP TO THIS POINT IN TIME. ONCE YOU BEGIN TO HARNESS YOUR INTERNAL POWER AND CONSCIOUSLY REGULATE YOUR THOUGHTS AND FEELINGS SO THAT THEY ARE EVER-INCREASINGLY ALIGNED WITH ONLY THAT WHICH YOU DESIRE YOU WILL EVER-INCREASINGLY SEE THE EXTERNAL SHIFTS WITHIN YOUR EXTERIOR REALITY. YOU WILL BEGIN TO EVER-INCREASINGLY KNOW AND FEEL THAT YOU ARE IN FACT THE MASTER DESIGNER OF YOUR LIFE. FALL IN LOVE WITH THIS INNATE POWER WITHIN YOU. BLAMING EXTERNAL PEOPLE AND CIRCUMSTANCES WILL NOT CHANGE ANYTHING, DOING SO ONLY ATTRACTS MORE THINGS TO FEEL THIS WAY ABOUT. IT TAKES SELF-DISCIPLINE TO STOP BLAMING AND CONSCIOUSLY SHIFT YOUR INTERNAL PERSPECTIVES, BUT IT MUST BE DONE. THIS IS THE ONLY WAY TO HARNESS YOUR INNER POWER AND DIRECT IT INTO WHAT YOU DO IN FACT DESIRE. THERE IS POWER IN CLEAN AND TIDY: REMOVE ALL PEOPLE, PLACES AND THINGS FROM YOUR LIFE THAT BRING YOUR FEELING STATE INTO WHAT YOU DO NOT WANT, ONLY KEEP THE PEOPLE, PLACES AND THINGS THAT BRING YOU FEELING STATES YOU DO WANT MORE OF. DEEP CLEAN, ORGANIZE AND DECORATE YOUR HOME, VEHICLE, WORKSPACE, SACRED SPACES AND ANY OTHER SPACES IN YOUR LIFE WITH THINGS THAT IGNITE THE THOUGHTS AND FEELINGS OF GENUINE GRATITUDE FOR YOUR DESIRES FULFILLED. CREATE SPACE FOR YOUR DESIRES TO ENTER YOUR LIFE THROUGH LETTING GO OF OLD CLUTTER, PLACES AND PEOPLE WHO DO NOT SERVE YOUR HIGHEST GOOD AND DESIRED LIFE DESIGN. EVOLVE. YOUR VIBRATIONAL FREQUENCY AND INSPIRED ACTION STEPS ARE EFFECTS THAT CAUSE THE MANIFESTATION OF YOUR DESIRED LIFE DESIGN.

6. THE LAW OF ATTRACTION.

YOUR BELIEFS CREATE YOUR REALITY.

EVERYTHING IN THE UNIVERSE IS ENERGY, AND ENERGY ALWAYS ATTRACTS THE SAME FREQUENCY OF ENERGY. THIS IS EXACTLY HOW AND WHY EACH PERSON WILL ALWAYS RECEIVE PROOF OF EVERY SINGLE BELIEF THEY INTERNALLY HOLD AS TRUE.

'WHEN YOU CHANGE THE WAY YOU LOOK AT THINGS THE THINGS YOU LOOK AT CHANGE'
- DR. WAYNE DYER.

WHEN YOU SHIFT PERSPECTIVES AND / OR CHANGE YOUR BELIEFS

ABOUT ANYTHING / EVERYTHING YOU WILL RECEIVE PROOF

THAT YOUR NEW PERSPECTIVES AND / OR BELIEFS ARE IN FACT TRUE.

SWITCH FROM THE PERSPECTIVE OF CAUSE AND EFFECT

TO THE PERSPECTIVE OF CAUSING AN EFFECT.

CREATE A NEW STORY FOR YOUR LIFE. CREATE THE LIFE DESIGN YOU DO DESIRE TO LIVE.

7. THE LAW OF COMPENSATION.

OUR SOURCE PROVIDES US WITH PHYSICAL MANIFESTATIONS AS RESULT OF OUR FEELING STATES WE HAVE EMBODIED IN COMBINATION WITH THE INSPIRED ACTION STEPS WE HAVE TAKEN. THE PHYSICAL REALITY SURROUNDING YOU IS THE PROOF OF WHAT YOU ARE / HAVE BEEN INTERNALLY EMBODYING AND THE INSPIRED ACTION STEPS YOU HAVE OR HAVE NOT BEEN TAKING. IT IS ALL IN PERFECT HARMONY WITH THE FEELING STATES [VIBRATIONAL FREQUENCIES] YOU EMBODY AND EMANATE. LEARN FROM YOUR EXTERNAL LIFE, WHAT DO YOU NOT WANT TO SEE IN IT ANYMORE? WHAT DO YOU WANT TO SEE IN IT? RECOGNIZE THAT IN ORDER TO CHANGE THE EXTERNAL YOU MUST FIRST INTERNALLY MATCH THE FREQUENCY OF WHAT YOU DO WANT. EMBODY THE FEELING STATE OF HOW IT FEELS TO ALREADY HAVE THIS IN YOUR EXTERNAL REALITY, ONCE YOU MASTER DOING SO INTERNALLY YOUR EXTERNAL REALITY WILL REFLECT. YOU CAN SEE EXACTLY WHERE YOU ARE AT INTERNALLY BY CURIOUSLY AND PLAYFULLY EXAMINING YOUR EXTERNAL LIFE. DO SO NON JUDGMENTALLY, WITHOUT SELF-PUNISHMENT. JUST OBSERVE AND TRULY HONOR THE PLACE YOU ARE RIGHT NOW INTERNALLY. RECOGNIZING THAT YOU WILL SOON BE IN AN ENTIRELY DIFFERENT PLACE, BUT FIRST YOU MUST ACCEPT WHERE YOU ARE. THEN, BEGIN TO ADJUST ACCORDINGLY INTO WHAT YOU DO DESIRE INTERNALLY AND EXTERNALLY. IT DOES TAKE TIME AND PRACTICE, SO BE GENTLE WITH YOURSELF. EVOLVE AT A PACE THAT IS COMFORTABLE TO YOU. YOU WILL EVOLVE TO EXACTLY WHERE YOU DO IN FACT WANT TO BE. JUST KEEP AT IT, AT THE PACE YOU FEEL IS RIGHT. REMEMBER: THERE ARE NO LOSSES, ONLY WINS AND ONLY LESSONS. EVERY SINGLE THING IN YOUR LIFE SERVES A PURPOSE. KNOW THIS AND SEE EVERY THING AND EVERY PERSON IN THIS LIGHT. ALL THINGS ARE LEADING YOU INTO YOUR DESIRED LIFE DESIGN. WHEN YOU SET INTENTIONS THE ENTIRE UNIVERSE CONSPIRES ON YOUR BEHALF TO CREATE A PATH FOR THIS DESIRE TO COME INTO YOUR LIFE. TRUST THIS PROCESS, ALLOW YOURSELF TO RELAX AND TUNE INTO YOUR INNER GUIDANCE.

8. THE LAW OF PERPETUAL TRANSMUTATION OF ENERGY.

WE HAVE THE INNATE INNER POWER TO CHANGE OUR EXTERIOR LIFE DESIGN. HIGHER VIBRATIONS ALWAYS DISSIPATE LOWER VIBRATIONS. APPLY THE SELF-DISCIPLINE TO SHIFT YOUR PERSPECTIVES AND BELIEFS, AND YOU WILL EVOLVE YOUR ENERGETIC VIBRATION TO A MUCH HIGHER LEVEL. THUS, DISSIPATING ALL LOWER VIBRATIONS YOU NO LONGER WISH TO SEE AND EXPERIENCE WITHIN YOUR LIFE. FOCUS INWARDS, ON YOURSELF AND ONLY FOCUS ON CHANGING YOURSELF — NOT OTHERS. ALLOW YOURSELF TO CHANGE AND EVOLVE INTERNALLY. ONLY FOCUS ON YOUR INTERNAL THOUGHTS AND FEELINGS AND YOU WILL SEE YOUR EXTERNAL REALITY CHANGE AS YOU DESIRE IT TO.
DON'T CONTRADICT YOUR THOUGHTS AND FEELINGS.
EVER-INCREASINGLY REMOVE ALL CONTRADICTING BELIEFS, PERMANENTLY.
ENERGY FLOWS WHERE ATTENTION GOES. WHAT YOU FOCUS ON EXPANDS.

9. THE LAW OF RELATIVITY.

ONLY 10% OF OUR LIFE IS DETERMINED BY OUR CIRCUMSTANCES,
THE REMAINING 90% IS DETERMINED BY THE ATTITUDE WE PERSONALLY CHOOSE TO EMBODY WHILE PERCEIVING AND REACTING TO THE CIRCUMSTANCES.
RECOGNIZE THIS & BE MINDFUL IN EACH AND EVERY MOMENT OF LIFE.
EACH SOUL EXPERIENCES CHALLENGES DURING THEIR HUMAN LIFETIME. NO ONE IS EXCEPT. THIS IS A SOUL EVOLVING EXPERIENCE. CHOOSE TO LEARN AND EVOLVE THROUGH THE CHALLENGES AND NOT BE STUCK IN A VICTIM MENTALITY. BREAK THROUGH THIS PERCEPTION AND SEE CHALLENGES AS OPPORTUNITIES TO DEFINE WHAT YOU DO AND DO NOT WANT IN YOUR LIFE. EMBODY HAVING WHAT YOU DO WANT. THE QUANTUM FIELD OF OPPORTUNITIES IS ABUNDANTLY FULL OF SOLUTIONS, DO NOT CHOOSE THE WORST ONE BY FOCUSING ON FEELING THE WORST CASE SCENARIO. KNOW YOUR DIVINE LIFE SOURCE, AND YOUR HIGHEST VIBRATIONAL ANGELS AND GUIDES ARE WILLING TO HELP YOU THROUGH — ASK FOR GUIDANCE AND BELIEVE YOU WILL RECEIVE IT. BE PRESENT. EMBODY FAITH IN YOUR MIND AND IN YOUR FEELING STATE.

10. THE LAW OF POLARITY.

EVERY SINGLE THING IN OUR EXISTENCE HAS ITS ENERGETIC OPPOSITE.
THIS IS HOW WE ARE ABLE TO DEFINE 'GOOD' AND 'BAD' AND 'LIGHT' AND 'DARK', ETC.
CHOOSE TO SHIFT YOUR PERSPECTIVE ON 'NEGATIVE' OCCURRENCES.
TRUST THAT IN THE BIGGER PICTURE THIS IS TRULY BENEFITING YOU. EMBODY FAITH
RATHER THAN FEAR. WHEN WE ARE CONSCIOUSLY EVOLVING WE WILL EXPERIENCE THE
REMOVAL OF THINGS THAT ARE NOT SERVING OUR DESIRES, WE ARE BECOMING ALIGNED
THROUGH REMOVAL OF THAT WHICH DOES NOT SERVE OUR DESIRED LIFE DESIGN.
DO NOT RESIST CHANGE, EMBRACE CHANGE AND ALLOW TRANSFORMATION TO FLOW.
THIS WILL ALLOW ALL OF YOUR DESIRES WILL ALIGN MUCH FASTER.
FLOW, DO NOT RESIST CHANGE. TRUST AND KNOW YOU ARE BEING
DIVINELY GUIDED INTO YOUR DESIRED LIFE DESIGN, ALWAYS.

11. THE LAW OF RHYTHM.

ALL ENERGY VIBRATES AND MOVES ACCORDING TO ITS OWN RHYTHM.
DO YOU SEE THE PATTERNS OF ENERGY REPETITION WITHIN YOUR LIFE?
EVENTS, CIRCUMSTANCES AND PEOPLE WITH SIMILAR ENERGY FREQUENCIES.
THIS IS YOUR POWER OF MANIFESTATION AT WORK, ATTRACTING TO YOU THE ENERGY
FREQUENCIES YOU CONTINUOUSLY EMBODY. CONSCIOUSLY CHOOSE TO SHIFT OUT OF THE
FAMILIAR AND HARMONIZE WITH THE ENERGETIC VIBRATIONS OF YOUR DESIRES FULFILLED
AND YOU WILL ALLOW THE PHYSICAL MANIFESTATION OF THESE THINGS TO FLOW INTO
YOUR LIFE AS YOU TAKE INSPIRED ACTION. OBSERVE YOUR ENERGETIC VIBRATION, IS IT
TRULY ALIGNED WITH THE ENERGETIC VIBRATION OF YOUR DESIRES FULFILLED?
YOUR ENERGY WILL NOT BE BLAND WHEN YOU EXPERIENCE YOUR DESIRES FULFILLED,
YOUR ENERGY WILL BE VIBRANT, RADIANT AND VERY APPRECIATIVE.
TRAIN YOURSELF TO EVER-INCREASINGLY EMBODY THIS HIGH VIBRATIONAL ENERGY OF
YOUR DESIRES FULFILLED, HARMONIZE YOUR ENTIRE LIFE WITH THIS ENERGY FREQUENCY
AND YOU WILL INEVITABLY ATTRACT THE PERFECT MATCH,
AS THIS IS UNIVERSAL LAW APPLYING TO US ALL.

12. THE LAW OF GENDER.

YIN — FEMININE ENERGY, YANG — MASCULINE ENERGY.
INTERNAL BALANCE OF THESE ENERGIES REFLECTS INTO OUR EXTERNAL REALITY.
WHEN WE MASTER THE BALANCE OF OUR INTERNAL ENERGY WE CONSCIOUSLY HARNESS
OUR INNATE POWER OF MANIFESTATION BETTER THAN EVER BEFORE
AND SEE THE MANIFESTED RESULTS IN OUR EXTERNAL REALITY.
DETERMINATION AND PATIENCE TOGETHER BRING BALANCE AND HARMONY TO OUR
INTERNAL STATE OF BEING. THUS, BRINGING THE FRUITION OF DESIRED LIFE DESIGN.
WE MUST MASTER THE YIN AND YANG THROUGH EVER-INCREASINGLY HARMONIZING
OUR ENERGY FREQUENCIES WHILE ALSO TAKING INSPIRED ACTION AND HOLDING FAITH
THAT OUR DIVINE LIFE SOURCE WILL WORK ITS MAGICK
IN PROVIDING THE EXACT HOW AND WHEN DETAILS.

BEING SPIRITUAL

DOES NOT REQUIRE ANYTHING OTHER THAN YOU SIMPLY BEING

AND RECOGNIZING THAT YOU ARE SPIRIT

HAVING A BEAUTIFULLY CREATIVE HUMAN EXPERIENCE

AND EMBRACING THE UNIQUENESS EMBEDDED WITHIN THAT.

ADVENTURE AND EXTERNAL MATERIAL ITEMS ARE HERE WITHIN THE JOURNEY

TO BE ENJOYED, TO BRING IN EXCITEMENT, VITALITY AND PLEASURE.

THERE IS NO CRITERIA FOR HOW TO BE SPIRITUAL,

SIMPLY DO THE THINGS THAT YOU SO DEEPLY LOVE TO DO.

CONNECT WITH THE DEPTHS OF YOUR OWN SOUL.

BEING SPIRITUAL IS IMMERSING YOURSELF

SO

DEEPLY

INTO ALL THAT YOUR SPIRIT LOVES.

THAT WILL DIFFER FOR EVERYONE,

WHICH IS WHY THERE ARE SO MANY OPTIONS AVAILABLE ON PLANET EARTH.

DO NOT ATTEMPT TO CHANGE ANOTHER'S INTERESTS, VALUES OR BOUNDARIES,

AND DO NOT EVER STRAY FROM YOUR OWN.

JUST TAKE A FEW MOMENTS TO PAUSE FROM THE CONSTANT FLOW OF LIFE, DROP EVERYTHING AND JUST FEEL ~ EMBODY UNCONDITIONAL LOVE IN YOUR HEART-SPACE AND SEND THIS LOVE OUT INTO THE SPIRITUAL REALM SURROUNDING YOU ~ THIS REALM, ALBEIT INVISIBLE TO THE HUMAN EYE, IS ALWAYS PRESENT, LOVING AND SUPPORTING YOU ~ GIVE THANKS TO YOUR HIGHEST VIBRATIONAL ANGELS AND SPIRIT GUIDES, LOVED ONES AND ANCESTORS ~ FEEL THIS GENUINE GRATITUDE EXPENDING OUT TO THEM ~ YOU MAY RECEIVE INSIGHTS, MESSAGES AND OTHER LOVING GESTURES DURING THIS TIME, OR AT A LATER TIME ~ MANY TIMES OUR MINDSET TOWARDS THE SPIRITUAL REALM AND ALL THINGS 'NORMALLY' UNSEEN BY THE HUMAN EYE HAS BEEN SHAPED AND DISTORTED BY THOSE WHO CAME BEFORE US .. CONSCIOUSLY OR UNCONSCIOUSLY TEACHING US TO FEAR THESE THINGS, SIMPLY BECAUSE THEY ARE UNFAMILIAR TO WHAT WE ARE ACCUSTOMED TO SEEING, FEELING, ETC. IN OUR EARTHLY LIFE. HUMANS FEAR WHAT THEY DO NOT UNDERSTAND. IN OUR OWN PUREST STATE WE ARE IN FACT FORMLESS ~ THE SPIRITUAL REALM IS TRULY MORE 'US' THAN THE PHYSICAL REALM IS ~ WE ALL WILL INEVITABLY SHED THIS HUMAN BODY ONE DAY AND RETURN TO OUR FORMLESS STATE, REALIZING THIS HUMAN EXPERIENCE WAS .. SOMETHING LIKE A DREAM .. A BEAUTIFUL GIFT .. THAT WE HAVE THE POWER TO CONSCIOUSLY TRANSFORM WITH OUR PREDOMINANT FEELING STATES ~ LINEAR TIME IS A HUMAN CREATED CONCEPT, OUR HUMAN MIND ACTS A BLINDFOLD, WE ARE UNABLE TO FULLY COMPREHEND THE INFINITE NATURE OF OUR SOUL WHILE WE ARE STILL RESIDING WITHIN THIS BODY THROUGHOUT THIS HUMAN LIFETIME .. WHEN WE CONSCIOUSLY CHOOSE TO RESIDE WITHIN THE PRESENT MOMENT WE TASTE INFINITY AT ITS PUREST ~ THE PRESENT MOMENT IS FOREVER A GIFT ~ WE ARE ALWAYS ABLE TO TUNE INTO THE REALM OF SPIRIT, ESPECIALLY WHEN WE CENTER OURSELVES IN THE PRESENT MOMENT. QUANTUM PHYSICS SHOWS US THAT EVERYTHING IS MADE OF ATOMS, AND AS YOU GO DEEPER AND DEEPER INTO THE ATOM YOU FIND THAT IT IS ONE-HUNDRED PERCENT COMPOSED OF ENERGY. ENERGY COMPOSES EVERYTHING IN OUR EXISTENCE ~ AND EVERYTHING VIBRATES AT ITS OWN UNIQUE FREQUENCY, ALL IS ENERGY ~ EVERYONE IS CAPABLE OF SEEING ENERGY ~ SOME INDIVIDUALS HAVE ALWAYS BEEN TUNED INTO THIS ABILITY, WHILE OTHERS SIMPLY NEED TO REIGNITE THE ABILITY ~ IF YOU ARE UNFAMILIAR WITH SEEING ENERGY: IT LOOKS A BIT LIKE STATIC DOES COVERING THE TELEVISION SCREEN. IT WON'T BE IDENTICAL TO THIS, BUT YOU GET THE IDEA. I SAY THIS SO THAT YOU WILL NOW KNOW YOU ARE SEEING IT .. WHEN YOU SEE IT. ~ DO THIS SIMPLE EXERCISE: GO INTO A DARK ROOM AND SOFTEN YOUR GAZE, FOCUS ON YOUR BREATHING AND THE PRESENT MOMENT. YOU SHOULD BEGIN TO SEE THE ENERGY PARTICLES VERY, VERY QUICKLY. IF YOU DO NOT .. YOU ARE MOST LIKELY TRYING TO HARD TO SEE ~ SO, SOFTEN YOUR GAZE. ONCE YOU SEE THEM AND ARE FEELING FAMILIAR WITH THEM YOU CAN THEN MOVE INTO A LIGHTED AREA. OR EVEN BETTER, GO OUTSIDE AND LOOK INTO THE SKY: DO THE SAME PROCESS AS WITHIN THE DARK ROOM. THE ENERGY PARTICLES IN THE SKY WILL APPEAR DIFFERENT THAN IN THE DARK ROOM BECAUSE THEY ARE FILLED WITH SO MUCH DAYLIGHT. CONTINUE TO PRACTICE [PAUSING AND BECOMING STILL AND PRESENT] TO SEE ENERGY PARTICLES THROUGHOUT EACH DAY. AS YOU CONSCIOUSLY DO YOU WILL BEGIN TO INCREASINGLY DO SO ALL THE TIME OUT OF HABIT ~ THIS STRENGTHENS YOUR ABILITY TO NOT ONLY SEE ENERGY BUT TO ALSO DETECT SPIRIT MOVEMENT ~ REMEMBER, THE SPIRITUAL REALM IS FORMLESS .. POWERFUL, HIGH VIBRATIONAL ANGELS AND GUIDES CAN EXIST IN THE 'SMALLEST' PARTICLES ~ SIZE DOES NOT DEFINE POWER WITHIN THE REALM OF SPIRIT ~ ALSO, ALWAYS EMBODY FAITH AND KNOWINGNESS OVER FEAR AND DOUBT. JUST AS YOUR FREQUENCY ATTRACTS OTHER HUMANS ON THE SAME FREQUENCY ~ YOUR FREQUENCY ALSO ATTRACTS SPIRIT ON THE SAME FREQUENCY ~ ALWAYS INTEND TO BE SURROUNDED BY YOUR HIGHEST VIBRATIONAL ANGELS AND GUIDES ~ ALWAYS ~

SPIRITUAL TOOLS:

SPIRITUAL TOOLS ARE BENEFICIAL IN CHANNELING GUIDANCE AND INSPIRATION.
BUT, RECOGNIZE THAT THEY ARE NOT YOUR POWER SOURCE.
THEY ARE TOOLS.
YOUR PUREST FROM OF POWER RESIDES
WITHIN YOUR ABILITY TO BE MINDFUL IN THIS PRESENT MOMENT.
IN DOING SO, YOU ARE CONSCIOUSLY HARNESSING
YOUR FEELING STATES IN EACH PRESENT MOMENT,
THEREFORE, YOU ARE FULLY HARNESSING YOUR INNATE POWER OF MANIFESTATION
IN EACH MOMENT. THAT IS WHERE YOUR POWER RESIDES: IN THE PRESENT MOMENT.
**YOUR DIRECT CONNECTION TO YOUR DIVINE LIFE SOURCE
IS RESIDING WITHIN YOUR CONSCIOUS
[MINDFUL OF YOUR INNER POWER IN-THIS-MOMENT] SPIRITUAL PRACTICE.
YOU DO NOT NEED TOOLS IN ORDER TO HAVE THAT CONNECTION.**
THEY ARE BENEFICIAL IN SERVING SPIRITUAL PRACTICE,
THEIR PURPOSE IS TO ENHANCE YOUR CONNECTION AND POWER.
I AM SO GRATEFUL FOR ALL OF THE AMAZING SPIRITUAL TOOLS.
AND YET, I RECOGNIZE THEY ARE NOT MY SOURCE OF POWER,
THEY ARE TOOLS, ENHANCERS.
I ENCOURAGE MAKING THE CONNECTION TO YOUR OWN INNER POWER
AND WISDOM FIRST. THEN, CONNECT INTO MOTHER EARTH
AND YOUR DIVINE LIFE SOURCE. VISUALIZE A VIOLET FLAME
ENCOMPASSING YOU AND YOUR AURA, PROVIDING SUPREME PROTECTION,
ONLY THE HIGHEST ENERGY FREQUENCIES MAY EXIST WITHIN THE VIOLET FLAME.

ONCE INNER GUIDANCE HAS BEEN ESTABLISHED / RECEIVED,
ONCE THE FULL CONNECTION HAS BEEN MADE AND YOU TRULY FEEL YOUR INNER POWER
EMANATING THROUGHOUT EVERY FIBER OF YOUR BEING:
UTILIZE ANY SPIRITUAL TOOLS YOU ARE DRAWN TO, IN THE WAY YOU DESIRE TO.

DOING THE ABOVE WILL SERIOUSLY AMPLIFY YOUR EXPERIENCE,
LEAVING YOU FEELING TRULY EMPOWERED AND CONNECTED.
KNOWING YOU ARE THE CREATOR OF YOUR REALITY,
YOU ARE THE HOLDER OF THE WISDOM YOU WISH TO RECEIVE.
ENHANCE YOUR CONNECTION AND POWER BY UTILIZING TOOLS AFTER
THE MINDFUL CONNECTION HAS ALREADY BEEN MADE.
THERE IS SO MUCH POWER IN THIS REALIZATION ALONE,
BECAUSE YOUR TOOLS CAN NOW PROVIDE YOU WITH SO MUCH MORE
AMPLIFICATION OF YOUR INNER POWER AND CONNECTION TO
YOUR DIVINE LIFE SOURCE.

MY METHOD WITH SPIRITUAL TOOLS IS TO HAVE THEM WITH ME AS MUCH AS POSSIBLE SO THEY
ARE FAMILIAR WITH THE ENERGY OF ME. I LOVE TO DISPLAY THEM IN MY SPACE AND IF I FEEL
DRAWN TO ANY OF THEM I WILL THEN ACT ON THAT INTUITIVE, GUT FEELING AND UTILIZE
THEM. IF NOT THEN I JUST MEDITATE WITH THEM BY MY SIDE ..
OR HOLD AND OBSERVE THEM, APPRECIATING THEIR BEAUTY AND PURPOSE.
I BELIEVE IT IS IMPORTANT TO ONLY UTILIZE SPIRITUAL TOOLS WHEN TRULY FEELING IT.

HAVING A RITUAL IS GREAT,
BUT SOMETIMES THIS CAN LEAD TO FEELING LIKE WE ARE JUST RUNNING THROUGH THE
MOTIONS, AND WE CAN EASILY BEGIN TO DISCONNECT FROM OUR INNER POWER
AND WISDOM WHEN THIS HAPPENS.

ALSO CONSIDER:
WHENEVER YOU ARE USING ANY SPIRITUAL TOOLS
IT IS WISE TO INTEND THAT YOUR OWN THOUGHTS AND DESIRES
WILL NOT HINDER THE TRUE ANSWERS / GUIDANCE YOU ARE ASKING TO RECEIVE.

CANDLES CAN BE A GREAT MEDITATION TOOL OR INTENTION SETTING TOOL.

YOU CAN USE CANDLES WHILE SETTING INTENTIONS [TO DEEPEN YOUR RITUAL]
AND DURING YOUR INTENTION SETTING RITUAL YOU CAN ALSO BLESS ANOTHER CANDLE
[OR CANDLES] TO BURN LATER ON, SIMPLY TO REMIND YOU TO IGNITE THE FEELINGS OF YOUR DESIRE
FULFILLED. OR YOU MAY DESIRE TO MEDITATE ON THEM WITH FOCUS AT A LATER TIME, TO RECEIVE
ADDITIONAL GUIDANCE AND A DEEPENING OF CONNECTION TO THE FEELINGS OF HOW YOUR DESIRE
WILL FEEL AS ALREADY MANIFESTED WITHIN YOUR LIFE.

YOU CAN CREATE YOUR OWN CANDLES
AND MEDITATE ON YOUR INTENTIONS WHILE CREATING THEM,
OR PURCHASE CANDLES FROM COUNTLESS PLACES.
MAKE SURE IF YOU DO PURCHASE CANDLES THEY ARE FROM A TRUSTWORTHY SOURCE,
SINCE YOU WILL BE USING THEM FOR MEDITATION / INTENTION SETTING.
IF PURCHASING CANDLES:
CLEANSE THEM [SAGE OR PALO SANTO WORK VERY WELL] AND THEN BLESS THEM AS YOU INFUSE THEM
WITH YOUR INTENTION BEFORE LIGHTING THEM.
DIFFERENT COLORS HOLD DIFFERENT MEANINGS.
YOU CAN RESEARCH WHICH COLORS ARE BEST FOR THE INTENTION YOU ARE SETTING,
OR SIMPLY FOLLOW YOUR INTUITION.
WHITE IS CONSIDERED UNIVERSAL FOR ALL PURPOSES.

ONCE YOU HAVE COMPLETED THE ABOVE:

SET YOUR SPACE: IGNITE YOUR SENSES AS YOU PLEASE
[LIGHTING, MUSIC / TONES / FREQUENCIES, SMELLS, COMFORT, DRINKING WATER AVAILABLE]

BEGIN BY ENVISIONING PROTECTIVE WHITE LIGHT / A VIOLET FLAME ALL AROUND YOU,
A GENTLE MIST OR FLAME EMANATING THROUGHOUT EVERY FIBER OF YOUR BEING
AND YOUR AURA.
BREATHE DEEPLY ~ INTO THE DEPTHS OF YOUR BEING
~ PAUSE ~
TUNE INTO THE ENERGY, THE MAGICK, AROUND YOU AND WITHIN YOU.
~ EXHALE ALL THAT DOES NOT SERVE YOUR HIGHEST GOOD ~
— FEEL YOUR INNER POWER —
FEEL YOUR CONNECTION TO YOUR DIVINE LIFE AND POWER SOURCE,
KNOW YOU ARE PROTECTED, GUIDED AND SUPPORTED BY YOUR CREATIVE LIFE SOURCE.
THIS ORGANIZED INTELLIGENCE IS INFUSING YOU,
PROTECTING YOU AND FUELING YOU WITH ITS CREATIVE POWER,
~ YOU ARE PERFECTLY ALIGNED RIGHT NOW ~
AND IN EACH OF THE FOLLOWING MOMENTS.
HOLDING ABSOLUTE FAITH, TRUST YOUR INTUITION ENTIRELY.
THIS IS YOUR POWER WORKING MAGICKALLY AND BEAUTIFULLY WITHIN YOU.

KEEP YOUR MINDSET AND INTENTIONS PURE,
FOCUS ON THE VIBRATIONAL FREQUENCIES YOU ARE EMBODYING.

FEEL INTO THE PUREST NATURE OF YOUR SOUL.
AS YOU GAZE INTO THE CANDLE FLAME [WITHOUT JUDGEMENT] CONCENTRATE ON
OBSERVING THE MOVEMENT OF THE FLAME WITHIN EACH MOMENT.

HOW LARGE OR SMALL IS THE FLAME? IS THE FLAME MOVING? OR NOT MOVING?
THE FLAME REPRESENTS THE VITALITY AND MOVEMENT OF THE INTENTION YOU ARE FOCUSING ON.
TUNE INTO YOUR OWN INTUITION
WHAT DOES IT HAVE TO SAY?
DO YOU FEEL ANY GUIDANCE, MESSAGES OR SYMBOLS SURFACING?
IF SO, JOURNAL THEM DOWN. DO NOT SPEND TOO MUCH TIME WRITING,
JUST NOTE THEM DOWN AND CONTINUE GAZING.

IF YOU ARE EXTINGUISHING THE CANDLE:
DO SO WITHOUT USING THE BREATH OF LIFE.
IF YOU ARE LETTING YOUR CANDLE BURN MAKE SURE IT IS IN A SAFE LOCATION.

ONCE YOU HAVE FINISHED: GIVE GENUINE THANKS,
AND ALLOW YOURSELF TIME TO RELAX MENTALLY AND PHYSICALLY.

EVERY SINGLE HUMAN ON PLANET EARTH IS UNIQUE.

ALTHOUGH MILLIONS OF PEOPLE SHARE THE SAME SUN SIGN

IT IS IMPORTANT TO UNDERSTAND THAT THERE IS FAR MORE DETAIL THAT GOES INTO EACH HUMAN'S NATAL CHART. WE EACH HAVE OUR SUN SIGN, ASCENDANT SIGN, MOON SIGN, ETC, ETC, ETC.. AND THAT IS JUST IT, THERE ARE MULTIPLE ASPECTS TO EACH HUMAN, NOT JUST ONE. USUALLY PEOPLE KNOW THEIR SUN SIGN, THE SIGN THAT PEOPLE WILL SAY 'I'M A ____'. AN INCREASING AMOUNT OF PEOPLE ARE AWAKENING TO THE FACT THAT THERE IS FAR MORE DEPTH TO EACH OF OUR NATAL CHART'S THAN JUST OUR SUN SIGN. NO ONE ELSE HAS YOUR EXACT NATAL CHART, EVEN TWINS WILL HAVE SLIGHT DIFFERENCES IN THEIR CHARTS. HAVING A PROFESSIONAL NATAL CHART READING IS A REALLY BENEFICIAL INVESTMENT IN YOURSELF AS THIS READING WILL ALLOW A PROFESSIONAL TO PULL AND INTERPRET YOUR ENTIRE NATAL CHART FOR YOU. THEY WILL ELABORATE ON EACH ASPECT OF YOUR CHART, AS WELL AS WHAT SIGNIFICANCE EVERYTHING COMBINED HOLDS WITHIN YOUR LIFE. FOR A NATAL CHART READING IT IS CRUCIAL TO HAVE YOUR BIRTH DATE, BIRTH TIME [THE EXACT HOUR AND MINUTE] AND BIRTH PLACE. THIS INFORMATION IS CRUCIAL BECAUSE THE ALIGNMENT OF THE PLANETS IS ALWAYS IN MOTION AND CHANGING .. AND EVEN SOMEONE WHO IS BORN ON THE EXACT SAME DAY AND YEAR AS YOU WILL HAVE A DIFFERENT CHART THAN YOU, EVEN IF YOU WERE BORN ONLY MINUTES APART THE CHARTS CAN BE TOTALLY DIFFERENT! THE DETAILS OF YOUR BIRTH TIME DO MATTER, SIGNIFICANTLY .. SO DON'T GUESS. THERE ARE FREE SERVICES ON THE INTERNET THAT ALLOW YOU TO PULL YOUR OWN NATAL CHART AND SEE WHAT THAT ENTAILS, WHICH IS FUN TO DO WHEN YOU FIRST REALIZE YOU DO HAVE MORE THAN ONE SIGN APPLYING TO YOU. BUT, I DO HIGHLY RECOMMEND INVESTING IN A PROFESSIONAL, QUALITY CHART INTERPRETATION, BECAUSE IT IS VERY COMPLEX AND INVESTING IN SOMEONE FAMILIAR WITH NATAL CHART READINGS WILL ALLOW YOU TO UNDERSTAND THE MEANING OF IT ALL SO MUCH MORE IN DEPTH THAN YOU EVER COULD WITH AN AUTOMATED RESULT ON THE INTERNET. TAKE THE TIME TO FIND A QUALIFIED AND TRUSTED SOURCE AND MAKE SURE YOU VIBE WITH THEIR VIBE BEFORE INVESTING IN THEIR NATAL CHART SERVICES. ALSO, ON ANOTHER NOTE, WHENEVER YOU ARE SEEKING EXTERNAL ADVICE FROM ANYONE [EVEN IF THE SOURCE IS HIGHLY RECOGNIZED AND TRUSTED FOR THEIR INTUITIVE ADVICE, OR EVEN IF IT ISN'T IN RELATION TO INTUITIVE GUIDANCE AT ALL] USE DISCERNMENT AND ULTIMATELY FEEL WHAT IS TRUE FOR YOU. WHAT RESONATES WITH THE CORE OF YOUR OWN SOUL? TRUST YOURSELF! YOU ARE YOUR OWN GREATEST SOURCE OF INTUITIVE WISDOM WHEN IT COMES TO YOU AND YOUR LIFE. YOU HOLD THE MOST POWER AND WISDOM WITHIN YOU FOR WHAT IS ULTIMATELY BEST FOR YOU AND YOUR LIFE. IF YOU EVER ENCOUNTER ANOTHER WHO CLAIMS TO KNOW WHAT IS BEST FOR YOU AND YOUR LIFE: BE SKEPTICAL!!! ANY INTUITIVE PERSON OR GUIDE [OR ANY OTHER PERSON, PERIOD] WHO TRULY INTENDS FOR YOUR HIGHEST GOOD WILL ALWAYS TURN YOU INWARDS AND GUIDE YOU INTO SEEKING YOUR INNERMOST WISDOM AND INTUITIVE INSIGHTS. THEY MAY TELL YOU WHAT THEY INTUITIVELY FEEL OR SEE BUT THEY WILL NOT TELL YOU WHAT SHOULD OR SHOULD NOT BE DONE, AND IF THEY ATTEMPT TO DO SO .. BE VERY SKEPTICAL OF THIS. LISTEN TO WHAT THEY HAVE TO SAY [POLITELY], BUT BE SKEPTICAL AND DON'T TAKE IT ALL TO HEART. NO ONE OUTSIDE OF YOU EVER KNOWS WHAT IS ULTIMATELY BEST FOR YOU. INTUITIVE INSIGHTS FROM OTHERS CAN BE BENEFICIAL, FUN AND HELPFUL IN SHIFTING PERSPECTIVE, BUT ALWAYS .. ALWAYS .. ALWAYS .. USE DISCERNMENT AND TRUST YOUR INTUITION ABOVE ALL ELSE. YOUR PATH YOU ARE ON IN ANY PRESENT MOMENT IS ALWAYS ABLE TO CHANGE. REMEMBER: YOU ARE THE CREATOR OF YOUR REALITY.

OTHER PEOPLE CAN ONLY TRIGGER YOUR INNER KNOWING, SERVING AS A GUIDE ..

YOU TRULY DO HOLD ALL OF THE POWER YOU NEED WITHIN YOU, ALLOW IT TO BE UNLEASHED.

'TO BE HAPPY WITH YOURSELF IN THE PRESENT MOMENT

WHILE MAINTAINING A DREAM OF YOUR FUTURE

IS A GRAND RECIPE FOR MANIFESTATION.

WHEN YOU FEEL SO WHOLE THAT YOU NO LONGER CARE WHETHER "IT" WILL HAPPEN,

THAT'S WHEN AMAZING THINGS MATERIALIZE BEFORE YOUR EYES.

I'VE LEARNED THAT BEING WHOLE IS THE PERFECT STATE OF CREATION. I'VE SEEN THIS TIME

AND TIME AGAIN IN WITNESSING TRUE HEALINGS IN PEOPLE ALL OVER THE WORLD. THEY FEEL

SO COMPLETE THAT THEY NO LONGER WANT, NO LONGER FEEL LACK, AND NO LONGER TRY TO

DO IT THEMSELVES. THEY LET GO, AND TO THEIR AMAZEMENT, SOMETHING GREATER THAN

THEY ARE RESPONDS—AND THEY LAUGH AT THE SIMPLICITY OF THE PROCESS.'

— JOE DISPENZA, YOU ARE THE PLACEBO

I AM CONSTANTLY GROWING, AND THAT IS BEAUTIFUL.

THERE IS NO 'FINAL DESTINATION' I AM GOING TO ONE DAY FIND MYSELF AT.

MY HAPPINESS AND SUCCESS RESIDE WITHIN MY PASSIONATE AND FULFILLING LIFE JOURNEY.

MY JOURNEY TAKES FORM EXACTLY AS I DESIRE,

BECAUSE I AM ALWAYS IN THE BLISSFUL MINDSET OF EXPERIENCING THE GRATITUDE

THAT COMES WITH MY DESIRES FULFILLED.

REFLECT ON THE EXPERIENCES YOU DESIRE TO HAVE IN YOUR LIFETIME--

ARE YOUR BEHAVIORS CONGRUENT WITH YOUR DESIRED LIFE DESIGN?

HOW CAN YOU BETTER ALIGN WITH YOUR DESIRED LIFE DESIGN?

ARE YOU GROWING IN THE DIRECTION OF YOUR DESIRED LIFE DESIGN?

WHAT CAN YOU DO TO NOURISH YOUR GROWTH IN THAT DIRECTION?

DO ONE THING EVERY DAY THAT SCARES YOU. - ELEANOR ROOSEVELT

'SUCCESS IS MEASURED BY YOUR DISCIPLINE AND INNER PEACE.'— MIKE DITKA

DREAM. LIVE. BE GRATEFUL. GIVE.

LOVE THE GODDESS LIFE DESIGNER?

INSPIRE OTHERS VIA REVIEW &
SHARE YOUR FEEDBACK WITH ME!

ARE THERE ANY POTENTIAL ADDITIONS / ALTERATIONS YOU WOULD LOVE TO SEE?

IG:
I CHECK IN PERIODICALLY & I POST INSPIRATION / RECOMMENDATIONS
I AM FEELING. @ZAEYLINSATYA

THE KINDLE EBOOK VERSION IS ALSO AVAILABLE FOR PURCHASE ON AMAZON.

THE 2020 VERSION WILL BE AVAILABLE IN NOVEMBER 2019.

SENDING BLESSINGS TO YOU AND YOUR CREATIVE JOURNEY.

Made in the USA
Lexington, KY
10 April 2019